AN ALERT,
WELL HYDRATED

ARTIST

IN NO ACUTE DISTRESS

AN ALERT, WELL HYDRATED

ARTIST

IN NO ACUTE DISTRESS

CATHERINE ARMSDEN

 Torchflame Books

Published 2023, by Torchflame Books
www.torchflamebooks.com

Paperback ISBN: 978-1-61153-535-8
E-book ISBN: 978-1-61153-536-5
Library of Congress Control Number: 2023920733

Cover design by Jori Hanna
Cover Artwork by Hadley Ferguson

This book is a truthful recollection of actual events in the
author's life. Some conversations have been recreated. The
names and details of some individuals may have been changed
to respect their privacy.

All royalties from the sale of this book will be donated to
Summit for Parkinson's, a non-profit founded by Hadley
Ferguson in 2011 to serve people in Montana who are living
with Parkinson's and related conditions.

To those who don't look away

CONTENTS

FOREWORD

C atherine Armsden came into my life just as I was ending three years of intense secret-keeping. We both had been recently diagnosed with Parkinson's disease (PD), and because I was a practicing physician, the stigma of PD had kept me silent.

With San Francisco and Cleveland geographically distant and no established buddy system in place for the newly diagnosed, it was my good fortune that because we were both computer competent fifty-somethings, a girlfriend match took place in a Facebook (FB) PD chat room that was only clicks instead of miles away.

Now sixteen years into this journey, I come to this honor of writing a foreword for Catherine's book with a unique perspective: first and foremost, as a friend to both Catherine and Hadley, women who continue to amaze and inspire me, and secondly, through the eyes of a person living with PD.

Additionally, I am a physician who believes that the doctor-patient relationship requires not only textbook knowledge of diseases and their treatments, but also a keen understanding of their impact on the human condition. I appreciate the challenges physicians face: more patients, less time, and an ever-increasing volume of knowledge to keep up with. But medical providers must be READY to respond to what is playing out in the moment, be ready to look Catherine in the eye, and be prepared to greet Hadley with empathy rather than indifference. In the big scheme of things, we are in this business to help heal those around us who are suffering.

In 2011, several of us from our FB group traveled to Portland, Oregon, for NBA star, now a Person With Parkinson's (PWP), Brian Grant's first fundraiser. Enter Hadley Ferguson, a young, bubbly woman newly diagnosed with PD. She was lovely and poised, and her optimism seemed part of her inherent nature. Hadley caught our attention with her "glass is half-full" attitude and became a welcome addition to our all-women chat group, adding to our organically growing buddy system.

Through this group, Catherine, an architect and published novelist, and Hadley, an accomplished painter, developed a friendship that encouraged both women not to let PD derail their work.

Some readers may not be aware that PD can and often does "look" different from one patient to the next. However, within a year or two of an official diagnosis, most of us settle into what neurologists call "garden-variety PD."

But Hadley didn't take long to see and experience things the rest of us did not, compelling her to search for her medical truth with Catherine at her side.

Catherine is a marvelous storyteller, drawing the reader in as she masterfully intertwines the chronicle of her own PD journey with Hadley's more uncertain one. Along the way, Catherine takes us into the workings of Hadley's art world while dutifully dispensing a steady dose of Parkinson's disease education, which she cleverly ties to the story at hand.

An Alert, Well-Hydrated Artist in No Acute Distress (a title that steals from the shorthand physicians use in their medical records to give an impression of a patient's overall affect) will be instantly familiar to any family touched by PD and the physicians caring for them. Catherine is an honest raconteur, balancing the stories of two determined women in need of a diagnosis with the efforts of their doctors to provide them with one, albeit often less than successfully.

Patients with PD and their care partners are sure to find inherent comfort in the shared PD stories, especially when a story can find humor in the absurdities of PD that we all endure.

As a physician reading this book, I have thought a lot about Catherine recounting her and Hadley's medical interactions. She describes them with a tempered matter-of-factness, not disparaging the providers they encounter that fall short of "Do no harm," yet allowing us to feel their frustration when their doctors are not hearing them. Catherine's chapter on empathy provides a poignant reminder that a physician's choice of words and actions does matter. Once again, the human condition is utmost.

It has been nearly fifteen years since Catherine and I first met in that chat group. The group no longer gets together, but some relationships have been maintained. None more so than mine with Catherine. We still talk almost weekly as we try to decipher the meaning of our ever-changing and intensifying PD symptoms.

Our talks are more wide-ranging than strictly narrow PD issues. Politics, culture, and child-rearing make frequent appearances, while the greater medical world is constant fodder. Catherine is not a physician, but she thinks like one. That's why it's great that she leaves space in this book to address important topics such as environmental toxins and PD, cognitive errors doctors make when diagnosing, and deep brain stimulation surgery (DBS). In doing so, she puts some of her frustrations aside to illuminate our medical system and society's role in creating a man-made disease that leading scientists are now calling a pandemic.

The publication of Catherine's novel *Dream House* and the broadening of Hadley's artistic répertoire, which includes intimate landscapes alongside her prominent historical murals, are testaments to their talent and perseverance and are proof that their PD experiences do not define them.

Catherine and Hadley's journey will lead you to consider your own journey and connection with medicine, whether it involves a chronic illness or nothing more than an annual check-up. In doing so, I hope you gain as much perspective as Catherine has. It can only help to better our collective human condition.

—Karen Jaffe, Cleveland, Ohio, 2023

PROLOGUE

"**D**o you think it's all in my head?"

Hadley takes off her glasses and sets them on the varnished burl table. Her brown eyes are huge and searching, brimming with tears. For the first time, it hits me that at thirty-seven, she's only eleven years older than my daughter, and I flood with a maternal urge to reach for her hand and tell her everything's going to be okay. But this is probably a lie, and the truth is the reason she's here.

At four o'clock in Rochester, Minnesota, in late November 2012, it's eighteen degrees outside and already dark; we're in a pub full of people who haven't warmed up enough to shed their down jackets. Hadley's drinking her favorite, a mojito, and I am, too, in a gesture of solidarity. The mojitos are midwestern-generous and lack fresh mint but taste of someplace warm and vacation-like, not here. We're determined to make this night as fun as possible. After drinks, we'll see a movie and then have dinner, since Hadley has just finished her sixth grueling day at The Mayo Clinic. Before she'd asked me her difficult question, "Do you think it's all in my head?" I was wondering whether, after the super-sized mojito, I'd be able to find the Galaxy 14 Theater in my rental car. Now, all my attention is on how to answer her.

"No," I say, feeling my way toward a response. It has never occurred to me that the myriad symptoms Hadley was experiencing, many of which I shared, could be anything but a serious neurological disease. "I don't think it's all in your head. But if it were, I'd be relieved because it would mean that you have something treatable."

This observation sounds leaden with hopefulness even to me, but it seems to sink Hadley into a slump behind the table. She's pale, her long, auburn hair limp and without the shine I remember. But I know she's not one to give up or give in. She pulls a Kleenex from her cloth purse, blows her nose, puts her glasses on, and peers at me. "So, you do think there's some possibility that all this could be psychological?"

"No, no," I say, doing a quick mental review of some of her symptoms, like orthostatic hypotension (abnormally fluctuating blood pressure) and urinary difficulties, both things that the mind couldn't possibly cook up. "Your physical illness is real; the question is just what's causing it. I mean...this is The Mayo Clinic, and they can't leave any stone unturned. Right?" I ask, hoping I'm not saying anything she hasn't thought of herself.

When Hadley tilts her face down and sips from her tall mojito, I know I've said exactly the wrong thing. I've flown across the cold continent to be helpful, and I've managed to mess up in the first twenty-four hours.

Hadley wants the truth about her medical condition, yes. And just as much, she wants people to believe her illness is real.

ONE:
SOMETHING IS NOT RIGHT

I n bed at night, while the rest of me was ready to melt into the mattress, my right leg refused to relax. I was missing bits of dialogue in movies I was trying to watch as I squirmed to reposition my leg so the muscle contractions would stop. If this isn't a textbook case of restless leg syndrome, I consoled myself, I don't know what is.

I am neither an excessive worrier nor a denier. I was fifty-two in 2007 and had read enough about medical conditions to know that symptoms don't always point to the most common diagnosis. Nowadays, when your doctor won't address your fears, you go straight to your computer, where Dr. Google will let you leap into the mouth of the dragon without assuming you're a hypochondriac.

Deep in the click-hole, you can plug in symptoms and pull up diseases that make your fingers sweat on the keyboard. Only someone in deep denial wouldn't have been concerned when learning about illnesses like multiple sclerosis (MS) and amyotrophic lateral sclerosis (ALS), both of which involve the kind of symptom I was experiencing. I remember being haunted by the post of a thirty-year-old man on an MS forum: "If you have progressive MS, understand that how you feel today is the best you'll ever feel because this disease only gets more horrible." But it was ALS I was most afraid of because it runs its course so quickly and cruelly.

I knew that the constant muscle contractions in my leg, if not indicative of a disease process, had to at least have a structural cause. Thinking they might be caused by what felt like a pinched nerve in my lower back that acted up now and then, a couple of months later, I saw a spine specialist. He ordered an MRI of my lumbar spine and found nothing worth following up on. A few weeks later, I consulted with an orthopedist. He referred me to a physical therapist who detected a distinct area of immobility in my spine and prescribed stretching exercises.

A month later, I noticed in the shower that the toes on my right foot curled under and that I would stand on the outside of that foot. Aha! Perhaps the problem could be with my foot! I consulted a podiatrist who prescribed custom orthotics. But he also noted the tingling I felt in the top of my foot and my shin when he brushed his fingers over them and referred me to a physiatrist.

By now, it was November, ten months after I first felt something was off. The physiatrist was a delicate young woman who suggested a nerve conduction (NCS) study and electromyogram (EMG), which would detect which nerves in my leg or back were affected. I gleaned from her cheerful recommendation that these tests would be no big deal. On the day of the testing, she opened an impressive toolbox and plugged in a wand that she touched to my leg. When I flinched from the electric shock, she asked me if I was okay. I said yes. After all, I'd given birth twice without anesthesia; isn't that the pain against which we measure all other pain? Up and down my leg, she zapped, and when she was done with my bad leg, she went after my good one.

Then she said, "Now for the tough part."

No one had ever described to me what an intramuscular EMG entails. Simply put, the doctor sticks a thick needle straight into your muscle and then stirs it. Imagine acupuncture performed by cavemen. While the needles in your flesh are twisted, the nerve signals in your muscle are transmitted to the doctor's oscilloscope, creating an unpleasant radio static—the perfect soundtrack for torture. The louder the static, the more abnormally worked up your affected muscle is. Stabbing her needle up and down my leg, the physiatrist and I began to talk, a welcome distraction. She told me about how, as a girl, she'd come to the U.S. from Vietnam after the war.

"My father," she explained (stab!) "suffered from a neurological disease" (stab!) "due to his exposure to Agent Orange" (stab!). Her cheerfulness faded as she continued to plunge her needles into my flesh. I felt her pain, compounded by a degree of guilt; coverage of the Vietnam War had played on our family TV every night when I was growing up. I would be lying if I said the word "retribution" didn't cross my mind as I lay at her mercy on the table. I was afraid to ask her the name of her father's disease, as if knowing would make it contagious.

The physiatrist diagnosed me with L4-L5 radiculopathy, a spinal impingement on the nerves by my lumbar vertebrae. "No big deal," she said, and recommended physical therapy. A couple of weeks later, a physical therapist confirmed her diagnosis, saying I needed to lengthen my spine to work out the compression. This also conformed to what the first physical therapist had observed.

The diagnosis of radiculopathy was accurate, but it would turn out to be a red herring. Within a couple of months, I knew it couldn't explain everything I was feeling, like the lack of coordination when I walked, as if my upper and lower body weren't talking to each other. I remember demonstrating to a friend that while I could tap my left hand on a table rapidly and at length, my right hand would peter out and stall after a few moments. My friend didn't tell me I was worrying about nothing. I could see in her furrowed brow that she was genuinely troubled by what she'd observed.

For the next year, I continued to consult with doctors and tried various types of bodywork and alternative medicine, including Pilates, Feldenkrais, chiropractic, and acupuncture. Nothing helped. I shared my symptoms freely with everyone I knew, picking their brains, hoping they'd have a hunch or know a miracle worker who could treat me.

In July of 2008, I made an appointment with an integrative medicine physician who had been very helpful to me ten years earlier when I was sick with something my primary care physician had no idea how to treat. I was confident Dr. Norton would take my wayward leg seriously. And, like many doctors I've known, he radiated self-assurance—as if self-assurance itself had healing power—and this time, he was not at all concerned about my symptoms. He shook his head at my worrying.

"Catherine, there's nothing physically wrong with you. But you're very anxious. I want you to think about this yoga retreat."

He handed me a flyer with an illustration of rolling hills, trees, and a bodhisattva. The bodhisattva really pushed my buttons: I'm sure she was a lovely woman, but with fifty-three rational, intelligent years under my belt, didn't I deserve a little respect, too? I was angry but afraid to show it.

I started taking an interest in people on the street who were limping. I noticed the man who owned the audio equipment store next door to my office limping awkwardly, just like me, while he was crossing the street. I screwed up the courage to ask him about it. "Pinched nerve in my neck," he told me.

Hopeful that this could be my problem, too, I had a cervical spine MRI done. It was normal. More good news, I supposed, but I was no closer to understanding why, when I walked, my right leg wasn't keeping up. Trudging uphill—unavoidable in San Francisco—I felt like I was battling a headwind while walking through deep snow.

And now I had a new problem: a frozen shoulder, aka adhesive capsulitis, caused by the vigorous tree and bush pruning I'd done over a few summer days. Unlike my neurological symptoms, my abused shoulder caused pain—the teeth-grinding type. I took it to a new physical therapist who assured me that most of his clients were women over fifty with frozen shoulders—a message, I assume, that was supposed to reassure me. In fact, it offered a comforting distraction until I showed him my walk.

"Swing your arm!" he called out.

What? I wasn't swinging my arm? We practiced walking in place, which took a lot of concentration for me to do properly. "You just need re-training," the PT said as if people forgot how to walk every day. He was certain that the cause of my symptoms was a slipped SI joint. "Trust me," he said with doe-eyed sincerity. "Nothing terrible is happening to you."

A couple of months later, I saw Dr. Norton for a follow-up. This time, I persuaded him to leave his building so he could watch me walk. After all, if walking was becoming my main difficulty, how could he possibly make an assessment while I was sitting in a chair? Out in the parking lot, he seemed jittery and mole-like; I felt my belief in him diminish, as if the bright daylight had illuminated his mere mortality.

Back in his office, his air of authority was restored. "What will it take to convince you!" he exclaimed. Do you want me to order you a brain MRI?"

"A brain MRI won't diagnose all neurological conditions," I said.

"Yes, it will."

I was pretty sure he was wrong, but there are times we defer to our doctors when it would serve us not to. We want to believe in them, and we want them to believe we believe in them because we need them; they hold the keys that unlock the mysteries of our bodies.

"Okay," I told him. "Let's do a brain MRI."

"You again?" the MRI technician said when I walked in, blasé about the procedure now that I was a regular in this lab. I felt a little macho lying calmly in the tube of terror, wondering why we could take a picture with our phone of piranha sushi we're eating in Venezuela and text it to people in Wyoming, but no one can figure out how to stop the ear-splitting soundtrack inside an MRI machine.

"See?" Dr. Norton said when the MRI came back normal. "Feel better now?"

I wanted to slap him, though I've never slapped anyone in my life. "No," I said. "But at least I know I don't have a brain tumor." In a few minutes, I would be dragging to my car with no explanation for my sloppy walk.

All the people I'd consulted about my symptoms had been so very optimistic! They seemed, actually, *aggressively* optimistic. I wanted very much to believe them, but I wasn't feeling it. When you're moving in a way that makes your family and closest friends wince with barely concealed terror, it's not human to assume the best-case scenario. You don't think, oh, the fact that I can't coordinate my arms with my legs when I walk is probably because my kids are stressing me out.

Far from reassuring me, the optimism of these health practitioners made me lonely and afraid in the body that was becoming a stranger to me.

TWO:
NOT THE WORST THING

People often describe someone who's risen above great challenges as having an "indomitable spirit." For those with a serious illness, I believe indomitability might begin organically, not by choice, during a drawn-out diagnostic process. Shunted from doctor to doctor, we develop emotional muscle by chasing something we don't want to catch while fear dogs us, nipping at our heels. It takes determination to face unpleasant tests and to cope with doctors who tell us things we know in our gut are, at best, incomplete. We build courage keeping the dogs at bay for however long it takes to get a diagnosis.

In late 2008, after nearly two years of stuffing my burgeoning fear and armed with my nerve conduction study and electromyography test results—a wad of paper with curvy graphs and charts—I went to see a general neurologist at one of the nation's top ten hospitals. He had me sit on the edge of the table and put me through a drill designed to distinguish between different neurological conditions. Little did I know I would soon be subjected to many of these same tests two or three times a year for the rest of my life.

First, the neurologist asked me a couple of questions: "What is today's date?" "Where are we?"

With a bright light, he examined my pupils, then had me stare straight ahead as he stretched his arms sideways and asked me to tell him on which hand his fingers were wiggling. Keeping my head still, I followed his finger with my eyes as he swept it around and up and down.

Then, he asked me to:

1. Touch my left ear with my right hand, stick out my tongue, and repeat after him, "Today is a cloudy day in San Francisco."

2. Close my eyes and hold my arms straight out in front of me for several seconds. Then, with my eyes open, he instructed me to resist as he tried to push down my outstretched hands.

3. Tap my index finger together with my thumb on each hand as fast as I could, then rapidly tap each foot against his hand.

4. Relax each arm and then each leg while he moved them around like Gumby.

5. Reach my finger out repetitively to touch the finger he was holding up, then my nose, then his finger.

He tested my elbow, knee, and ankle reflexes, ran his fingers along the back of my hands at the same time, and then both calves, asking, "Can you feel this, and does it feel the same on both sides?"

I followed him into the hallway, where he watched me walk away from him and back and then again on my tiptoes, on my heels, and finally heel to toe, as if on a balance beam.

He did a "pull test": He stood behind me and yanked my shoulders. When a healthy person experiences a threat to their physical stability, the brain will trigger a rescue reaction to keep them from falling. In people with some neurological diseases, there is often a loss of these postural reflexes.

Finally, back in the exam room, he asked me to write my name—the most mysterious of all his requests. My handwriting, he said, was normal, and I thought, *whatever that means.*

I'd passed all of his other tests, too. He told me to return in a year if my symptoms worsened. Leaving the neurologist's office, I felt relieved—until I was reminded of my wacky gait, which, strangely, hadn't made an impression on the doctor.

A year in limbo felt like a very long time. In the fall, I returned to see the neurologist. He put me through the same neurological drill. When he was finished, he said nothing, turned his back to me, and scribbled in my chart.

Finally, he said, "The only thing I can think of is that it could be Parkinson's." He turned suddenly, as if it had just occurred to him that maybe he should look at me. "It's not the worst thing," he said.

This may have been true for him, in the context of the many neurologically impaired patients who pass through his exam room, and had he taken the time to explain to me where Parkinson's stood on the neurological disease spectrum—or anything about Parkinson's, for that matter—I might have been reassured. But he hadn't, and now icicles were forming in the air between us. He tore a piece of paper from his pad—a prescription for levodopa, which I learned when I got home and looked it up is the gold standard Parkinson's medication that all patients end up taking. "Take it for five days," he said. "Call me on the fifth day and tell me how you feel when you walk. If you have Parkinson's, this should help." He ushered me out the door. "I don't want you leaving here thinking you have Parkinson's."

⁂

"I have Parkinson's," I told my husband, Lewis, at home that night. He said, "No, you don't." Relentlessly optimistic, he could've been a doctor.

⁂

I began taking the levodopa and waited to see whether it would normalize my gait.

"You're walking better! Your arm's swinging!" Lewis said cheerfully on the fourth day. He didn't get that this was not good news.

Was I walking better? I wondered. I knew that in some hard-to-describe way, I felt better. On the fifth day of taking the levodopa, I left a message for the neurologist as he'd instructed. When he didn't return my call, I called again on the sixth day, and the seventh. The weekend came and went. I had no idea whether I was supposed to keep taking the scary-as-hell brain drug that might have been treating a scary-as-hell brain disease. By the end of Monday, when he still hadn't called back, I was not only scared, I was furious. He was messing with my brain!

On day ten, after I'd told the receptionist to let the neurologist know how I felt about his negligence, he called. His greeting was brusque. Having felt my dissatisfaction was fully justified, now I found myself stumbling over my words, reminding him that I had been following his instructions to call him. "I'm a very busy doctor," he broke in. "This is a busy clinic. I can refer you to a movement disorders specialist here, but if you need more attention, you should look for a doctor in private practice."

His hostility shocked me, and I felt left out at sea. Impulsively, I decided to avoid his highly esteemed clinic altogether and look elsewhere for a Parkinson's neurologist, known as a movement disorders specialist (MDS). I made an appointment with one in a Parkinson's center an hour away. Two days before Christmas, I drove there, vibrating with the probability that I was in the fast lane, hurtling toward something terrible.

In the exam room, a nurse took my history and gave me a list of eight words—house, bread, blender, dog, milk, church, spinach, lawn—to remember for the duration of my appointment. Was she kidding? My blood pressure alone was probably enough to erase my short-term memory. But when she left the room, I sat waiting for the doctor, reciting the words in my head. It seemed important.

The door burst open, and the MDS, a woman in her forties who appeared flushed and harassed, introduced herself and took a seat behind her laptop. Reading over my intake information, she glanced up only occasionally to peer at me. Then she rolled her chair over and put me through some of the same drill the *very busy* neurologist had. Turning my arm over in her hands, she muttered, "Cogwheeling." She stood. "Okay, let's walk." She led me out of the exam room.

I walked down the short hall and back just once, and she motioned me back into my chair. We'd been together less than five minutes. Sitting down, she said, "You have Parkinson's. Any questions?"

I suddenly felt like a kid who had planned to walk slowly into frigid ocean water but had been cajoled into diving off the rocks. "Um..." I started. "Actually, since I only learned two seconds ago that I have Parkinson's, I haven't had time to think of questions. But I am wondering, how do you know?"

"I've been looking at people with Parkinson's for twenty years. You have a gait disturbance and cogwheel rigidity in your arm. You're affected on only one side—which is typical at first—and already have some facial masking."

I thought about my face. She was wrong about that part, I was sure; that's just how my face is. "What should I do?" I asked.

She rolled her chair back behind her laptop. "So basically, there are dopamine agonists like Mirapex and Requip, and there's levodopa, which everyone ends up taking sooner or later, and then there's the MAO-B inhibitor, Azilect. The first line of defense is usually the agonists, and most people tolerate them okay, though they can cause insomnia, weight loss, hallucinations, sexual disinhibition, and addictions to shopping and gambling. Levodopa can cause some problems like dyskinesia, so I'd want to start you on Mirapex and also Azilect because it's the only drug that some studies have shown might slow disease progression, but uh oh, I see you're taking Remeron, which you can't take when you're taking Azilect, so I'd want you to stop taking that."

She looked hard at me. "Do you think you can stop taking the Remeron?"

I was reeling. So many names! Like the first chapter of a Russian novel. And I had the other list of words to worry about house, bread, blender... "Sorry?"

"Do you think you can stop taking this one medication so you can start taking Azilect?"

"I don't know."

"Well." She closed her laptop. "You can think about it. And we'll want you to have a tremor soon."

This seemed like the oddest thing she'd said so far. "Why?"

"Because we don't want you to have atypical Parkinson's, which can be much worse."

"Oh," I said. I didn't want to hear more, but this mysterious bit of information, so carelessly dispensed, would come back to haunt me.

"What else?" she said.

"Do people my age often get Parkinson's?"

"Yes, they do!" This seemed to excite her; she smiled for the first time. "In fact, I'll want to introduce you to a group I started—all women around your age and even younger who have Parkinson's but who're all go-getters—active, fun, creative. I don't tell a patient about the group if she's the type who feels sorry for herself. No self-pitiers in this group. I think you'd love it. They're called the Parkinson's Princesses."

Astounded that I'd found a second neurologist even more insensitive than the first, I smiled broadly, so she wouldn't think I was for one second feeling sorry for myself.

She told me to make a follow-up appointment, but I knew I wouldn't. "What about the words?" I asked.

"Pardon?"

"Milk, dog, bread, blender, church, spinach, house, lawn."

"Terrific!" she said. "Have a great holiday!"

During the long drive home, I felt at once stunned and strangely liberated. I'd been given a serious diagnosis, yes, and I'd need to find an MDS with a modicum of emotional intelligence. But it seemed clear I wasn't going to die of a deadly neurological condition, and I didn't need chemotherapy or other drastic interventions.

For the first time in two years, I had no doctors' or physical therapy appointments or tests on my calendar. The big, hairy question in my head was gone. Doctors would stop telling me I was worrying about nothing, and friends would stop asking me why I was limping.

It wasn't the worst thing.

By the time I'd reached the off-ramp for San Francisco, though, I realized that before the end of the day, I'd be paying a visit to Dr. Google to see what he had to say about Parkinson's. The once undefined future of my body soon would be circumscribed by words that wouldn't easily be forgotten: stumbling, lurching, shaking, freezing, mumbling, drooling.

The nipping dogs had caught up with me. I would need to tame them.

THREE:

NEW DISEASE, NEW FRIENDS

I n January 2010, running from the "no self-pitiers" MDS who had diagnosed me, I met Dr. Bright, who would become my MDS. I was immediately drawn to his welcoming peppiness and warm smile. Four days after our first appointment, when the plastic travel cup I'd left in his office showed up on my doorstep, I was over the moon about him. In what universe does a doctor stop on the way to his daughter's school to return a patient's stupid travel cup?

Dr. Bright connected me with a Facebook group started by a woman with Young Onset Parkinson's Disease, which I'd never heard of. Since I'd never known of anyone with PD who was as young as I was, fifty-four, I believed YOPD described me. Soon, I would learn that about 1-2% of people over sixty-five are affected by Parkinson's, and the 10-20% of people with Parkinson's who are diagnosed before the age of fifty are designated as having YOPD. I guess Dr. Bright thought I was close enough, and thankfully, no one in the group has ever challenged me on this point.

When I joined the YOPD Facebook group, there were seventeen members. I was the oldest. I was dismayed to discover there were others as young as twenty-six as well as those who were in their forties who'd had PD since their twenties. My heart hurt as I read about careers interrupted, raising children, and taking care of aging parents—or facing their disease alone. I couldn't imagine dealing with a shaky body, a stumbling walk, or worse, while shuttling between the office, kids' sports practices, and music lessons. Not only is it physically strenuous to meet these demands, but also, putting on a good face for your kids and work colleagues is an enormous challenge when you're sick. Many in the group have realistic concerns about frightening their children, who are too young to understand the nature of their disease or are worried about being fired from their jobs. Imagining all they had to deal with, I suddenly felt very lucky to have made it to my mid-fifties before being diagnosed. My youngest child had just left for college, my parents had died without knowing I was sick, and I had the luxury of working at home.

Within five years, our YOPD Facebook group grew to 370 members. Facebook has been given a bad rap for many good reasons, but for the millions of people who suffer from chronic disease, are housebound, or simply live alone, it is a tremendous gift. For me, the community has provided a place where my physical and experiential anomalies are considered normal.

Typically, Parkinson's patients meet with their movement disorders specialists two to three times a year, but since we experience a daily cornucopia of symptoms that continue to change, having a support group to spontaneously consult about symptoms and medications is a lifeline. No question, large or small, is dismissed by the group: "Who can tell me about applying for disability?" "Does anyone else feel like they're more uncomfortable than they used to be in hot weather?" We discuss and debate the latest research as well as helpful therapies, all in impressive, sometimes gory, detail.

We complain, get outraged, share our joys, and cheerlead. In the middle of the night, when one of us loses our courage, someone is always online to commiserate and help.

Hadley was a member of the YOPD group when I joined. She was thirty-three, a painter, married with a three-year-old daughter, and living in Montana. As an artist-turned-architect-turned-writer, I was immediately drawn in by a photograph she'd posted of herself, sitting atop a high scaffold in front of a huge, complicated mural she was painting inside a school, just one of a few large mural commissions she'd been given. The photo told the story of a talented artist with a remarkably big life who didn't seem to be letting a serious diagnosis get in her way. But I also saw in that image a young woman dwarfed by the immensity of her work and of the struggle she had ahead of her, reconciling her ambition and motherhood with her Parkinson's.

At the time, Hadley's Facebook posts conveyed a surplus of optimism and enthusiasm, punctuated with smiling emoticons and exclamation points. When someone in the group shared good news, she was one of the first to exclaim, "So exciting!!!" She was sympathetic and compassionate, regularly posting encouraging words. Months after I joined the YOPD group, another member would tell me, "The first time I met Hadley in person, she was like, 'Hi! I'm Hadley, and I have Parkinson's!' She was so cheerful I thought she was nuts!"

I knew Hadley was anything but, because we had already taken our conversations from Facebook to the phone. We broke the ice by comparing notes on the YOPD membership: who was funny, who was scaring us with their reports of bad falls or medication side effects, who seemed nice, naughty, or narcissistic. We were both armchair analysts, fascinated by human behavior. Hadley's insightfulness made it hard for me to believe she was only thirty-three. For the first time, I understood what the term "old soul" means. (Later, I would learn about her past and understand why she seemed wise beyond her years). I admired her authenticity and positive-but-realistic outlook and quickly recognized that in her career as an artist, business owner, and organizer, she was unusually capable—one of those people whose left and right brains both operate at full throttle.

We had inspired chats about Hadley's painting and my writing. I remember one especially fun conversation about a painting in which she was incorporating her deceased aunt's ashes—at her request—into the pigment. "I imagine my aunt in the painting on the wall, looking out at my life, watching," Hadley mused, sparking a conversation in which we imagined what could be a fantastic short story.

And, of course, Hadley and I compared notes on our experiences with Parkinson's. Still early into our diagnoses, we were annoyed but not yet impaired by our symptoms. When we talked to each other, the fear of what loomed ahead with our illness lightened—as if together, we became two pillars that could more easily hold the future aloft. We laughed a lot. An outsider listening to our calls might have been mystified by our jauntiness and silliness at times, but it could be explained by something important that we shared: Before our diagnoses, both of us had been searching for years for what was ailing us and having read up on all the more deadly diseases that could have been causing our symptoms, we were both giddy with relief when told we had Parkinson's.

Parkinson's: an incurable neurological disease, but a disease that one lives with for many years. It's a testament to the human spirit how quickly we can sometimes adjust our outlook by regarding our struggles in relative terms.

In July 2011, six months after meeting Hadley online, we had a chance to meet in person. She and her husband, John, were traveling to Portland, Oregon, for a fundraising event organized by the Brian Grant Foundation, and I decided to go with Lewis. Hadley travels to Portland often, as John's family is there, as well as a gallery that represents her work. Within weeks of her diagnosis, she had befriended Brian Grant, a retired NBA basketball star who also has YOPD, so that she could contribute to the work of his foundation.

Brian's gala was the first Parkinson's event I'd attended, and I was excited and nervous to meet several other women from our YOPD Facebook group. Though we are as different as any four random women can be, I felt an instant connection with them as I stole curious glances at how their bodies moved. Alyssa, I noticed, had a gait disturbance that looked like my own, but unlike me, she was very stiff. Soania, who was forty at the time and has had PD since she was twenty-six, held her tremoring hand with the other and rocked gently in her high heels. The swaying—not itself a symptom of PD, but rather a side effect of PD medication—was integrated with her willowy beauty and mellifluous voice, giving her the appearance of a graceful dancer. Hadley's Parkinson's was invisible since, like me, she has no tremor.

On our first night at the elegant Nines Hotel, where it seemed everyone was either a basketball player, an ex-basketball player, or someone with Parkinson's, we four "Parkies" stood in the crowded elevator like shrubs in a redwood grove and rode to the top to start a delightfully warm evening in the rooftop bar. At the table, we were a squirmy bunch, legs shifting, hands trembling. I felt an affection for these women that I knew was tied to the enormous relief of being with vibrant, high-functioning people who shared my weird disease. I might have expected the occasion to be sobering, but instead, it felt celebratory; I found myself wanting us to get drunk and go dancing somewhere. Alas, none of us drank too much. But when the check came, we must have appeared drunk anyway as we fumbled with cards and bills– a task particularly hard for people with PD. We laughed because although we were all carefully groomed, our wallets were, uniformly, a mess.

Throughout the weekend, Hadley's energy astonished me. Radiant and svelte in her floor-length black dress, she worked the Brian Grant Foundation gala like a pro. Her genuine, gentle, and down-to-earth manner made her an especially magnetic networker for the cause of PD. She stayed at the party long after Lewis and I returned to the hotel. In the morning, she left early for the golf course with her easel and paints; as part of Brian's fundraiser, she'd committed to making a painting of the golf tournament, which would be auctioned off that evening.

Meeting Hadley and three other women from our Facebook group in a roomful of at least a hundred others with Parkinson's, was both exhilarating and confusing. I've never belonged to a community other than the schools I attended; I don't go to church and have never been a member of a club. I most enjoy seeing my friends one-on-one rather than in groups. But being with the women from the YOPD group in Portland gave me a heady sense of belonging. At a time when I'd assumed my life had grown nearly as big as it would, something powerful had suddenly been made available to me because of my Parkinson's. I felt a new part of myself open, like a second pair of arms that could embrace more of the world: new friends with whom I shared something vital and intimate, a new personal challenge. Also, I had a new interest to focus on—neuroscience, which I found fascinating.

During the Portland weekend, I also learned that Hadley, Soania, and Alyssa were putting an enormous amount of time and energy into the Parkinson's cause, sitting on advisory committees, running marathons to raise funds, and serving as spokespeople. When Hadley returned to Missoula from the gala event, she hit the ground running, throwing herself into the nonprofit she'd founded almost immediately after her diagnosis, Summit for Parkinson's. Along with her many commitments as a mother, wife, and artist, she skillfully and enthusiastically made Summit a critically important resource for Montanans living with PD.

My new friends were inspiring. They made me want to join in the activism. Yet, because I had only recently arrived at a quieter phase of life in which my empty nest afforded time to focus on my creative work, I felt fiercely protective of my hours of introversion, aka, my writing.

There was this novel, *Dream House.* The novel I'd been rewriting for too many years to admit seemed on the cusp of being published—*would* be published after one last push on the manuscript. After all, I had just landed a top literary agent.

FOUR:
A HEART IS OPENED

After our fun weekend together in Portland at the Brian Grant Foundation gala, Hadley and I texted nearly every week throughout the fall of 2011. At times, when she talked about her painting commissions and plans for Summit for Parkinson's, her high energy and spirits seemed almost like euphoria, raising a small red flag inside me.

In December, she called and said soberly, "I met this pharmacologist at a Christmas party, and he said to me, 'You don't have Parkinson's.'"

I contemplated what this meant, if anything. "Can you believe he said that?" she pressed.

I was struck by her agitation. For the first time, her extraordinary equanimity in the face of our disease seemed to falter. But why? I wondered. She'd been diagnosed by a Parkinson's specialist. Why should she concern herself with the unsolicited opinion of some know-it-all who'd only just met her?

The longer we lingered on this interaction, the more the little red flag waved.

Parkinson's Disease, first identified in 1817 as "the shaking palsy" by English physician James Parkinson, is a progressive, degenerative disease of the nervous system. It's called a "movement disorder" because of its hallmark signs and symptoms of reduced motor function, such as slow and imprecise movement (bradykinesia), muscular rigidity, stiffness, and tremor. Most of these motor symptoms are caused by the death of dopamine-producing neurons in the basal ganglia (which includes the caudate, putamen, and globus pallidus), areas of the brain that control movement and coordination. Scientists believe Parkinson's develops over many years or decades; most symptoms don't appear until a patient has lost about 80% of these neurons.

Tremor is the most common motor symptom associated with PD, but a large fraction of people with the disease do not have one. Bradykinesia is required for a clinical diagnosis of Parkinson's, and many people will also experience balance problems and facial "masking" that makes them appear less animated. Speech can be altered for some people, creating a lower, hoarser, or even an unintelligible voice.

In addition to this full menu of motor symptoms, there are many "non-motor" symptoms that are not caused by the loss of dopamine but by the depletion of neurotransmitters due to cell death in other areas of the brain. Constipation, in particular, is very common in Parkinson's and can precede motor symptoms by many years. People with PD can be affected by mild cognitive impairment, and as many as 50-80% of patients will develop dementia in the later stages of the disease. Hallucinations, mostly visual, can occur with or without dementia and may be related to Parkinson's medications, especially at higher doses. Other common non-motor symptoms can include mood changes (depression, anxiety, apathy), insomnia, restless legs, and fatigue.

In addition to these afflictions, about 75% of Parkinson's patients will experience some dysfunction of the autonomic nervous system that controls "automatic" body processes, including heart rate, blood pressure, salivation, swallowing, digestion, and sexual arousal.

With the wide range and number of symptoms associated with Parkinson's, it's easy to see why diagnosing the disease can be tricky. This is especially true when a patient like me doesn't present with a tremor or in the early stage of the disease when other symptoms, like my lack of arm swing and asymmetrical gait, are not yet obvious. Diagnosis relies on a clinician's keen eye and careful listening. As I discovered, there are also psychosocial hurdles to clear in the diagnostic process, including bias or dismissiveness on the part of a doctor, or inadequate communication on the part of a patient. I remember clearly telling more than one of the first doctors I consulted that "I just feel weird when I'm moving through space." I'm sure it sounded vague to them and certainly not urgent, but it was precisely how I felt. In fact, I've come to believe that when a patient describes what they are experiencing as "weird," they probably have a neurological disease!

In the more than one hundred years since James Parkinson discovered the disease, no blood or imaging test was established that could confirm it. Finally, in 2023, the Michael J. Fox Foundation announced a major breakthrough for the future of PD diagnosis. Their study, which involved hundreds of volun-heroes with and without Parkinson's who subjected themselves to lumbar punctures for multiple years, confirmed the presence of an abnormally formed protein, alpha-synuclein, in the spinal fluid of 93% of people with Parkinson's who participated. Very few tests for neurologic disorders are over 90% sensitive for disease. The test will provide a PD biomarker not only in people diagnosed with

Parkinson's but also in individuals who have not yet been diagnosed or shown clinical symptoms of the disease but are at a high risk of developing it. Alpha-synuclein is such an important player in the story of Parkinson's that I have given it its own Chapter 26 Alpha-Synuclein: The Mental Marauder.

An estimated seven million people worldwide have Parkinson's disease, more than a million of them in the U.S. Medications and interventions can treat symptoms, but there is no known therapy that can stop or even slow disease progression, the rate of which varies from person to person. Although it is typically indolent, PD can make life extremely challenging and can be fatal if it creates complications such as pneumonia related to swallow dysfunction causing aspiration, or falls with significant bodily injury. Parkinson's is the fourteenth leading cause of death in the U.S.

Many people with PD have the same average life expectancy as people without it. In this way, the general neurologist who first suspected I might have PD was right: It's certainly not the worst thing.

As Hadley and I became closer, I learned that getting her diagnosis had been even more of a trial than it had been for me. She seemed to somehow share the blame for this, referring to herself as a "complicated case." Curiosity piqued, I wanted to know more about her past. She began sharing pieces of her history and I was drawn in by its richness and complexity. Later, when I decided to write this story, I asked her to put hers down on paper.

How do we choose to tell the story of our life? The story Hadley wrote down first—the one that slid easily off her fingertips was the one that tracked her movements on the planet, her accomplishments, the things that caught her eye and imagination during the years until she gave birth to her daughter, Sarah.

Hadley was born in Missoula, Montana, in 1976. Her mother, Jana, taught seventh- and eighth-grade English; her father, Fred, was a professor at the University of Montana. Hadley was born with pulmonary stenosis, an obstruction to the flow of blood from the right ventricle of the heart to the pulmonary artery. Congenital cardiac abnormalities are not rare, and Jana and Fred were told that Hadley's defect would eventually require surgical intervention. By the time she was four, Hadley's color was often bluish, and Jana began driving her to a cardiologist in Salt Lake City. At one appointment, Hadley's resting heart rate measured 200 beats per minute— the highest number on the monitor. The cardiologist recommended immediate surgery.

On May 18, 1980, the day Hadley's family left Missoula to drive to Salt Lake City for her open-heart surgery, Mount St. Helens erupted, the deadliest and most destructive volcanic event in the history of the U.S. Because the air was filled with ash, Hadley had to wear a mask all the way to Utah. Her heart surgery was a success, and she recovered well. When she could be active again, Jana and Fred took her on a yearlong adventure to live in Bratislava, Slovakia. Hadley remembers walking along the Danube River to a preschool where no one spoke English, having pneumonia a few months later, and "suddenly" becoming fluent in Slovak.

Hadley's parents' marriage was faltering during the year in Bratislava. In retrospect, she's sure she sensed their struggle and developed a way to act out her distress: stealing. She began squirreling away her schoolmates' belongings in her backpack. At the end of a year, when her family moved back to their house in Missoula, she continued this habit, telling her parents that she'd found her pilfered goods—a gold locket, a pair of mittens in the street on the way home.

She also developed a talent for fibbing whenever she found herself in situations she didn't want her parents to know about. She was always confident that she could come up with a creative story to escape punishment.

When Hadley was nine, Jana announced that she and Hadley would be moving to New York City, where Jana would finish her master's degree in English as a second language. Hadley's father would stay behind in Missoula. For the first several months in New York, Hadley was miserable; she often felt like an outsider since many of her schoolmates hadn't even heard of Montana. To soothe her loneliness, she focused on the opportunities she had in New York that she hadn't had in Missoula. She and Jana frequented the city's museums, sparking Hadley's love of the visual arts. She took her time in front of paintings, studying light and shadow, marveling at how brushstrokes and color could make elements like buttons and cloth folds appear fully three-dimensional.

When Hadley's father came to New York at Christmastime, it was clear to Hadley that things weren't right between her parents. A few months later, Jana confirmed that she and Fred were splitting up. Hadley was upset, but by the next morning, she'd resolved that all three of them would be happier if her parents weren't together. She continued to thrive in New York. Her world expanded with the exposure to art and music; she felt she grew and matured more than in any other year of her childhood. By the time she and her mother returned to Missoula, lying and taking things from her friends had become a thing of the past.

The summer Hadley turned thirteen, Jana accepted a two-year teaching position at Kumamoto University in Japan. Hadley was nervous about leaving Missoula again, but gave herself a pep talk: "Hadley, you need to go into this as a blank slate. You need to be flexible and do whatever you can to learn about this new culture and blend in."

In a matter of days after arriving in Japan, Hadley was attending a public school where she was the only American student. She didn't speak a word of Japanese, and halfway through her first day, she realized she was wearing her uniform's skirt backwards—mortifying for a thirteen-year-old. Her first few months in Japan were much like other times she'd had to adjust to a foreign place, but now that she was a teenager, the separation from her Missoula friends felt unbearable.

By her second year in Japan, Hadley had become fluent in Japanese and had picked up all the mannerisms of a Japanese girl. She played the flute in the Kumamoto Youth Symphony and studied piano. Though she was occasionally homesick, she was mostly happy and savored her independence. Meanwhile, Jana fell in love with Charlie, a fellow Missoulan who was doing an exchange professorship in Japan, and they were married in a garden later that year.

When Hadley, Jana, and Charlie moved back to Missoula two years later, Hadley found she had to adjust to yet another culture, this time her own. She was a shy ninth grader who'd learned at her Japanese school that submissiveness was respectful. Gradually, though, as she moved through high school, she became more confident and social. She poured herself into music, joining the school band and orchestra. Her senior year, she decided to trade some of her musical activities for art classes, which she loved.

When it came time to apply to college, there was no question in Hadley's mind that after all the moving around she'd done, she would attend the University of Montana in Missoula. There, she shed the remains of her shy self and took full advantage of all college had to offer. An accomplished pianist, she had always believed she would become a musician, but her burgeoning interest in visual art compelled her to switch her major from music to fine arts.

As she worked through her art degree, Hadley found she struggled with how to use color and did everything she could to avoid painting, settling on a concentration in sculpture. The summer after her freshman year, she traveled to visit Charlie, who was spending time in Japan. The trip inspired her to live there again. She was especially excited about the possibility of continuing her art studies in Japan, where she knew she would receive excellent instruction in technique and form. The next year, the University of Montana awarded her a scholarship to study sculpture at Kumamoto University for her junior year.

At the University, Hadley sculpted clay figures and busts that she cast in plaster. The plaster forms would then be cast in epoxy resin, a material that could be painted to look like any material—wood, marble, or bronze. Looking back, Hadley shakes her head at the hours she spent working without a mask, breathing the resin's toxic fumes. It's hard for her not to wonder whether this known toxin is at the root of her neurological disease.

Hadley spent much of that year in Japan traveling, revisiting Nagasaki and Hiroshima, which had haunted her since being there with classmates as a teen. Jana and Charlie were spending the year in the Czech Republic, and Hadley visited them, traveling to Plezn and Prague as well as to Terezin, where she was moved by an exhibit of drawings and poems created by children in the concentration camps during the war.

The exhibits inspired her senior art thesis for the University of Montana, The Children's Peace Crane Project. Working with the idea that cranes are a symbol of peace, she had children from Japan, Montana, and Europe fold 50,000 paper cranes, which she strung on hundreds of strands to form the walls of an 8'x12' room. Six "story boxes" displayed stories and poems written by children from around the world who had been victims of violent conflict. When Hadley talks about The Children's Peace Crane Project, she glows with excitement and pride.

The summer before she left for Japan, Hadley had met John Ferguson, a law student at the University of Montana. They stayed in touch, he visited her in Japan, and they fell in love. John finished law school and spent another year at the University to complete a master's degree in environmental studies, while Hadley finished her senior year. In 1999, after graduation, they moved to Portland, Oregon, John's hometown.

In Portland, Hadley applied for a job at McMenamin's, a company that owns hotels, breweries, pubs, and theaters in Oregon. The company employed a team of artists who were painting its buildings with scenes depicting the histories of the areas where they were located. Hadley, who considered herself a sculptor, not a painter, was delighted when she was hired. At McMenamin's, she learned how to paint and discovered she was very good at it.

In 2001, a little over a year after Hadley had started working for McMenamin's, she and John moved back to Missoula, where they were married. Hadley built her business as a freelance artist and in 2005 received a commission to paint seven murals illustrating the history of Missoula on the exterior wall of a prominent downtown building. She was thrilled with the opportunity to create a work of significance for the city where she'd grown up. After that project, her commissions increased, and she enjoyed a consistent flow of work and income.

In 2006, Hadley and John's daughter, Sarah, was born, marking a turning point in Hadley's life. In the personal history she wrote for me, she observed:

> Having Sarah brought perspective. My focus
> was no longer on John and my needs, dreams,
> and plans. She meant more than all the other
> things in our life, and I would do anything to
> make sure she had all the love and support we
> could give her. In the past, I might have been
> able to smile or ignore things that made me
> upset or uncomfortable, but once I had Sarah,
> I was no longer passive. She needed me to be
> strong. She made me a better person.

The change in perspective that Sarah's birth gave Hadley resonated with my experience when my children were born. For those who faced circumstances that made us guarded and hypervigilant as children, becoming a parent offers a chance to love fearlessly with an open heart. In her last sentences, Hadley also revealed that she welcomed a new imperative to be strong, to stand up for herself in ways she hadn't in the past. I was struck by the potency of this sentiment since it seemed to me she'd been remarkably resilient and independent as a young girl. I wondered whether there were other forces in her life that had contributed to her feeling weak, passive, and like "a complicated case."

It turned out Hadley had another, more difficult, story to recount—one lying between the lines of the one she'd written down for me.

FIVE:
EVERY BODY TELLS A STORY

Anyone can dash off an account of their childhood, told in hindsight with gratitude for the opportunities and challenges that helped them grow. But to convey not only what we've done and where we've been but also who we are, we sometimes need also to tell the history that's lodged in our bodies. Hadley's history is short—a mere thirty-nine years, but the story of her body is long, packed with plot twists and mystery.

At the end of their year in the Czech Republic, Hadley, Jana, and Fred returned to their house in Missoula. Showering one day when she was five, Hadley became very dizzy, and her ears started ringing. Bright spots danced before her eyes, then she slipped into darkness and fainted. This was the first of about a dozen fainting episodes she would experience throughout her life, events that doctors considered to be unrelated to the pulmonary stenosis that had been surgically corrected.

Hadley experienced many periods of feeling unwell while growing up. Because her pediatrician often made her feel as if she was wasting her time, she was embarrassed when she went to see her for health problems like recurring gastrointestinal distress. In her twenties, when Hadley was having trouble breathing one day, she debated all day and night whether to go to the doctor, worried she might seem like a hypochondriac. When she finally went in, her doctor took an x-ray that revealed a collapsed lung—the result of a powerful reaction to a pain medication she'd taken after her recent wisdom teeth extraction. "I guess you really do have something going on," the doctor said, seeming to confirm for Hadley that the doctor had usually disbelieved her.

Also, in her twenties, Hadley developed daily abdominal cramping that was so intense it would stop her in her tracks. For more than a year, she shuttled between doctors, most of whom told her the pain could be attributed to being young and female. She'd begun to feel that once again, she might be making a big deal out of nothing when a doctor finally discovered a cyst on her fallopian tube as well as other small, benign growths on her ovaries. After he surgically removed them, Hadley remained pain-free for about a year before the cramps returned. She was frustrated and still exhausted by the year of appointments leading up to surgery and had assumed the cyst removal would've taken care of the problem. She didn't return to her doctors, deciding the pain would be easier to cope with than the humiliation of being made to feel she was overreacting.

While Hadley was pregnant with Sarah, the cramps went completely away, confirming in her mind that they had been real. But her pregnancy was not easy. Eight weeks before her due date, she experienced abdominal pain that she downplayed at her doctor's appointment. When her doctor discovered she was in preterm labor, she was admitted to the hospital. By the next day, the contractions had stopped. Hadley was discharged and put on bed rest for a week. She had a painting commission due, a large wall piece that involved carving designs in wood pieces and then painting them. She brought all the pieces to bed with her and carved for days, leaving wood shavings in the sheets. This determination to honor her commitments is one of Hadley's strongest character traits and one that has persisted through her toughest times.

The first day Hadley was allowed to get out and walk around, she was gripped by a cramp more excruciating than any she'd had; this time, she was certain she needed to go to the hospital. The pain turned out to be a kidney stone, which she passed the next morning. She was given a dose of pain medication, and when she got home the same day, she began to have the breathing difficulty she'd experienced years earlier when her lung collapsed. Worried that the medication had triggered the same reaction, she stopped it. She waited three days for her breathing to correct itself, telling herself not to worry because she'd learned that at the end of a pregnancy people commonly experience breathing problems. When her breathing didn't improve, she finally went to the ER, where they discovered she was experiencing mild congestive heart failure. It turned out that Hadley's history of pulmonary stenosis made her vulnerable because, during pregnancy, a woman's blood volume increases by nearly 50%. The extra plasma was overburdening her heart.

From then on in her pregnancy, Hadley was closely monitored. She was induced ten days early and given an epidural so that while she was in labor, her heart wouldn't be further strained. Sarah was born healthy, weighing five pounds and three ounces. Hadley was thrilled. But she'd intended to breastfeed as long as she could, and Sarah had trouble latching on. On top of that, after the birth, Hadley continued to bleed. She convinced herself the bleeding was normal, but at her six-week follow-up, her gynecologist was alarmed and ordered an ultrasound that revealed some of the placenta from the birth had been left behind. After everything Hadley had been through with her pregnancy, hearing she needed yet another procedure to remove the placenta nearly put her over the edge. She was ready to be at home enjoying Sarah.

For the next two years, Hadley's only physical complaint was unrelenting exhaustion. She told herself that it was probably because she had a newborn, then a one-year-old, then a two-year-old. Finally, she rationalized that she was simply getting older.

Hadley would still faint from time to time and since doctors were not concerned, she became nonchalant about it herself, often announcing to the person she was with, "I'm going out now!" Fainting, or vasovagal syncope, is often a symptom of orthostatic hypotension, a sudden drop in heart rate and blood pressure that leads to reduced blood flow to the brain. After an episode in 2008 when Hadley had been "out" for an alarming forty minutes, she underwent a tilt table test to diagnose the cause of her fainting. For this test, a patient is outfitted with monitors to track vital signs, including heart rate and blood pressure, then strapped to a table that tilts until they feel lightheaded or faint. Typically, a patient will feel symptomatic from the tilting around the twenty-five-minute mark; it took Hadley only eleven minutes. Her heart rate in the moment before she fainted fell from eighty-five to sixty-two beats per minute and then plunged into the twenties. Once she was out, there was an interval of six seconds when there was no heartbeat. Her blood pressure dropped drastically, from 108 to 60. A delta of thirty is considered significant orthostatic hypotension, and Hadley's proved to be extreme. She was advised to stay well hydrated, increase her salt intake, and be careful when rising from a sitting or lying position.

In 2009, when Sarah was three, Hadley's obstetrician reassured her that she could try for another baby. A couple of bad viruses that fall deterred her, and then, during a family vacation, she developed severe sciatica. An x-ray showed she had degenerative disc disease, and she was prescribed physical therapy. When the therapy didn't help, and she noticed her right leg was dragging, the PT suggested she have a neurological workup. By the end of November, she'd lost twenty pounds with no change in her eating or exercise habits. Her hands were falling asleep while she was working, and she was experiencing tingling, otherwise known as paresthesia, in various parts of her body. Occasionally, she would drop objects for no apparent reason. She began having difficulty with fine motor movements.

In January 2010, Hadley had her first appointment with Dr. Sherry Reid, a neurologist in Missoula who would prove to be a loyal, dedicated advocate for Hadley throughout her medical ordeal. Dr. Reid immediately made Hadley feel she'd be well cared for, telling her, "You've come to the right place." She ordered a lumbar puncture and MRI tests to rule out diseases like multiple sclerosis. When the results were normal, Hadley and Dr. Reid agreed she should go to The Mayo Clinic in Arizona, where she had extensive blood work, underwent a spinal tap, brain and spine MRIs, CT scans, nerve conduction studies, and electromyography. All tests appeared normal, with the exception of brisk reflexes or hyperreflexia, including a positive Babinski reflex. A Babinksi reflex occurs when the bottom of the foot is stroked, the big toe extends upwards, and the other toes fan out. In young children (<2 years of age), it can be normal since the brain and spinal cord are not fully developed. In an adult, it's a sign of damage to the nerve paths connecting the brain and spinal cord. Hyperreflexia is manifested by an overactive response to bodily stimuli.

The Mayo Clinic's findings were inconclusive:

> IMPRESSION/REPORT/PLAN: Multiple symptoms with no evidence of organic neurologic disease. Her hyperreflexia does not likely reflect central nervous system disease. It is longstanding and can be seen in persons who are anxious. At this time, I have recommended that she resume low-impact exercise, maintain a well-balanced diet, and address any potential stressors that could worsen her physical condition. She could also potentially benefit from a referral to an occupational therapist for improvement of hand strength and coordination.

The Mayo Clinic neurologist's suggestion that anxiety and stress might be causing Hadley's symptoms demoralized her. She returned to Missoula, devastated that she still didn't know what was wrong with her. To make matters worse, she sensed that some people around her thought she was imagining her illness and that she needed to stop seeking help and get on with her life.

For many people, health issues consume a huge amount of time and energy and occupy a lot of psychic space. Patients with complicated health histories get road-weary as they recount these histories over and over to doctors. And sadly, doctors are not immune to tuning out when the history begins to read like an epic war story. But Dr. Reid, Hadley's neurologist in Missoula, never stopped believing Hadley was suffering from an organic disease process happening in her body and not merely anxious. After The Mayo Clinic evaluation, at their next appointment, she surprised Hadley by having her perform the same neurological drill I was put through by the general neurologist. She noticed Hadley's dragging gait, the telltale Parkinson's cogwheel rigidity when manipulating Hadley's arm, and how she didn't swing her right arm when she walked.

"Hadley," Dr. Reid said, "I think we've been going about this the wrong way. Maybe you have Parkinson's disease."

Hadley was shocked—she was so young! Like me, she thought Parkinson's was a disease for older people, like her stepfather Charlie, who'd just been diagnosed the year before. She was prescribed levodopa to take for a week, as I had been. Right away, the levodopa significantly boosted her energy, a change that confirmed she was dopamine deficient and suggested she might be dealing with Parkinson's.

There was not a single movement disorders specialist in Montana, so Dr. Reid referred Hadley to an MDS in another state. At first, because Hadley was so young, Dr. Youngman suspected Hadley had Munchausen Syndrome, a serious psychological disorder in which a patient pretends to be sick or injured to get attention. (Fortunately, he didn't tell her about this concern until over a year later.) After examining her, however, Dr. Youngman seemed to easily confirm Dr. Reid's diagnosis of Parkinson's.

Hadley remembers crying in her car after the appointment, both because, in her words, "I felt Parkinson's was the true answer" and because she didn't know how to break the news to her mother, who was still adjusting to Charlie's PD diagnosis. Hadley's family members were distressed but supportive and relieved that her years of searching were over.

For Hadley, the diagnosis marked a new start: She would no longer be preoccupied with what was ailing her or spinning with self-doubt about the validity of her illness. Instead of facing a life-threatening condition that could prevent her from seeing Sarah grow up, she saw her life stretching out before her, however imperfectly. At last, she could direct her energy outward with a sense of purpose as a mother, wife, daughter, friend, and artist.

SIX:
FIGHT OR FLIGHT

I n 1969, Swiss-American psychiatrist Elizabeth Kubler-Ross introduced the hypothesis that people, when faced with a terrible diagnosis, will often pass through five emotional stages: denial, anger, bargaining, depression, and acceptance. A scientist in our Parkinson's Facebook group, Sara Riggare, has come up with another version of the stages of grief that describes the pro-activeness I associate with my friends with PD: shock (at hearing the news); sorrow (mourning the future you won't have); searching (for information); sharing (supporting your patient community); and shaping (creating a new future for yourself).

Judging by how quickly Hadley embraced her diagnosis and reached out to contribute to the PD cause, it would appear that she arrived at Rigarre's sharing and shaping stages almost immediately. Perhaps because she had dealt with disturbing symptoms for years, she'd already experienced denial, anger, depression, shock, and sorrow before getting her diagnosis. We know she often was forced into denial about her illness because of the inconclusive, sometimes dismissive, feedback she received from doctors. Denial sometimes worked to manage her fear. When not in denial, she experienced depression not only because she lacked the energy she needed for work and family but also because she knew something was very wrong with her health. She'd had a painfully long time to contemplate worst-case scenarios, so when she learned she had PD, it was hardly a shock. Instead of thinking, "why me?"—the question that would inevitably come up in Kubler-Ross's anger stage, Hadley considered herself lucky that it wasn't a more terrible disease.

Something besides the ordeal of her diagnosis allowed Hadley to arrive quickly at acceptance: the resilience that is both part of her nature and was nurtured by her life experience. As she bounced between cultures, Hadley learned to observe and adjust to new situations, memorizing details that would help her fit in and focusing on positive experiences to maximize her comfort. She learned to accept frightening and unhappy experiences as a teenager, deeming them "character builders." And then there was her body: How can we measure the long-term emotional (let alone physical) impact of open-heart surgery, a collapsed lung, or congestive heart failure? To the majority of us who've never fainted, it seems impossible that a person could become so familiar with passing out that she could joke about it. Coping with the traumas affecting most of Hadley's vital organs would require a robust relationship with fear. By the time she was in her twenties, she had developed a strong survival instinct, having learned, like a creature in the wild, to appear strong in times of weakness. Striving to rise above her physical and emotional challenges has clearly served Hadley's aspirations for a full and remarkably productive life.

There's a cost to armoring up your already injured being, as Hadley had been doing for a long time. I learned this when

I was forty-three, just a few years older than Hadley, during the relentlessly rainy winter of 1998 that put figure skater Tara Lipinski and Washington intern Monica Lewinsky on the world stage. The insomnia that had been chronic since my mid-twenties had become acute; I had gastrointestinal problems, and my muscles burned. Despite consuming twice as much food as my six-foot-three husband, I was unable to gain much-needed weight and was plagued with a deep, gnawing hunger. Some days, it was tough to even push a cart around the supermarket.

I told my new primary care physician, who seemed more thorough than my old one that I believed years of sleep deprivation had finally caused me to "crash." She was skeptical, and when every blood test she ordered came back normal, she declared that I was "as healthy as a horse." She added, smiling almost playfully, "Rest assured that insomnia has never killed anyone." I had heard this refrain before, and now it rang even more brutally false. She prescribed an anti-anxiety medication for sleep that didn't help me sleep and made me depressed, and then we were finished. There was nothing more she could do.

I consulted a sleep specialist who educated me about "sleep hygiene." I followed his instructions faithfully: Never do anything but sleep or have sex in your bed, make the room dark, don't watch TV or have stimulating conversations before bed, exercise, and get plenty of daylight beginning first thing in the morning. The most frustrating rule of good sleep hygiene was "don't nap during the day." It made me want to cry—I hadn't been able to nap in twenty years. Maybe if I could nap, I thought to myself, I wouldn't have a sleep problem. Oh, to be able to attain the divine sensation of sleepiness! In fact, the more tired I was, the more awake I felt. In bed at night, I had a buzz, as if an engine were keeping me hovering just above my mattress.

For my digestive problems, I saw a gastroenterologist who told me I had irritable bowel syndrome (IBS) that would be fixed by eating more fiber. The added fiber, the kind that you stir into orange juice, made me feel like I'd ingested steel wool. Over two decades of seeking help for poor sleep and digestion, I had heard the one-size-fits-all prescriptions "fiber" and "sleep hygiene" so many times that they triggered a silent primal scream.

Later, after I was diagnosed with Parkinson's, I would learn that sleep and G.I. disorders often precede a PD diagnosis by more than a decade. At the time, though, I was scared. If I couldn't sleep and couldn't process food properly, how would I stay alive?

I had a loving and helpful husband, wonderful family and friends, two sweet kids, and access to the best healthcare in San Francisco. Because Lewis and I owned our architecture firm, I had a very flexible work situation. But with no doctor to guide me, I had no idea what I should do to get well. For more than a year, I awoke with one question: How will I take care of my children? I worked hard to hide my struggle from them, rising to fix breakfast before school and maintaining a cheerful countenance after school until they went to bed. I thought I was putting on a pretty good charade until one morning at breakfast when our eleven-year-old burst into tears. I hugged her and asked her what was wrong, even though I was pretty sure I knew.

"I'm afraid you'll die," she sobbed.

Although I felt as if I might, in fact, be dying, I remember how at-the-ready my protective instincts were, and how easily I called up my most reassuring tone. "No, no," I told her. "I'm not going to die. I promise."

Since no doctor could find a reason to think I was even sick, I felt fairly secure in my promise even though my body was telling me otherwise. Without a name to call my illness, though, I worried about how to explain it to friends and family. To make matters worse, the medication my doctor had prescribed didn't help me sleep and created a new problem: rebound anxiety. I became plagued with the fear that my intractable insomnia and G.I. problems were symptoms of a mental illness that I wasn't strong enough to overcome. A generation before, would what I was going through have been called a "nervous breakdown"—words gossiped across suburban fences? I tried to calm myself by meditating, but no amount of listening to "loving myself, healing myself" tapes could persuade me to feel compassionate toward my body. It had stolen my life for no medically apparent reason.

Then, like a miracle, I found a therapist who seemed to be compassion personified. He grasped immediately the seriousness of my illness, offering me not only a safe place to expose the enormity of my fear and distress but also practical solutions. He referred me to a psychiatrist who prescribed Remeron, a medication that only just the year before had been approved by the FDA. For me, Remeron was a magic bullet for both insomnia and IBS. My therapist also recommended an integrative medicine doctor. It was the 1990s, the decade in which integrative medicine began to gain legitimacy in the U.S. The new approach emphasized treating the whole person rather than just a disease, using traditional Western medicine in combination with selective alternative therapies to promote wellness.

Integrative medicine acknowledges that if a person feels unwell, they *are* unwell. Whereas my primary care physician looked past my wraithlike appearance and wasn't concerned when I told her I felt like I was wasting away, my integrative doctor listened carefully to everything I described and told me, "You're seriously depleted, and things in your body have gotten out of balance." He went on to explain that the sympathetic nervous system uses energy to keep us vigilant and responsive to emergencies, speeding up heart rate, increasing blood pressure, and stopping digestion. In contrast, the parasympathetic system works to counter the sympathetic system, kicking in when we're eating, sleeping, or meditating to help the body relax and conserve energy.

"Your sympathetic system is in overdrive, and your parasympathetic system is unable to counter it. You're stuck in emergency 'fight or flight' mode, causing inflammation, insomnia, and anxiety. And the understandable fear you feel about what's happening to you is further fueling your sympathetic nervous system."

Fight or flight. He'd nailed it! His explanation made visceral sense to me: a bird, terrified and in the crosshairs of a powerful predator—my insomnia. He told me that it had taken me years to drive my body into this state and it would therefore take years for me to heal, but he was going to help me every step of the way. He launched an exhaustive study of my hormones and gut bacteria, tweaking them with medicine and supplements to restore balance. Very gradually, with his steady accompaniment, my health vastly improved. After a couple of years, I began to feel I could count on my body to be strong enough to support my busy life; my body, in turn, could rely on me to know how to take care of it.

This was doctoring at its very best. I would argue that the first step in healing is feeling confident that you will be listened to and cared for. Although all of us are grateful to be living in an age when most diseases are understood, technologies are advanced, and treatments are plentiful, we sometimes still wish for the days we've read about when the village doctor knew and attended to his patients almost like family. Most patients don't expect medical miracles from their doctors. Still, they do hope for basic assurances from them.

1) I believe you when you tell me you are sick.

2) I don't know yet what's ailing you, but I will do my best to find out and am going to share with you everything I learn.

3) even if I can't reach a precise diagnosis, I'm going to help you because I care about your health.

Because of this positive experience with my integrative physician, I was frustrated ten years later when he didn't take a more investigative approach to my neurological symptoms. In retrospect, I realized I'd come up against his limitations. He had told me early on that he'd suffered on and off for years from chronic fatigue syndrome; this no doubt drove his career as an expert on CFS and related conditions like mine. While he was able to stand in my shoes when I presented with symptoms he recognized, when I came to him with neurological abnormalities, instead of explaining that he didn't know how to help, he defaulted to a paternalistic mode, telling me I was anxious about nothing.

Once, Hadley was a fellow Parkie and a kindred spirit; after she told me her health history, I understood we shared much more. Growing up, we both suffered a kind of emotional and physical erosion that we worked very hard to keep from interfering with our lives. But it's true of everyone that however well we've coped or covered up, whatever rational sense we've made of our histories and whatever we believe we've made peace with, our experiences have shaped who we are physiologically. Conversely, the bodies we are given help define who we are. How different a person is who's never suffered a serious or chronic illness, whose body has never made them feel weak, ashamed, or afraid, from the many of us whose bodies speak loudly to us on most days! The able-bodied can be tempted to accuse people like me of being too attentive to our bodies, as if they're children we're spoiling. But I know this: like a child, when your body steps out of the room with a smile and no complaint, allowing you to turn your attention elsewhere, you're thrilled to let it go.

I felt my friendship with Hadley deepen. I understood now that the pharmacologist at the party who'd questioned her Parkinson's diagnosis had struck at the muck of doubt she still carried from a lifetime of feeling unseen by doctors. I saw vulnerability beneath her cheerful acceptance of her diagnosis. It was as if she was waiting for the other shoe to drop. Was her tentativeness just a habit? I wondered. Had she moved past acceptance into another stage of grief called "doubt"? I wanted to reassure her. Because I'm twenty-one years older, I imagined I could help protect her from more uncertainty by advocating for her in ways I hadn't known how to for my younger self.

SEVEN:

DRUGS AND OTHER AGENTS

"**H**ave you been gambling or wanting sex constantly? Cleaning closets or shopping obsessively?" Dr. Bright asked me. "Sorry," he added, smiling. "I have to ask."

I laughed. There's a freshness and sincerity about Dr. Bright, as if he might feel his patients are the best thing about his work.

For a year following my diagnosis, my Parkinson's symptoms didn't bother me enough to treat them with medication. When I was finally ready to get some relief for my bradykinesia (slowness) and awkward gait, Dr. Bright thoroughly explained the treatment options, which mainly involve replenishing the brain's dwindling supply of dopamine with one or both of two types of medications. Often, the first line of defense is a dopamine agonist, which activates dopamine receptors in the brain that would normally be stimulated by one's own dopamine. In effect, it tricks the brain into thinking it's getting the dopamine it needs. Levodopa, the gold standard medication that every PD patient ends up taking sooner or later, is a chemical that's converted into dopamine by the central nervous system. Developed in the 1960s, it's considered to be one of the most important breakthroughs in the history of medicine. Because levodopa alone often causes nausea, it's always combined with carbidopa, which prevents levodopa from breaking down in the bloodstream so that more of it can reach the brain. On levodopa, a patient can enjoy many hours a day without symptoms like tremor, gait disturbance, and rigidity—and they might experience a sense of rejuvenation. Many describe the change in how they feel on the drug as "miraculous." In fact, without it, someone with advanced Parkinson's can be unable to take a step or even rise from a chair. The medication must be taken multiple times a day to keep symptoms at bay and more and more is needed as Parkinson's progresses. Unfortunately, there's a downside to levodopa: Prolonged use can bring on dyskinesia, spontaneous and sometimes relentless involuntary movements that can look like swaying, jerking, or writhing. People often mistake this movement as a symptom of the disease itself, but it's actually a side effect of levodopa that can be as disabling as the PD itself. In a small minority of people, dyskinesia can begin relatively quickly after beginning levodopa therapy. For this reason, many patients choose to delay taking it, relying on the dopamine agonists for as long as possible.

During our medication discussion, Dr. Bright and I settled on the dopamine agonist Mirapex. I asked if he was going to prescribe Azilect, the medication that the MDS who had diagnosed me had recommended. I expressed my concern about having to stop taking Remeron, the drug that had brought my insomnia under control twelve years earlier but which was contraindicated with Azilect. Dr. Bright swiveled his chair to face his laptop, pulled up the results of a study on Azilect, and carefully explained the graphs to me. "The results of the Azilect study are contradictory," he said.

"It seems unlikely that Azilect slows PD progression as we'd hoped. There's no reason for you to stop taking the Remeron in order to take Azilect." I was enormously relieved since, by that point, insomnia had been much more of a monster in my life than PD. I also appreciated Dr. Bright's respectful willingness to share the medical science with me.

Now, sitting in Dr. Bright's exam room months after starting Mirapex, I thought about his odd questions about sex and shopping. I knew that obsessive behavior was not an uncommon side effect of the drug. I told him that the Mirapex helped me walk normally. It also energized me mentally, and I was enjoying productive work on my novel, *Dream House*, which I was revising for the third—or was it the fourth or fifth time? "No," I told him. "No obsessive behavior."

But in truth, I was obsessed. I'd been working on the novel on and off for seven years. I had abandoned practicing architecture for something that felt more compelling and immediately gratifying: writing a work of fiction about a woman who practiced architecture. What did I know about writing a novel when I began? Nothing. But I believed I had a good story, that I was the only one who could tell it, and that I had to tell it. I took classes to support my new passion, joined one writing group and then another so I could get the feedback I needed to fuel me. For the first few years of writing, I had no aspirations to publish; it was fulfilling enough just to write. But after a couple of years, the story bulked up and became more refined. It began to have the shape of a book.

I was so infatuated with writing that when I was diagnosed with Parkinson's, one of my first thoughts was that being able to walk might be overrated. If I became housebound and frozen in my chair because of Parkinson's, so what? I could still be a writer. (This was before I learned that Parkinson's patients have a higher risk of developing dementia.) Two months before I was diagnosed, I had joined a writing group in which everyone but me had published one or two novels. Listening to their publishing tales, learning from their insightful critiques, and high on their encouragement, I began to allow myself to imagine my novel on a bookshelf. I had a dream. It felt huge. It made my Parkinson's seem like a puny troll beneath a bridge.

During my six months on Mirapex, I showed up at my computer every day, burying myself in the fictional world I'd created. Writers are disciplined and must be determined and at least a little obsessive to revise, revise, revise, and then revise again, never knowing whether their work will ever matter to anyone but them. It didn't occur to me at the time that Mirapex was contributing to my drive. But I was acutely aware that the medication had brought back the insomnia I'd mostly licked ten years earlier, even though I was still taking the Remeron. My exhaustion made it nearly impossible to exercise and socialize. With the guidance of a psychiatrist, I tried eight different supplements and medications for sleep, but none could counteract the powerful stimulation of Mirapex. I was wilted and bleary-eyed, yet during those months I felt blissfully drunk on the narrative of my novel.

In April of 2011, my writing group agreed my manuscript was ready to send to literary agents, and I sent it out to six, having no idea what to expect. Awake at 4:30 the next morning, I checked my email and was flabbergasted to find a message from an agent who said he'd been up until 3 a.m. reading and that my book was "really quite astonishing," and he would be in touch soon. I lay vibrating in bed, waiting for an acceptable time to crow the news to Lewis.

"I told you it's a great book," he said in that confident, sunny way of his.

The agent finished reading the next day and emailed to ask when we could meet. I asked if we could wait a week so I'd have the chance to hear from other agents. He was accommodating, and I alerted the agents that I'd had a show of interest so they'd read my manuscript sooner rather than later.

A few days later, on Mother's Day, blitzed from sleeplessness but high on hopefulness, I was weeding our daughter's bureau drawers, perhaps subconsciously seeking a way to re-experience motherhood while my children were living far away at college. My phone rang with a number I didn't recognize. Since it never occurred to me that an agent would call instead of emailing, I was unprepared for what happened next: a swooning, theatrical bid from the highest profile agent in the group to whom I'd sent my novel. She was calling from a cab in New York City, she said, on her way to lunch with (insert name of famous author here), "but I just wanted to tell you how much I love your book! It just screams FILM!"

Lewis could tell from the other room that I was having a stressful, though clearly not unhappy, conversation and appeared outside the bedroom. I gave him the thumbs up and closed the door. I needed to concentrate. Now, the agent was telling me how the descriptions in *Dream House* reminded her of the Edward Hopper show she'd just seen at the Metropolitan Museum. Where was she going with this, and why was she laying it on so thick? I wondered. After a full fifteen minutes of effervescing about her upcoming vacation in Maine, she delivered the punch line: "I've only read the first hundred pages, but Lila, my colleague, has read the whole thing, and she thinks it's terrific, and the two of us share a sensibility. I'm sure you know I've been in the business a long, long time, and I know what I like and what I like sells, and so if you're ready, Catherine, I'm ready to sign you on."

Blindsided! I tried to think. In two weeks, she said, she'd be on a long flight home from her vacation, and she expected to finish reading my novel then, but if I could commit to a contract now since she was there in The City for the next few days, she'd like to pitch *Dream House* to a few publishers. "So, what do you say?"

I felt a little dizzy, walking circles in my daughter's small bedroom. Did agents take on books they hadn't even finished reading? On the other hand, the other agent in her company, Lila, seemed to have fallen in love with *Dream House*. Was it possible I'd written a "hot" book without realizing it? I doubted it; it's a quiet novel, more water than fire. One hundred pages—what could this agent know about the story? Then again, I reasoned, she must know what she's doing. She's an expert.

I was confused, the way I had been when doctors were telling me, "Catherine, there's nothing wrong with you." How I wanted to believe them! The agent's gushing offer of representation felt like another dare to hope for something, even as a false note played in my head.

Sleep-starved and overwhelmed, I was in no shape to make snap decisions. But I wanted to throw caution to the wind, to let this powerful agent take *Dream House* into the world.

EIGHT:
FALLING AND FLYING

Journalist and documentary filmmaker Dave Iverson, who has Parkinson's, has described it as a disease of subtraction. It takes things away from you one by one— your arm swing, your walk, your balance, your smile, your voice. Because of this unstoppable subtraction, he's said, you need to keep adding things into your life.

By the time the effusive literary agent reached me on the phone that Mother's Day, I knew very well what I needed to add into my life: the publication of *Dream House*. I would never have said this out loud before publication began to seem possible; the stakes were too high.

As she waited for me to respond to her offer of representation, I drew a deep but silent breath. "Yes, okay," I told her.

"Terrific! I can already picture the cover for it! What do you think—one of those quintessential New England porches? Could you get some headshots taken? And we'll need a synopsis of the novel. Lila will contact you to work on manuscript revisions. My business manager will send you a contract. Please get that signed as soon as possible. I'll be in touch in about two weeks when I've finished reading. Oh, one more thing—how old are you, dear?"

"Fifty-six," I said. After an awkward little silence, I added, "I know. Not a typical age for a debut."

"Well, that's okay," she said. I felt the first twinge of regret and thought: Wait until she finds out about the Parkinson's.

When I hung up, I was almost afraid to open the door of my daughter's room. After years of crafting my book in the safety of my house-cocoon, I felt like both of us, my book and I, were stepping out onto the freeway.

The agent's contract arrived three days later, thirteen pages of the most byzantine language I'd ever read. The lawyer I showed it to was astonished by its overreach and negotiated for two weeks with the agent's business manager. Lila and I had several delightful and productive editing conversations. Everything seemed to be on track; still, while my lips formed utterances of excitement when family and friends congratulated me, inside, I restrained myself from celebrating.

"If it's too good to be true, it probably isn't," the adage goes. Two weeks later, right on schedule, I received my manuscript from the agent with the comments she'd made during her flight home. Reading through the notes, I knew immediately that she regretted having taken me on. Her notes had a lilt of disappointment—"I'm afraid... Honestly, this is just..." as if she felt I'd made a promise to her in the first 100 pages and had broken it in the remaining 220. Among other things, she'd hoped it was a book about sisters. It wasn't. Within a few days, I learned the magnitude of the problem: She'd disagreed ("very rare," she noted) with Lila to the degree that she couldn't let Lila work with me to "fix all the problems." She recommended I hire an independent editor. "And then, Catherine dear, I truly hope you will let us see it again."

I could spend a paragraph breaking out all the special little horrors contained in the agent's kiss-off, but I'll focus on its basic capriciousness: We had a contract! Did a contract that had attempted to claim the rights to all of my creative work, whether a book or a building, for fifty years after my death exempt her from any responsibility to me? A couple of months later, I would ask to be released from our contract. Because even if I could revise the manuscript to her satisfaction—difficult considering she wouldn't comment on what she wanted from the book—I realized I'd lost all respect for her. She'd behaved sleazily by making a pre-emptive strike on my book, grabbing it before the other agents had a chance to finish reading it.

Now, I had to come to terms with the fact that my book, which had "screamed film," had failed in some major way. It had attempted its first flight from the nest only to splat below the tree.

The black cloud of Parkinson's disease hovered over me, blotting out the beacon of my book.

Having a degenerative disease lends a melodramatic quality to life's twists and turns that might otherwise feel par for the course. I was aware that my feelings of failure were out of proportion and premature, based on one unfortunate encounter. But I heard the loud ticking of the clock. Parkinson's was building a kind of cage around me, reducing the space I was taking up. One of the exercise routines prescribed to Parkinson's patients, LSVT BIG, involves repetitively and emphatically thrusting our limbs outward to remind our body how to reclaim that space. Writing and having my work read was another way for me to keep expanding, stretching myself out into the world.

Sitting in Dr. Bright's office, the agent mishegas still fresh, I thought my Mirapex-induced insomnia might just finish me off. Dr. Bright was glad the Mirapex didn't seem to be causing obsessive behavior but was concerned about my pharmaceutical experiments for sleep. Maybe he thought it ironic that the last time I'd seen him, I'd been taking two drugs for insomnia, and since then, I'd been seeing a psychiatrist who'd prescribed several others to try, yet I was afraid of switching from a dopamine agonist to levodopa because of the risk of developing dyskinesia down the road.

"Not everyone develops dyskinesia from levodopa," Dr. Bright told me. "Does it make sense to sacrifice the quality of your life now in hopes that it will guarantee a better quality of life much later? Your life is now. Look at you. You're completely exhausted."

Dr. Bright was right. I needed to sleep now. I stopped the Mirapex and started the levodopa. In three days, I was sleeping as I had been before my diagnosis. Levodopa was so much more effective than the Mirapex for my symptoms that I felt years younger. And just in time. I needed all the help I could get to salvage my confidence and get back on track with my writing.

Hadley was also taking Mirapex, but unlike me, she'd made friends with her wakeful life. Her career as an artist was thriving. Her paintings were represented by galleries in both Missoula and Portland, Oregon, and Missoula was graced with more and more of her work as she continued to take commissions for murals in public spaces. She'd completed murals for a pancake parlor, a sushi restaurant, a pub, a juice bar, a medical research office, and the Fort Missoula Historical Museum, among others. Also finished was her largest work to date, the Heart of Missoula Murals, seven paintings of historic Missoula covering 2400 square feet of the Allegra Print and Imaging building's exterior. The murals depict the development of Missoula's railroad, the founding of the University of Montana, and the city's industrial beginnings in the early 1900s.

The paintings that best represent Hadley's work are mostly Montana scenes. Her collectors are struck by how powerfully she captures the shapes, light, and colors of the Western landscape. Soon after she was diagnosed with PD, Hadley considered what it would mean for her art if she lost mobility in her dominant hand, so she decided to make a painting using only her left. The image was of John, Sarah, and herself walking on a woodsy path flooded with warm light and brilliant fall color. Dudley Dana, who has represented Hadley's work at the Dana Gallery in Missoula, said of the piece, "It's absolutely incredible. Just sheer emotion."

Hadley began work on her largest project to date, the Missoula Catholic School Heritage Project, for which she'd create four eight by twelve-foot panels as "a visual representation of the story of pioneering Jesuit priests, innovative Sisters of Providence and dedicated families whose early vision and passion for justice helped shape the landscape of western Montana." In April of 2011, the first two panels were unveiled to great excitement, and Hadley began work on the third.

Founding Summit for Parkinson's and planning the non-profit's first fundraising event were exciting and deeply satisfying for Hadley. Through the organization, she'd made many new friends with and without Parkinson's. Summit's first three-day event in October 2011 was ambitious, including an all-day conference featuring a panel of neurologists and psychologists, workshops on creative movement and expression, and a fundraising art auction and gala. The event raised over $140,000.

Hadley's full life would have been a tremendous amount to juggle mentally and physically for anyone, let alone someone with a degenerative neurological disease. Yet when I talked to her on the phone, she seemed on fire about all she was doing.

"The wacky thing," she laughed, "is that I seem to suddenly only need four or five hours of sleep at night, and I'm not tired. I can get so much done! I finished three paintings last night!"

I'll admit I was a little envious. Mirapex, while keeping me up at night, didn't make me need less sleep. Hadley wasn't alone in her nocturnal bliss. In our Parkinson's Facebook group, there was a gang who regularly posted back and forth at two, three, and four in the morning. One of them, Hadley's and my friend, Karen Jaffe, a physician and mother of three, was always up until the wee hours doing crossword puzzles, sudoku, or even spinning. Like Hadley, she was taking a dopamine agonist. She slept three or four hours each night and claimed that was enough. "It's not that I can't sleep if I go to bed," she explained to me. "I just don't want to sleep." In the 16 years since her diagnosis, Karen has been enormously busy as a physician, mother, and grandmother. She has served for many years on the Michael J. Fox Foundation Patient Council, and she and her husband, Marc, have hosted a highly successful annual fundraiser for PD, "Shaking with Laughter." Since retiring from her medical practice in 2013, Karen has co-founded a non-profit Parkinson's wellness center in Cleveland that offers speaker forums on PD, exercise, and movement programs designed specifically for Parkinson's patients and an in-house Movement Disorders Specialist. I often joke that Karen, a master networker, knows everyone on the international Parkinson's who's-who list.

Even just recounting all that Hadley and Karen have accomplished since their diagnoses leaves me breathless.

When I first got to know them and a few others in our group, I was in awe of and also somewhat mystified by their boundless energy and drive. They're not all Type A's, born athletes or extroverts. But being diagnosed at a young age with a degenerative disease, if it doesn't crush you, can spark a fire under you to make the most of your life. Those with YOPD are also driven by the compelling race to find a cure within our lifetimes. To that end, hosting galas, art auctions, tennis tournaments, Zumbathons, and other events to raise money for PD research became an annual, impassioned undertaking for many in our Facebook group.

There was something about Hadley's and Karen's energy that worried me, though. It had that careening quality associated with machinery built for speed and power—enormously satisfying but likely to damage the machine in the long run.

All of us Parkies were driving under a potent, sometimes seductive, new influence we would rely on for life: dopamine.

NINE:
THE DOPAMINE DIARIES

I n recent years, the brain, with its nearly one hundred billion neurons that make at least one hundred trillion connections, has become hot scientific territory, yet another final frontier. And dopamine, the chemical messenger that becomes depleted in people with Parkinson's, is the media darling, once called "the Kim Kardashian of neurotransmitters" by neuroscientist Vaughn Bell because it's often discussed in the context of risky behavior involving sex, drugs, or gambling. Dopamine stimulates thrill-seeking or addictive behaviors in the brain's reward circuit, which controls a person's response to natural rewards such as social interactions, food, and sex.

Dopamine also acts in four or five other circuits of the brain that profoundly affect functions essential for survival, including motivation and drive, attentiveness, learning, feelings of well-being, and movement. In people with Parkinson's, the brain's motor circuit is the intended target when levodopa and dopamine agonists are prescribed. Ideally, enhanced dopamine availability in Parkinson's patients would only occur in the motor pathways, facilitating movement. But sometimes the effect is not so localized, and some of the agents that are aimed at the motor system will also increase dopamine in the reward system. When this occurs, a person with Parkinson's can experience addictive urges and decreased impulse control; a big dopamine spike in the reward circuit functions as a major motivator for them to "do that again," whatever "that" is. There are many accounts of Parkinson's patients taking dopamine agonists who've developed an addiction to gambling or impulse buying.

Not everyone prone to experiencing dopamine spikes will develop dangerous addictions; a Parkinson's patient might experience the spike as a drive to, for example, stay up all night painting, playing video games, or obsessively cleaning their house. Karen Jaffe is especially familiar with the powerful effect dopamine can have when it wanders into the reward circuit. Her husband Marc, a comedian and humor writer, wrote a play, *Side Effects May Include*, that exaggerated her experience with dopamine to a hilarious degree. Performed in many U.S. cities, the play chronicles the life of a fictional married couple dealing with typical middle-age issues, including a waning interest in sex. When the wife is diagnosed with Parkinson's and begins taking the dopamine agonist Requip, the couple is thrown a curveball—she develops an insatiable libido:

> Before Parkinson's and Requip, there were certain requirements for sex: Work had to be going well, our daughter couldn't need our attention, the house had to be clean, the temperature had to be between 74 and 84 degrees, and I think the Democrats had to control at least one house of Congress.
>
> Now the requisites for sex are: She has to have a job, our daughter has to be alive, the house

has to be standing, the temperature needs to be between 0 and 100 degrees, and the Democrats have to control at least one house of Congress.

And these things happen all the time! The dining table!

The bathroom floor!

A friend's dark patio during a party! The backseat of our Prius!

The front seat of a Prius! We didn't even know whose car it was! All those Priui look alike!

The story, which was also published in *The New York Times*, is funny and brave, reflecting the buoyancy with which Karen and Marc face her disease.

Another intriguing aspect of Parkinson's disease is the impact of dopamine depletion and subsequent dopamine augmentation on creativity. In addition to stimulating reward seeking, dopamine is known to increase novelty seeking, which can be a precursor to creativity. This doesn't mean that more dopamine always equals more creativity. In fact, naturally high dopamine levels are found in people working in less creative fields who are inclined to have lower thought variety, stick to the task at hand, and get things done in a predictable fashion. In problem-solving work, we rely heavily on the dorsolateral prefrontal cortex (DLPFC), the part of the brain responsible for working memory, reasoning, impulse control, and executive function. Creative work involves the default network, the brain region that's active when we're not focused on a specific task and our mind is wandering, generating spontaneous thought. As dopamine goes up, it enhances function in the DLPFC, but it throttles down activity in our default network. (Interestingly, brain

MRIs done on jazz musicians have revealed that when they are improvising, their DLPFCs are deactivated.) Conversely, very creative people with low dopamine levels experience impaired functioning in the DLPFC; they have a hard time deactivating their default network in order to get from point A to point B and finish projects. At the extreme end of the low dopamine spectrum are those whose thoughts are so relentlessly spontaneous and creative that they become chaotic, as in the case of schizophrenia.

Creativity, then, requires a well-balanced brain chemistry—low enough dopamine that the default network can create novelty and high enough that the DLPFC can manage the complexity of creative thoughts so that a person can follow through on their ideas. To turn up productive creativity, theoretically, people who start with a naturally high dopamine state would need to lower their dopamine, and those who start with a low dopamine state—people with bipolar disorder, ADHD, schizophrenia, and Parkinson's, for example, would need to raise their dopamine.

There's no easy way to measure a person's dopamine level, so people who wish to be more creative or better problem solvers aren't running to their doctors asking to have their dopamine levels tweaked! But, studies of those who are treated with dopamine have found that it can often boost creativity and even artistic skill. In some cases, Parkinson's patients have begun to excel at an entirely new creative pursuit. One woman, despite never having written before, became an award-winning poet. In another example, a graphic designer treated for PD made a sudden switch to painting, discovering that the change from tightly controlled, contained work to broad sweeps of the paintbrush not only unleashed a new aspect of his artistic sensibility but also temporarily relieved him of his rigidity, freezing, and tremor.

In other cases, artists treated with dopamine have found themselves working obsessively. A 2014 piece in *The Atlantic Monthly* about creativity and Parkinson's described the experience of a forty-one-year-old woman with PD who, after starting levodopa treatment, developed what her doctors called an addiction to painting:

> Her home became a gathering place for artists, and she began compulsively buying painting materials. She described the spiral earlier this year in a medical journal: "I started painting from morning till night, and often all through the night until morning. I used countless numbers of brushes at a time. I used knives, forks, sponges ... I would gouge open tubes of paint—it was everywhere. But I was still in control at that point. Then, I started painting on the walls, the furniture, and even the washing machine. I would paint any surface I came across. I also had my 'expression wall,' and I could not stop myself from painting and repainting it every night in a trance-like state. My partner could no longer bear it. People close to me realized that I crossed some kind of line into the pathological, and, at their instigation, I was hospitalized. Today, my doctors have succeeded in getting my medication under control, and my creativity has become more tranquil and structured."

A question I asked my Parkinson's Facebook group about whether they'd experienced a spike in creativity since being diagnosed yielded many posts naming a wide variety of artistic pursuits, from publishing a first book to repurposing furniture. One member posted that she'd taken on all kinds of creative endeavors: putting together marketing and advertising campaigns for several non-profits, designing and constructing costumes for several plays, teaching classes on closet makeovers, consulting on interior design, creating photo books for special occasions, and writing poetry. Joe Narciso, an actor in our group who appeared in *Law and Order*, among other TV shows and films, shared his dangerous ride on dopamine medication:

> I was (am) an actor. When I started taking PD meds, I also started writing. I wrote TV shows and actually sold 4. When I started taking Mirapex, I stopped sleeping, gained 50 pounds, and almost ruined my marriage and family. I was so compulsive. About everything. EVERYthing. Added levodopa and Comtan, and my creativity was in overdrive. Still no sleep. I mean, maybe 2 hours a night for eight years, despite trying every sleeping pill and sleep aid out there. My health was a wreck. Falling down stairs. Breathing issues. Apnea. Choking. Weight. Then, I had DBS (deep brain stimulation surgery). I came off meds completely. Lost 40 pounds. No apnea and breathing fine. No choking. No falling. Sleep like a rock EVERY night. Health is way better. Creativity is comparatively non-existent. Obviously, I'll take health. But I miss being so creative.

It's not yet clear to scientists whether a new creative drive is related to the dopamine dysregulation that occurs in people with Parkinson's or is caused by dopamine therapy itself. Perhaps the death of dopamine neurotransmitters in PD patients leaves them in the low-dopamine state typical of highly creative people. It could be that a spike in dopamine reduces their inhibition, making them more inclined to try new things, or makes them better able to follow through on creative ideas that have been percolating but haven't yet been brought to light.

I've wondered whether dopamine was a factor in my career shift from architecture to writing. A very creative field, architecture nonetheless relies heavily on that logical, puzzle-solving area of the brain, the DLPFC. I began to write in earnest in my forties during the year when my health was failing. Because I didn't have the energy to do much more than take care of our two kids, I stopped going to work at the architecture practice Lewis and I shared. There was no question that my DLPFC, and therefore my executive function, were compromised by my illness, but I needed a creative outlet. During those first years of writing, I didn't do the important planning or plotting that goes into a good work of fiction, both because I didn't know what that was yet and because I didn't have the focus. Instead, I spent much of my day at the computer putting words to the images and ideas that floated up from my brain's default network. Sometimes, writing felt so fluid and full of novelty that it was like being in a waking dream state. Years later, with my DLPFC in better shape, I was able to do the hard work of structuring my parade of impressionistic paragraphs into a novel.

I still experience what I now think of as "default network moments." Like most artists, when my hands are busy holding the dog leash, the garden hose, or the toothbrush, some of my best ideas—the perfect adjective, a livelier turn of phrase, a metaphor or a plot point that has eluded me while sitting at my laptop—will surface.

Dopamine spikes clearly lit up Karen's libido, but we can only speculate that they've been partly responsible for her and Hadley's almost superhuman productivity. As for me, since learning about the mysteries of multifaceted dopamine, it's hard not to visualize the chemicals in my brain working their magic, even as they struggle against the tide to keep my brain alive.

TEN:

IS THE HONEYMOON OVER?

The consonants in the word "parkie" give the word a derogatory bite, but it's a diminutive that those of us with PD generally don't mind. The first time I heard someone in our Facebook group call herself a "parkie," I cracked up. A few weeks later, because my arms don't swing when I'm walking unmedicated—a classic PD characteristic, I laughed even harder when a fellow Parkie referred to people without Parkinson's as "arm swingers."

I've felt buoyed, belonging to a club in which laughing at our serious disease is allowed, encouraged, even prescriptive. One of the reasons we like to make fun of ourselves might be that PD is, in some ways, a goofy disease. I feel goofy in my body much of the time, like when my right leg drags and then, as my foot comes reluctantly forward, it does a fishtail, as if it's become unhinged from my ankle. A plain old limp isn't funny, but a body part with a mind of its own attracts attention. Beverly Ribaudo, who maintains the website Parkisnonshumor.com, writes: "Parkinson's will make you walk funny, talk funny, write funny, think funny, and make funny faces, so you might as well have fun with it and laugh."

In 2013, Michael J. Fox appeared in his own sitcom to make people laugh with him about his life with Parkinson's. He inspired the rest of us not only to find the humor in our plight but also to focus on who we still can be despite our disabilities.

Within weeks of my diagnosis, an old friend emailed me a link to a rap written and performed by Sharon Kha, a former vice president of the University of Arizona who has PD. Ms. Kha has regularly performed her raps about Parkinson's:

Yo! Homies! Listen up!

My name is Sharon Kha, and they all knew me

I used to be the spokesman for the University.

You know you have a problem when your writing gets small

And you have a little tremor and a tendency to fall,

And your posture is rigid, and your pace is slow,

And your irritated colleagues say, "Come ON, let's go."

...Well, our hands are shaky, and our speech is slow

And we have hallucinations, and our feet won't go

But if we can laugh at ourselves without much fuss

We may have Parkinson's: It'll never have us...

Another reason people with PD—especially younger people—may have developed a sense of humor about it is because our disease is typically indolent. We are probably going to be living with it for many years. This means we have a lot of time both to be fearful of what's to come and to find ways to cope with that fear. Peter Dunlap-Shohl, a former editorial cartoonist for the *Anchorage Daily News* who was diagnosed with Parkinson's at forty-three, is the best example I know of someone who's been able to make people laugh even when touching on the darkest aspects of having a degenerative disease. After years of caricaturing world leaders, politicians, and bureaucrats, Peter turned his laser-sharp satire on himself, chronicling with cartoons and illustrations his adventures with PD in his brilliant graphic novel, *My Degeneration*. In 2013, he addressed a Parkinson's convention with these remarks:

> ...humor can decrease the power that something or someone has over you. This is why Syrian authorities kidnapped political cartoonist Ali Ferzat and broke his hands. It's why the caricaturist Daumier was thrown in jail. Twice. Why does this undermining of power work? Because much of the power any force has is the power we give it through our fear. Humor can disarm fear thoroughly and permanently.

Hadley and I spent a lot of time on the phone laughing about our Parkinson's. I appreciated how our joking took the edge off the anxiety and loneliness that come with having a progressive disease. In the late fall of 2011, she told me she'd fallen a couple of times, laughing as she explained, "It's the weirdest thing—if someone touches me from behind, I keel right over!" I laughed, too, because I didn't want to reveal my alarm. But after our call, I was distracted with worry. I knew from our Facebook group that falling was often part of having PD, but I felt certain that it usually came later in the disease.

In January and February, Hadley managed to work at her usual record-setting pace to complete twenty-three paintings for a show in Portland, Oregon, that would open in March. In late February, she wrote that she felt she was exiting the "Parkinson's honeymoon phase," an expression used by the PD community that refers to the early years, when symptoms are typically mild. Hadley had been exhausted for years, but now she was feeling the fatigue in all of her muscles—when she walked, ate, spoke. Every movement felt slow. Her hands were cramping when she held a paintbrush. The miracle of Mirapex had worn off and she wondered why she was feeling as bad as she had been before she began taking it. Still, she insisted she felt optimistic that she would get some relief when she next saw her Movement Disorders Specialist, Dr. Youngman. After all, there were still PD medications she hadn't tried, like the gold standard, levodopa. Following our Facebook group, I knew all of us were experiencing our individual Parkinson's journeys, but this didn't stop me from imagining worst-case scenarios—in Hadley's case, more serious neurological diseases that can start with Parkinson's symptoms.

By March, Hadley had finished the paintings for her show, but her energy was seriously faltering. She'd caught several viruses from Sarah and had minimal energy to work on the Missoula Catholic Schools mural project. She was in desperate need, she told me, of something that would help her get her work done. That month, at her semi-annual appointment with Dr. Youngman, he suggested she start levodopa. Hadley was reluctant; like all young onset Parkinson's patients, she wanted to delay taking levodopa as long as possible to avoid dyskinesia. So Dr. Youngman switched her medication from Mirapex to Requip, hoping the different dopamine agonist would be more effective. He also gave her a prescription for levodopa in case she changed her mind and wanted to try it. Then Hadley asked him a question that had been nagging her since the pharmacologist at the Christmas party had questioned her Parkinson's diagnosis.

"Do you feel certain I have Parkinson's?"

"You have Parkinson's," Dr. Youngman said. "But if by next year you still don't have a tremor, we'll do a brain MRI to rule out atypical Parkinson's."

Hadley felt satisfied with this. She didn't know what "atypical Parkinson's" was, but in some way, it sounded better than Parkinson's. When she got home, though, Google turned up information that terrified her. Atypical Parkinson's was not the benign variation she had assumed, and its symptoms mirrored hers to a T.

She wrote to me with this news. I read her email twice, filled with dread. One of the several conditions sometimes referred to as "atypical Parkinson's" is so terrible Hadley hadn't been able to bring herself to name it in her email: multiple system atrophy. MSA is very rare, but had been on my radar from the time I first started having neurological symptoms because a woman from my small high school had died from the disease when she was forty-seven. I called Hadley immediately.

"I know I shouldn't go crazy Googling," she said. "But listen to this—a list of symptoms that separate regular Parkinson's from atypical Parkinson's: 'falls at presentation or early in the disease course, poor response to medication, symmetry of motor signs, rapid disease progression, lack of tremor, early dysautonomia, like urinary urge or retention, persistent erectile failure, and symptomatic orthostatic hypotension.'" Hadley paused. "I have everything on this list! Well, everything except erectile failure."

We both laughed—or more like gasped. I was shocked. Besides her abnormally fluctuating blood pressure (orthostatic hypotension), I didn't know Hadley was experiencing dysautonomia. "You have urinary retention?" I asked, feeling shy about the intimate question.

"Yeah, I kind of do sometimes. Like, I can't go all day."

I tried hard not to react, though this new information was a blow. If Hadley had typical Parkinson's, it seemed too soon for her to have this symptom. I wanted to soothe her fear, but in her words, I heard nothing but reasonableness as she calmly synthesized what she was experiencing in her body with the medical information she'd uncovered. She'd done her homework; I could see no crack in her concern where I could wedge in an encouraging word.

In an email in April, Hadley shared with Dr. Youngman what she'd been reading about multiple system atrophy. She asked if they could investigate this possible diagnosis so that she could know sooner rather than later and prepare herself and her family. Dr. Youngman wrote back that as far as he knew, she didn't have the typical signs of MSA, and she shouldn't "obsess over it." He assured her that when he saw her at her summer appointment, they'd have a chance to check her progression and do necessary tests. In other words: Time will tell.

When Hadley told me about this exchange, I cringed. I knew how much she liked and trusted Dr. Youngman, so his telling her not to "obsess" seemed not only insulting but also like a betrayal—especially given that he had been the first to raise the possibility of atypical Parkinson's or MSA. Had he believed he could float out the suggestion of a deadly diagnosis without inciting her need to know more? Hadley was taking care of herself, doing what any intelligent person would do: looking for answers in a calm, methodical way. "In my book," I told her, "that's not obsessing." "I know," she said. "I don't know what to think about it all." The low tone of discouragement in her voice was new to me.

Requip, the dopamine agonist that Dr. Youngman prescribed for Hadley, made her tired, nauseated, and sometimes dizzy. At lunch with friends one day, fifteen minutes after taking a dose, she became increasingly dizzy and stretched out on the floor so she wouldn't faint. She lost consciousness. Her friends told her later that her lips and face blanched, and big beads of sweat dotted her chest. They carried her out and drove her to the ER, all of which she was unaware of until she came to in the hospital. She sent a text message right away to Dr. Youngman asking whether she could stop the Requip altogether or needed to taper. "I'm a pro at fainting," she wrote. "So today didn't bother me in that sense. I just don't want to have too many repeats."

The brave face she presented to Dr. Youngman, minimizing her concern about the fainting episode, was typical of the Hadley I had come to know. Because of her medical history, it's very important to her not to seem like she's overreacting. But her stoic message didn't help her get the response she needed from Dr. Youngman. It took him four days to answer her cry for help, and in his email, he didn't address the fainting at all; he merely advised her to discontinue the Requip. Hadley turned to her Missoula neurologist, Dr. Reid, for help. She told her Dr. Youngman's dismissal had made her reluctant to assert herself with him and ask more questions. Together, Hadley and Dr. Reid decided she should stop the Requip and start levodopa. Dr. Reid felt that the Requip, while not known to cause fainting, had probably aggravated Hadley's susceptibility to fainting events.

Levodopa, which had worked so magically for me, helped Hadley only minimally—more evidence that she could be dealing with MSA. Speaking with her on the phone, I knew she was scared. She understood that since there's no treatment for MSA, there was nothing physically to be gained by catching it sooner rather than later. Still, her urgency to know grew. I would have felt the same way.

I found myself internalizing Hadley's fear, and her plight became mine. Our bond had been established on the premise of a shared certainty—our Parkinson's disease; now, I would stay with her as she veered into this excruciating uncertainty. From there, our friendship would grow more complex, no doubt moving forward with less laughter.

ELEVEN:
THE DOPAMINE DIALOGUES

"**M**ake a follow-up appointment in six months," my Movement Disorders Specialist, Dr. Bright, told me at my first appointment with him. I walked out of his office with a life-changing diagnosis, relieved that I didn't need tests, medication, or other interventions, but in a kind of stupor, wondering how I was supposed to fold this new knowledge about myself into the fabric of my everyday life—for six months!

It reminded me of leaving the hospital with a new baby: Where were the operating instructions? What would happen tomorrow when I wouldn't be surrounded by health providers? Next week? Ten years from now? Fortunately, with a baby, a few weeks after the birth, there is that much-anticipated newborn checkup with the pediatrician who smiles reassuringly when you stumble to her, cradling the mysterious creature who will be your responsibility for the foreseeable future.

The six-month Parkinson's follow-up is standard. Patients typically see their MDS twice a year during the first five to ten years after diagnosis. At least after my diagnosis, I was confident I'd left the hospital with the right baby. Hadley couldn't be sure what she was carrying around now, and months would pass before she'd learn more. When fear is involved, time becomes the enemy.

Except for the hour or so we spend with our MDS, Parkinson's patients are left on our own to develop coping strategies. Over one million people in the U.S. are afflicted with PD, and about 90,000 new cases are diagnosed each year. Yet, we are only just beginning to see the kinds of resources for Parkinson's patients that are available at cancer centers, where a team approach promotes physical and emotional well-being from the time of diagnosis. Comprehensive PD resource centers that do exist largely have been created not by medical teams or hospitals, but by ambitious physical therapists or Parkinson's patients themselves. Three that were established by our Facebook group's members are Cleveland's InMotion, co-founded by Karen Jaffe; Atlanta's PD Gladiators, founded by Larry Kahn; and ParkinGo, founded in Victoria, Canada by physical therapist Jillian Carson. YOPD patients especially are not content to sit back and wait to see what another six months or six years will bring; they are determined and proactive about their disease. Centers for people with PD that offer PD-specific exercise classes, informational sessions, and a supportive place to come together are springing up around the world.

Three of the most prominent Parkinson's foundations in the U.S.—The Michael J. Fox Foundation, The Brian Grant Foundation, and The Davis Phinney Foundation were also started by people with YOPD. The Fox Foundation is a leader in funding drug trials, research into biomarkers, and the search for a cure, having raised 1.5 billion dollars since 2000. Davis Phinney, an Olympic medal-winning cyclist who was diagnosed with YOPD at age 40, started his foundation in 2004 with the mission to improve the quality of life for people living with PD. Diagnosed with YOPD at age thirty-six, NBA athlete Brian Grant founded his Portland, Oregon, organization in 2008.

Traditionally, patients have participated in clinical trials and haven't studied and managed their own health care, but that paradigm has shifted as patients have become better informed. Sara Riggare, a Swedish engineer in our FB group who was diagnosed with PD at age thirty-two, is dedicated to creating technology that will change how people live with PD. "My mission," Sara says, "is to give individual patients the tools to improve their own healthcare experience. I need to show that my research can change things for me and for the world and that it can make an immediate benefit, not in ten or twenty years."

Entrepreneurs have jumped into the self-care movement. In 2016, I was a tester for an app being developed by a local startup that streamed a personalized cycling protocol to my phone, then stored my workout data so I could track my progress and eventually, any benefits of the exercise. The workouts, which I did on a stationary bike, were based on the results of studies like one done by Dr. Jay Alberts at the Cleveland Clinic that demonstrated that cycling, when performed at a certain level of intensity, might be neuroprotective, i.e., might slow the death rate of dopamine-producing neurons.

Much of the information people with PD need to take care of ourselves can be found on our laptops. Our Facebook support group offers advice about all aspects of our disease—feedback that will be corroborated or debated among members with rigor and intelligence. There are no boundaries to the issues people will raise, whether it's how to talk about PD with their children, sexual dysfunction, or if they should accept a job offer.

Q: I'm wondering if anyone can offer some advice on what to do when you freeze in public. That happened to me tonight. My husband and I had gone out for dinner, and when we were leaving, I couldn't go out the door. I just stood there for the longest time. It was so embarrassing!

A: I have freezing episodes that can last a half hour. It is my most disabling symptom. Parkies have many different tips and gadgets, like laser pens or a sort of visual cue. You might find that if your husband taps you on the shoulder or otherwise distracts you, it may break the freeze. I find that if I see myself (mind's eye) as walking fluidly through the doorway, bam—no freezing.

Or this:

Q: Going through the procedure of trying to collect disability insurance. After review of my application and additional third-party questionnaire, they said they need even more medical evidence of my condition. (Records from two prestigious neurologists from highly regarded hospitals were sent.) I have had PD for eight years. Give me a break. But they have scheduled a bone and back examination. Not neurological. Is this common?

The ten responses to this post about disability were packed with useful information and encouragement.

Another important way in which our online group picks up where our health providers leave off is by comparing notes about our symptoms, histories, and responses to medications. Sometimes, we discover something together that might not have seemed significant to us individually. For example, a member in her late thirties posted that she experienced her first PD symptoms immediately after she stopped taking oral contraceptives, which she'd been on for seven years. Several years after diagnosis, she realized that during the week before her period, the efficacy of her PD medications was cut in half. She resumed taking The Pill and discovered that with the added hormones, she could cut way down on her PD medications. Within a few hours, thirteen women in our group had responded to her post, some reporting that immediately after going through menopause—especially in cases of early menopause—their PD symptoms began. Others wrote that they experienced big fluctuations in their PD symptoms that corresponded with their menstrual cycles. Scientists know that estrogen is, to some degree, neuroprotective and that this might explain why more men than women get PD. But our posts might suggest something more: that a precipitous drop in estrogen could trigger Parkinson's in people who might be genetically susceptible to the disease. Most neurologists are not yet addressing the effects of hormone fluctuations with their women YOPD patients. Still, some in our group have already pressed their doctors to prescribe hormonal treatment, with good results. This information sharing could be an important contribution to PD research; it seems inevitable that the effects of estrogen, progesterone, and testosterone on dopamine will become a factor in the study of PD.

One recurring topic in the Facebook group is deep brain stimulation surgery (DBS). As Parkinson's progresses, the increase of levodopa needed to control symptoms often, but not always, causes uncontrollable movement. When this dyskinesia becomes unmanageable, DBS can be an option. In 2014, Alim Louis Benabid, MD, PhD, and Mahlon R. DeLong,

MD, won the Lasker-DeBakey Clinical Medical Research Award—regarded as the Nobel Prize for medical research—for this breakthrough procedure. Since the 1990s, tens of thousands worldwide have undergone DBS, which involves implanting electrodes into the brain that target improperly functioning motor circuits. A stimulator similar to a cardiac pacemaker is implanted under the collarbone and sends electrical pulses to block the signals that cause some PD symptoms. With a controller the size of a TV remote control, the patient can change pulse amplitude or toggle between programs set up by their DBS programmer. DBS is not suitable for all PD patients, and it can't stop Parkinson's from progressing, but it has dramatically reduced symptoms. For those considering it, having access to many others who've gone through the procedure is vitally important. Whether or not to have brain surgery is not your run-of-the-mill decision!

> Q: To DBS or not to DBS? This is driving me crazy! Do the benefits outweigh the risks?
>
> A: For me, the answer is yes! I had DBS two years ago and it has given me my life back. In addition to controlling my tremors, I have drastically reduced my meds.
>
> Q: When you say, "got my life back," how bad were things? Just asking because I'm considering DBS but don't want to do it until I have no other options.

The responder had been having trouble with his medications, which led him to DBS. He was taking a lot of levodopa, which nauseated him. Only Mirapex controlled his symptoms, but it caused compulsive eating, shopping, and sex. He gained sixty pounds, and his house was full of things he'd bought and didn't need. He was unhappy, his wife was unhappy, and his kids were driving him crazy. After DBS, he got off the Mirapex, only purchased things he needed, lost forty pounds in one year, and started enjoying his family again.

Most Parkinson's patients probably imagine the possibility of needing DBS surgery someday and hearing firsthand the specifics of how it's helped others is very reassuring. But we're not always preoccupied with scary-as-hell decisions and drama; sometimes, members give us wonderful reasons to celebrate. I remember exactly where I was—in the Whole Foods parking lot when I read this joyful post on my phone:

Hi All!!! I'm a mama! 6lbs 4oz and perfect! It has been a rough five days, but we are going home TODAY!!! We couldn't be happier!

Perhaps the most important role our online support group plays is as a full-time community of empathizers. No concern is ever ignored, and there are no holidays or closing times. Occasionally, group members have the opportunity to meet in person, often at a Parkinson's event. When there's a group of us, a kind of team spirit light-heartedness prevails. It's different meeting one-on-one. The first two times I got together with someone in our group, we arrived at our meeting place as we would for any date with a stranger: smiling, exchanging polite greetings, slipping into chairs opposite each other, doing our best—as we do every day to appear as the "okay" youngish people we still were. Within minutes of starting our conversation, our eyes welled with tears, because it was okay to not be okay. Because even though we didn't really know each other, we *knew*.

Of course, being connected with so many people with Parkinson's can be frightening and painful, too. Occasionally, someone will post alarming news that will sock me in the gut if I'm having a particularly bad day: Their husband is leaving them, they can no longer hold the job they love, or they had a dangerous reaction to a medication. Feeling their pain can trigger my blackest fears: Will I lose my mental capacity? Will I end up alone? This is no surprise; when I joined the group, I understood that I would be face-to-face with every version of the beast that is Parkinson's.

But what I couldn't anticipate was the even beastlier beasts at the Parkinson's party:

Although all of us had been given a PD diagnosis, not everyone would turn out to have Parkinson's.

TWELVE:
TO MAKE A LONG STORY SHORT

About the time Hadley started questioning her Parkinson's diagnosis, I was struck by the difficulties of one of our other Facebook group members, a woman in her mid-forties. Jane had a flair for black humor; once, she got me laughing with her graphic description of the war she'd waged on cockroaches in her New York City apartment. She lamented the copious amount of Raid she'd deployed, which she suspected had caused her Parkinson's. Like me, Jane was an amateur researcher. When it seemed like our public posts were becoming too pedantic, she and I exchanged private messages about, for example, the neurotoxicity of certain pesticides.

Jane had undergone deep brain stimulation surgery for her PD, but within months of the procedure, she was falling again—"flat on my face," she posted. How could this be? Typically, DBS had more lasting benefits. Concerned, I sent her a private message. She wrote back and told me about the various falls over the past few years that had left her with six broken ribs and a fractured clavicle and vertebra. She'd also been treated with Botox for excruciating dystonia (involuntary muscle contractions typical in PD), and it had knocked out the muscles in her neck, necessitating a cervical fusion. She described this nightmare at length, with candor and remarkable humor.

I continued to worry about Jane over the next several months. She wasn't posting on Facebook and hadn't responded to a private message I'd sent her. Finally, six months after our first messages to each other, she wrote.

Dear Catherine,

In 2003, I started experiencing strange symptoms—balance problems, fear in the car, and an altered sense of space. I felt something was wrong, especially the driving phobia. After visits to a number of specialists and with worsening symptoms, I consulted my friend, a hospital nurse practitioner I really trust who knows all the doctors around. She recommended a neurologist. She told me people thought he was odd and that his bedside manner was atrocious, but she had the utmost respect for him.

He diagnosed me. He walked into the exam room, looked at me a moment, and said, "You have Parkinson's." "How do you know?" I asked. "Look at your face! You look like a judge!" And that was it, I kid you not.

He explained that he could give me a prescription now or try some tests that ruled out other things. I opted for testing, which ruled out the other things. So two weeks later, I was on levodopa. My body responded like magic. The stiffness disappeared, the mask with it, and I practically felt as good as new except that it confirmed Parkinson's.

Given that, I dived into research about PD and meds. I asked my doctor why he didn't put me on Mirapex, and he said adamantly, "You're still driving!" He considered the agonists too big a risk for sudden sleep. (I had narcolepsy as a child, so I considered it a pretty significant risk, too.) I started to talk to other doctors. I went to a movement disorders specialist, who confirmed my diagnosis but asked me why I didn't take an agonist. He thought they were safe and effective. He proceeded to tell me about two accidents in which his patients had sudden sleep attacks.

I went to yet another MDS. Discussing the diagnosis (Parkinson's) at the end of the session, he also asked why I didn't take a dopamine agonist. He thought I should, and that he also had heard of accidents. I was now definitely in the no-agonist camp.

I should say that all of these doctors also thought I had remarkably low-grade Parkinson's, almost invisible to the untrained eye.

The first doctor even predicted a mild course for me long term. I asked him how he knew, and he said, "Because I went to Harvard!" Possibly, this is one reason people thought he was odd.

Still, I felt I was getting worse and not getting enough answers. I asked my first doctor for a referral to another doctor, and he made one also for a psychiatrist he knew who specializes in Parkinson's care (he proved to be really important, another story). I started in with the other doctor, who had an even worse bedside manner and a more violent antipathy toward the dopamine agonists. She had taken all her patients off them, given the frequency of bad side effects.

We tried some of the other standard drugs. I was starting already to show fluctuations, and the idea was to smooth them out. Comtan made me sick. Tasmar seemed to affect my balance—I described it as "making me zoom everywhere," now I know it as festinating. That was the start of my falling career, one of the things I do best.

Another attempted smoother, levodopa CR (controlled release), made me crazy suicidal around the clock. I've since learned that others have terrible reactions to it and find it unpredictable and ineffective. That's my experience, for sure.

So, in all, I felt like I was getting worse. So was my doctor's bedside manner. She told me to shut up once (with my husband in the room) and was openly dismissive when I asked about a handicapped placard. After a second request, she sighed and said, "No skin off my nose," then wrote the letter.

About this time, I began to consider deep brain stimulation as an option. When I asked

Dr. M, she said she thought it would be worth a shot and referred me to (a surgeon she highly respected) for both surgery and programming.

The neurosurgeon proved to be charming, attentive, good at discussing the disease, and willing to look hard into my medication, so I also asked if he would take me on as his regular patient. He did. Though experiments like Azilect didn't work, my dosing was under better control, and I felt good. The only problem was worsening dystonia in my back and neck, which was becoming cripplingly painful.

At this point, I was still working. I wanted to be together for my clients. I told them all about my young onset Parkinson's as I wanted to be both authentic and ethical. That said, I really didn't want my symptoms to be a distraction. I depended on levodopa to keep me going. But I was in a double bind: I was taking a lot of levodopa to stay on, but that gave me dyskinesia. If I didn't take it, I was stiff, slow, and full of negative feelings. I was becoming obviously symptomatic either way, and dosing around my appointments was a full-time job. I had to start considering retirement. But I wasn't quite ready.

In February of 2009, I asked (my doctor) for a Botox shot to relieve the dystonia. He told me it was completely safe in his many years of experience. However, it knocked my neck muscles right out. The following day, I could not lift my head—either I was too sensitive or had too much. That was the final blow to my work. And my driving. I retired and went on Social Security disability. And my head hung off my shoulders for six months before the Botox wore off and the muscles came back.

To make a long story short, I changed doctors again. The doctor told me it was his belief that his role was to give his patients the best quality of life possible since there is no cure and that doing DBS early before my symptoms were bad would help most. He had also wanted to try Amantadine (which gave me scaly livedo reticularis) and Mirapex, which, at that point, I still didn't want. So, I returned to levodopa.

My symptoms were obviously worse and worsening. I finally did get DBS (again, another story), and after a brief, wonderful period of autonomy, I started falling again. I spent the year in and out of the hospital, recovering from a variety of fractures and an operation to fuse my cervical spine (an effect of the Botox months). But by early this summer, I was back where I started—really, seriously, obviously disabled.

This past June, my doctor re-diagnosed me. I have either "severe, advanced Parkinson's" or "multiple system atrophy with Parkinsonism" (MSA-P), also known as one of the "atypical Parkinson's" diseases. Obviously, I respond to levodopa, which points to Parkinson's. But I also had worsening autonomic symptoms all along—incontinence, difficulty breathing, swallowing, talking, bad body temperature regulation, profound lack of balance, all progressing really fast—the good stuff that goes with MSA. And to the doctor, it "looks like" MSA. There's a lot of overlap between PD and MSA, granted. The doctor has said to me the diagnosis is really an academic argument—it won't change the treatment. Unfortunately, the prognosis sucks either way.

Now, after DBS, my stabilized meds routine, and my is-what-it-is diagnosis, the main treatment is physical and occupational therapy. I'm pretty much wheelchair-bound at this point, but I depend on levodopa to be able to talk, eat, and sit up. It takes me about two hours to eat a meal now.

So, this is the end of my current story. Sorry, it took forever, but I'm pretty slow, as you've guessed. I hope it's of some use to you; go ahead and ask if not. I am sending you my best!

I was shaking by the time I finished reading Jane's message. It had been eight years since she experienced her first Parkinsonian symptoms, and she was now in a wheelchair. I had a dreadful feeling that she'd taken the time to write down a blow-by-blow of her experience because she realized she was facing an imminent demise. I felt honored that she'd told me her story but miserable that she was slipping away. I struggled with what to write back. I thanked her for sharing her story and told her I was stunned and saddened and that I hoped she'd keep writing. A month later, she wrote, "Promise me you won't get sad. I want to thank you for listening." A couple of months after that, she wrote:

My husband is helping me write a letter to my father. I have to talk to him about the fact that I'll probably die within the next four years, and I think that letter will be the first of many I need to write to explain to my family and friends. I've cried a lot, but I've also made it a goal to live well in whatever time I've got. I'll let you know how the letter turns out.

Several weeks passed. I wrote to Jane asking if she'd written the letter to her father. I received no reply. For months, Jane had no presence in the Facebook group. Finally, eight months after her last message to me, her husband posted on our Facebook page that Jane had died of complications from MSA. He thanked us for our support. He sent me a private message, saying how important it was to Jane to have had the chance to chronicle her disease in her messages to me so that she could think it through. He added that it took her forever because, by then, she could hardly type.

I was touched by his note and asked him if I could share Jane's letter with someone I knew who might be dealing with MSA and more recently, if I could publish it here. Both times, he wrote back, "Yes, Jane would want her story to be helpful to others."

Hadley and I had worried together about Jane before, but now that Hadley might be facing MSA, I thought long and hard about whether to share Jane's story with her. On the one hand, Jane's was a diagnostic journey that Hadley could relate to and contained information that could be useful. Also, Hadley was a give-it-to-me-straight kind of patient. On the other hand, even though I knew Hadley still felt vibrantly alive, I worried she would be overwhelmed by Jane's account of her struggle with MSA. I asked if she wanted me to send her the letter, and she surprised me by saying yes. After I sent it, I remained conflicted enough that I never asked whether she'd read it.

She never said.

THIRTEEN:
WANTING TO BELIEVE

After learning Jane's story, it occurred to me that because multiple system atrophy (MSA) often shares symptoms with Parkinson's, it was very likely that there were others besides Hadley in our Facebook group who might face Jane's prognosis. And, yikes—what about me? In the days after reading Jane's letter, the offhand comment made by the neurologist who'd diagnosed me kept popping into my head: "We'll want you to have a tremor soon so we know it's not something worse than Parkinson's." I sent an email to my MDS, Dr. Bright: "Should I be worried that I still don't have a tremor? Could this indicate something worse than garden-variety Parkinson's?" Dr. Bright responded within an hour: "About 25% of patients with PD do not have tremor. I am certain you have garden-variety PD." I remember how powerful his confident answer was. I trusted his every word—I needed to keep my anxiety in check.

But then there was Hadley. Could MSA be her fate? If so, judging by the course of Jane's illness, there were good reasons for Hadley to get a clear diagnosis as soon as possible so that she wouldn't be subjected to unnecessary or potentially harmful tests, procedures, or medications. Because Jane had been misdiagnosed, she endured DBS brain surgery, which is enormously helpful for many with Parkinson's but typically results in poor outcomes for people with MSA.

Hadley had a vacation planned for June of 2012 with John, Sarah, her mother, Jana, and her stepfather, Charlie, at the Russian River in California, a little over an hour from where I live in San Francisco. I suggested she have a consultation with Dr. Bright, and she agreed it was a good idea. I wrote to Dr. Bright explaining that Hadley had been diagnosed with Parkinson's, but there was some concern about MSA that was initially raised by her MDS. I told him she had orthostatic hypotension and some autonomic symptoms, as well as a positive Babinski reflex and hyperreflexia, signs not typical in Parkinson's but typical of MSA. Dr. Bright generously agreed to fit Hadley into his schedule when she was in California, as I knew he would.

From our first meeting in 2010, I trusted Dr. Bright almost blindly. Two and a half years later, when I asked him to meet with Hadley, I felt certain he would see her illness clearly and wouldn't dismiss her concerns the way her MDS, Dr. Youngman, had. I had fantasies that he would swoop in on the proverbial white horse and rescue her from a terrible fate, that fate being either MSA or continuing to live with uncertainty.

On the day of her appointment with Dr. Bright, Hadley drove to San Francisco from the Russian River vacation rental with her whole family. We ate lunch at my neighborhood sushi restaurant—Sarah's request and a very adventurous one, I thought, for a five-year-old from a land-locked state. Hadley was quiet and barely ate, instead helping Sarah to navigate her lunch. Jana, a lively and inquisitive seventy-one-year-old, was a delightful conversationalist. Charlie, mild-mannered and in late-stage Parkinson's, was suffering from the cognitive effects of PD that slowed his speech and made retrieval of words difficult. He sat quietly as Jana occasionally helped him eat. John, always sweet, sat in the middle, dividing his attention between us. Not exactly the carefree mood of a family on vacation, I thought a little sadly, but how could it be? After lunch, we dropped Jana, Charlie, and Sarah in Golden Gate Park, and I drove Hadley and John to Dr. Bright's office. Once in the waiting room, Hadley filled out forms, and we chatted nervously until Dr. Bright came to get her.

A little over an hour later, Dr. Bright, Hadley, and John returned to where I was in the waiting room. After Dr. Bright left us, I asked Hadley, "What did he say?"

"He says I don't have MSA."

Startled by the decisiveness of this news, I shivered and gave Hadley a big hug.

When I stepped back, she smiled. "I know—it's amazing!" she said.

But she was more reserved than I expected her to be as we rode the elevator and left the hospital. In the car, trying to cloak my skepticism, I asked her, "So what did he say were the reasons you don't have MSA?"

"I wish I had had the presence of mind to ask him. That's the thing about me. I get so nervous and distracted...and he was busy checking out everything. I should have asked him that. Darn."

With me, Hadley was always on top of her game, forthright, and articulate about her health situation. I knew she would want to know exactly what Dr. Bright saw or didn't see that made him rule out MSA. But I also knew how flustering a doctor's appointment could be; I've often kicked myself afterward for not asking more pointed questions. I told Hadley that Dr. Bright was great about emailing and suggested she write to him. That night, when I was home and she was back with her family at their vacation rental, she and I came up with the questions she wanted answered, and she emailed him.

A couple of days later, Lewis and I drove to the Russian River to spend the afternoon with Hadley and her family. The cottage they'd rented had a lovely patio and a lawn with large trees overhanging the water. But I was so preoccupied with wanting to know how Dr. Bright had responded to Hadley's email that the pastoral setting couldn't work its magic. Everyone seemed tense as we put lunch together, and Hadley didn't seem at all celebratory, like someone who'd just been released from a death sentence. I couldn't help noticing how much effort she was putting into making everyone happy— Lewis and me, Sarah, her mother, and Charlie, who was entirely undemanding but, with his limited ability to speak, required special attention. I could see how tough Jana's role was, caring for Charlie with his advanced Parkinson's. The scene in the kitchen was a sobering view of what lay ahead for Hadley, me, and our families.

Finally, after lunch, Hadley had a chance to show me the response she'd received from Dr. Bright. In it, he explained that Parkinson's can have many presentations and that he's had many patients who've had one atypical symptom and have "obsessed" as to whether this meant they had atypical Parkinson's. He warned her that this mindset could be "very destructive." He went on to say that her symptoms were typical of PD, that MSA was rare, and that, to his knowledge, there have been no cases of MSA diagnosed before the age of forty.

Ugh! There was that word again—"obsess"—that Dr. Youngman had also used. I looked up at Hadley, and she smiled. "I don't know, Catherine," she said. "I liked him, and I feel better knowing he doesn't think it would be possible for me to have MSA, but..." she trailed off.

"I can't believe this," I said. "Those are his reasons that MSA is rare? And not knowing of anyone under forty who has been diagnosed with MSA?" I stopped. It was the wrong place to vent.

"There sure are cases of people with MSA in their thirties," Hadley said calmly. "All you have to do is look on the Internet. I want to believe him, but I wish he had a better reason for saying I don't have MSA." She put her hand on my shoulder. "I don't want you to feel like this was a waste of my time," she said. "I'm glad I went to see him. This shouldn't come between you and Dr. Bright because you've liked him."

In her usual way, despite this upsetting chapter in her search for a diagnosis, Hadley was taking care of my feelings. "I just don't understand," I said, "why he would say such a confident 'no' when he could've said, 'I can't say that it's MSA for sure, especially since I've only seen you once, but it's possible.'"

"I know," Hadley said, sounding far away. "I guess time will tell."

I hated those maddening words of resignation: "Time will tell."

Hadley, her family, Lewis, and I piled into our cars and drove to a nearby vineyard, where we sat outside at a picnic table and had chocolate and champagne in the soft, early-June air. It was my birthday, and Hadley wanted to celebrate. I tried to soak in the wine-country afternoon: the warm sun and rippling green vineyard, the rose-covered pergola, the delicate sweetness on my tongue. But they would barely penetrate. I could think only of how fleeting such pleasures could be for Hadley.

FOURTEEN:
BRAINSTORMING

Every summer, my family drives to the northernmost part of California to a cabin on a pristine, spring-fed river known for its icy temperature and trout. I am no fisherman, but the ranch's seclusion and bucolic setting offer a sublime respite from city life. In July of 2012, several weeks after Hadley's appointment with Dr. Bright, Lewis and I took some friends with us to the cabin, where we reveled in heart-stopping dips in the river, canoe rides, baby back ribs, and margaritas.

One morning, I found myself thinking about Hadley because I knew she'd just met with her MDS, Dr. Youngman. I walked down the riverbank to a spot where there was cell phone service and called her.

Hadley was somber as she recounted her appointment. The news of Dr. Bright's denial of an MSA diagnosis had seemed, mysteriously, to revive Dr. Youngman's concern about MSA. Hadley had brought him the report of the 2008 tilt table test she'd undergone because she'd discovered in her MSA research that her results correlated with the signs of MSA. The tilt table test, done to diagnose the cause of her fainting, had revealed that she had extreme orthostatic hypotension, or a sudden drop in heart rate and blood pressure, when changing positions. Orthostatic hypotension, when it's severe and frequent, can indicate a dysfunction of the autonomic nervous system that controls heart rate and other "automatic" functions like breathing, digestion, and body temperature, most of which are eventually affected by MSA. Dr. Youngman found the results to be significant. Given Hadley's other symptoms, including urinary retention, balance issues, and her reported minimal response to levodopa, he concluded that it was not premature to be worried about MSA. He told Hadley to return to see him in the fall for more tests and talked with her and John about preparing to make the best of the time Hadley had left— typically five to ten years after diagnosis. "I will, of course always be here to help," Dr. Youngman assured her.

Hadley reported all this with her usual calm. "At least we know now," she said.

I understood how important it was for her to stop searching and empathized with her relief. Unlike her, and perhaps because I wasn't the one who'd been given this drastic diagnosis, I could allow the news to hit me head-on. It was a monster. Over the next couple of days, Dr. Youngman's acceptance of MSA as a likely diagnosis for Hadley also rekindled my frustration about Dr. Bright's easy denial of MSA. How would I address my feelings with him? If I did, would I jeopardize our comfortable relationship? I hated the thought; it had taken some time to find an MDS I liked.

On a sultry evening at the ranch, I was well into a margarita when I decided to walk down the river to check my email. The moment I saw that I had service, my phone rang. It was Dr. Bright. I took a deep breath and answered. It was Friday, past the end of his workweek, but he was in search of a last-minute replacement for someone who'd dropped out of a study he was working on. I told him I would help them out by getting a brain MRI the next week. I took in very little of what he said about the study—he could have told me they were looking for brain Martians because I was preoccupied with deciding whether I had had too much margarita or not enough to talk to him about Hadley. Then, the dam burst—there was too much I wanted to say.

Fortunately, the tequila and the view of the river from where I was standing made feeling angry impossible. After telling Dr. Bright about Hadley's latest diagnosis, I asked him my main question: How could he have ruled out MSA simply based on its rarity and her age? When it seemed he was about to respond, I lost cell service. There was plenty of time to feel regretful that I'd brought the whole thing up, and now I had to decide whether to call him back. I did. When he answered, he acknowledged my concern but remained firm that Hadley had idiopathic, "garden-variety" Parkinson's. When I pressed him on her symptoms that could point to MSA, he explained that he wouldn't call into question the diagnosis made by another doctor until he was certain it was incorrect "because doing so can perpetuate a patient's irrational fear."

We were cut off again. I walked back to the cabin. It wasn't just the poor phone connection that made me feel Dr. Bright wasn't hearing me; his words had sounded generic. Instead of talking about Hadley, the person, it seemed we'd been having a philosophical debate and that he was letting me know I didn't understand the rules of engagement. Or if I did understand them, I had somehow broken them.

As summer moved along, Hadley the patient was struggling. But Hadley the artist was in big demand. Burgerville, a chain of thirty-nine restaurants all over the Pacific Northwest that serves fresh, local, and sustainable food in environmentally conscious facilities, had hired her to paint a mural inside their newest restaurant outside of Portland. For ten days, she worked nearly twelve hours a day covering a wall with a scene from local history; she was exhausted the entire time, often stretching out on the tile floor to take short naps.

In Missoula, Hadley continued work on the murals for the Missoula Catholic Schools Heritage Project. She also received thrilling news that she was one of three semi-finalists chosen from among fifty-five mural painters across the country to submit a proposal for an eighty-square-foot mural inside the Montana State Capitol in Helena. All at once, she was awash in opportunities that are rare for artists. But how would she manage it all with her progressive medical condition? What would she tell her clients? They knew she had Parkinson's, but now she struggled with whether to explain her new diagnosis, especially since her illness had been a mystery for so many years that she was reluctant to come right out and say "MSA."

Her reluctance would prove to be well-founded.

While Hadley painted, I was still buried deep in my novel, *Dream House*. It had been a year since I'd rescinded the contract with the agent who'd made the preemptive grab for it. The silver lining of my unpleasant experience with her was that I took her advice to get some help from an editor rather than passing the manuscript on to the agent who'd initially wanted it. The editor she'd recommended turned out to be an excellent match for me and for *Dream House*; Jay enthusiastically admired the book and was excited to collaborate.

When Jay and I started meeting, I had no idea how an editor worked. After so many years of relying on instinct and sporadic feedback from my writing groups, I had the urge to hand the manuscript to him and say, "Have your way with it and call me when you're done!" Editing doesn't generally work that way. Editors have a nose for what works and what doesn't, and they offer insights to jumpstart the author's own revision process. I was happy to discover that Jay and I agreed on what was most important about the book and what made it unique. He was skillful at nudging me to improve my work without interfering with my creative process or the novel's sensibility. For a year, we'd been brainstorming about, among other things, how to sharpen and distribute plot points for optimal impact. We'd meet, I'd rewrite. It was exhilarating, and it was exhausting. There were times when I lost faith, such as one long night in December of 2011 when I emailed him:

> Hi, Jay,
>
> I've been awake fretting and just have to ask: how likely do you think it is that I'm going to be able to sell this book? Sometimes I feel like it's human and it's just getting older and more tired and I don't know if it's the book or just me. I have these total lapses of confidence every now and then and can't tell if they're rooted in the real possibility that this book could languish or just typical first-time author jitters and impatience.

> Hi Catherine,
>
> It's just middle-of-the-night jitters, which I greatly admire. I think the book is very strong and will sell and find a responsive audience. You got your revisions done without getting

bogged down or lost: you have a clear sense of what you want to do and can focus on it and do it well and relatively fast (a relative term).

What will happen next is that you will get completely sick and tired of the book, and that's when you'll know it's done. And then, after a respite, you'll forget that you ever had any doubts, and you'll get excited again.

So don't freak out, don't worry. Keep working, enjoy the holidays, and call me anytime for a reality check/reassurance.

Jay was right. After a year of revising *Dream House* with him (on top of the years of rewriting before that), I sometimes became nauseated when I opened the document on my laptop. My bad mood made it difficult to discern whether I was creating new problems or making progress on the book. Finally, in July, after my trip to the ranch, I sent Jay my latest revisions.

Hi Catherine,

I read the pages you sent, and you nailed it! Congratulations! I love what you did. It works, and it's wonderful.

I exhaled a big "YESSS!" into my empty house. I'd been trying to build a novel on my own, combatting my considerable fear of failure with sheer determination, and Jay's help felt like the best kind of nurture. I understand why editors are sometimes referred to as "book doctors," though "book therapists" might be more accurate. Not only was he great at helping me fix things, but Jay also fully understood my book's emotionality, which is not so separate from my own. Being able to share everything with him about *Dream*

House—from the psychology of its characters to its structure to the middle-of-the-night anxiety it caused—was not only intellectually stimulating and productive, it was a tonic for my mental and physical health.

A book is not a being; an editor is not an MD. As much as I am tempted to, I wouldn't dare to stretch these metaphors further. But there is this: An important part of what made working with Jay so effective was that we both understood that while he has doctored many, many books, *Dream House* was my book; therefore, my ideas and instincts about it were at least as important as his informed recommendations. We were both wrong at different times, and when we openly debated an editorial issue, something wonderful happened: It became perfectly clear to us what should be done.

The successful working relationship Jay and I maintained throughout the revision process for *Dream House* made me wish my doctor-patient relationship with Dr. Bright could enjoy the same sensitivity, respect, and openness. It seemed possible; I felt certain that Dr. Bright genuinely cared about me as a patient. But his approach to Hadley and our unfinished phone conversation at the ranch had left me disillusioned. In a couple of months, I would be face-to-face with him at my semi-annual check-up. Before then, I would have to figure out how to express to him what I was feeling. Otherwise, there would be three of us in the little exam room: Dr. Bright, the elephant, and me.

FIFTEEN:
WHIPLASH!

O n our calendars for fall 2012, Hadley had several appointments with Dr. Youngman, and I had my semi-annual checkup with Dr. Bright. Hadley was expecting more testing to confirm her MSA diagnosis while I was still stewing about how to follow up with Dr. Bright on our aborted phone conversation. Since he'd doubted Hadley had MSA, even knowing Dr. Youngman disagreed, I began to worry that he might be a "good news doctor" who didn't tell his patients what he didn't think they needed to know. Could I trust him going forward to be totally honest with me about my health?

I convinced myself that if I asked him this question in an open, heartfelt manner, Dr. Bright would be receptive. But, my emotions were running high; in addition to the trust issue, I was distressed about Hadley's MSA and still upset that he was dismissive of Hadley. In other words, I was pretty sure that if I tried to talk to him in person, I'd cry. Horrors! Then what? I would risk his feeling blindsided and reacting in a way that could make things worse. I chickened out and wrote him an email. I left Hadley out of the conversation because I wanted to make it clear that my chief concern was our own doctor-patient dynamic.

Hi Dr. Bright,

Because in our phone conversation in July, we were both caught off-guard, I want to follow up to be sure I convey what's most important to me as your patient.

For two years, while I was having PD symptoms, my various health practitioners told me I was anxious, that my symptoms were nothing serious. It felt demeaning to have them tell me not to "obsess" or "be so anxious" when I knew something was wrong. I didn't need their pats on the head or empty optimism; I needed them to take my concerns seriously, to delve in and investigate. As a reasonable patient who's informed and in touch with her body, if I have concerns about symptoms or medications and they're totally dismissed without clear, hard evidence, I'm neither consoled nor helped. For me, "I don't know" are better words to hear than "It's nothing" when I know that it's something.

I understand that for some patients, not being given information that's in a grey area might be helpful. If given the choice, they might even be grateful not to hear the scary black-and-white stuff about their health. I'm here to say that is not me! My body is a mystery, and my doctors, with their expertise, help me to solve that mystery. In the nature of a true mystery-solvers collaboration, I want them to share all the clues with me—scary or not—when they pop up on the horizon. You are the voice of my nervous system; I'd much rather get news from you than from Facebook or Dr. Google.

I know you care a lot about your patients and that you keep in mind their best interests. I figured since I opened this can of worms by talking honestly with you about Hadley, I might as well ask you: Will you take my worries seriously, knowing I'm never just looking for the easy-to-hear answer, and will you tell me "the scary stuff," even if it's not the strategy you've typically used? I might be asking something of you that you aren't comfortable with; if this is the case, I hope you'll be honest with me.

All the Best, Catherine

I'm sure that whatever frustration I thought I was tempering by writing carefully and from the heart was blaringly evident from the length of my email. While waiting for Dr. Bright to reply, I worried that I'd doomed our relationship. Would he be angry? I needed him. I felt helpless and childlike. A couple of days later, Dr. Bright wrote:

I try to help each patient with understanding their symptoms and condition. I answer questions with as much precision as I can provide, and I do not try to "hide scary stuff." On the contrary, with my patients with more advanced symptoms, I often let them know the specific concerns I have about their condition.

I found myself studying his words the same way that I sometimes peer into my refrigerator, searching for that one satisfying bite of nourishment. However, he'd replied, and I did not doubt his earnestness.

At my appointment several weeks later, I waited until we were done with the exam and told Dr. Bright how sad I was about Hadley's MSA diagnosis. Tears welled in my eyes despite my best efforts to hold them back.

"Is she still walking okay without a lot of falling?" he asked. I told him yes. He shook his head. "It's very hard to diagnose MSA, and I wouldn't give up on it being Parkinson's yet."

Part of me, I realized, was still eager to abandon my ship of sorrow for his optimism, and I had a brief fantasy that he'd been right all along. As I stood to leave, Dr. Bright gave me a hug. I understood that the embrace was his way of telling me that he cared and wanted to be the best doctor he could be for me. It also felt like a gesture that signaled closure, and since I sensed that I'd elicited the deepest response from him that he could give, I resolved to let the business with Hadley go. But from then on, I would be extra careful to always be clear about what I needed to know from him.

In September, Hadley underwent a brain MRI. The scan showed minimal atrophy in the cerebellum that correlated with the side of her body most affected by symptoms. While this finding could support an MSA diagnosis, the results were considered to be within normal limits. She also did a urodynamic study, which assesses how urine is stored and released by the bladder and the urethra. The test confirmed Hadley had a neurogenic bladder, which explained her occasional inability to void. Like her orthostatic hypotension, this condition was an indication that her autonomic nervous system was impaired, which could be a sign of MSA.

Dr. Youngman met again with Hadley in early October and spent three hours with her doing more testing. He ordered a Dopamine Transporter Scan (or DaTscan), a new imaging test that had been approved by the FDA only the year before. A DaTscan can be used to look at the brain's dopamine activity. When a patient's illness is uncertain, a DaTscan can help to confirm a Parkinson's or MSA diagnosis if the scan shows a clear depletion of dopamine in the brain. A patient's dopamine activity can vary greatly depending on age or length of illness, however. Importantly, although imaging can sometimes support a diagnosis made by a clinician, it can't be relied upon alone to make a diagnosis. Furthermore, because dopamine loss is associated with both MSA and PD, the DaTscan cannot differentiate between the two diseases.

As she was filling out the forms for her health insurance company to justify the very expensive DaTscan, Hadley was startled when she read that DaTscans were sometimes used to distinguish between an organic disease process and a psychological one. She felt an old fear take hold: If the scan was normal, might Dr. Youngman revert to thinking her symptoms were all in her head? She remembered how, at her very first appointment, he'd wanted to rule out Munchausen's syndrome, a serious psychological disorder in which a patient pretends to be sick or injured to get attention. Now, she found herself almost wishing the DaTscan would be abnormal.

To Dr. Youngman's surprise, the scan revealed a slight abnormality, but the results were within the normal range, possibly indicating that Hadley had neither Parkinson's nor MSA. Dr. Youngman then had Hadley do a levodopa challenge test that involves taking a very high dose. Generally, if a patient has Parkinson's, their symptoms will respond well to the flood of levodopa. Hadley had always felt somewhat better on levodopa, but her response to the challenge was not nearly as strong as Dr. Youngman had expected, which would seem to support a diagnosis of MSA rather than PD.

Dr. Youngman was flummoxed by the tests' inconclusiveness to the extent that at her third appointment with him at the end of October, he had Hadley examined by a neuromuscular specialist who administered an electromyography (EMG) to test her muscle nerve cells. As was the case with the EMG I was given more than a year before I was diagnosed with Parkinson's, Hadley's results were abnormal. Finally, an abnormal result! The specialist told Dr. Youngman that this could suggest an upper motor neuron disease or primary lateral sclerosis (PLS). PLS is a devastating disease that causes muscle nerve cells to slowly break down, resulting in weakness, but unless it develops into ALS (Lou Gehrig's disease), it's not life-threatening, like MSA.

Since Hadley hadn't experienced muscle weakness, she was puzzled by the test results and scrambled to make sense of what appeared to be Dr. Youngman's shift in focus from MSA to neuromuscular disease. What about all the symptoms she experienced that were typical of MSA? "Could I have had the same abnormal EMG results if I had MSA?" she asked Dr. Youngman. He conceded that this was possible. Yet, as Hadley sat in the exam room with John, Dr. Youngman, and the neuromuscular specialist, she watched as Dr. Youngman became won over by the diagnosis of PLS. The other doctor left the room. To Hadley, Dr. Youngman seemed flustered and had a hard time looking her in the eye. He explained that he would no longer be able to help her because he knew nothing about motor neuron disease and that she would now be in the care of the neuromuscular specialist. He told her to stop taking levodopa, asserting that since she didn't have

Parkinson's or MSA, any benefit she had been getting from it had to be a placebo effect.

"Well," he said to Hadley and John, "this is a much better diagnosis than MSA. Here, I had diagnosed her with Parkinson's, and she made all these friends who have Parkinson's, and now she'll have to say goodbye to them."

Hadley was stunned. He was dismissing her just like that? How could he have been confident in his previous diagnosis of Parkinson's and then MSA, only to reject them both based on new findings of another doctor and a DaTscan and levodopa challenge test, both of which are known to sometimes be inconclusive? The sudden change in diagnosis intuitively seemed ill-considered to her. Most painful, though, was that Dr. Youngman, the doctor she'd thought of as a friend and advocate, had abandoned her.

After her appointment, Hadley and John flew to the city where they'd left their car and started the long drive back to Missoula. They rode for miles in a dazed silence. Every now and then, John would ask, "If it's not Parkinson's or MSA, how does he explain..." and he would name a symptom of Hadley's. Hadley thought to herself, well, at least John's on the same page with me.

It was snowing when Hadley and John got to the mountain pass two miles from the Montana border and suddenly, they heard a loud pop—a tire blowout. In the dwindling daylight, John swerved but managed to pull over. They called AAA and waited vigilantly, fearful that an approaching car would skid into them. Hadley had had to stop taking the levodopa for her appointment with Dr. Youngman, so she was extremely stiff and exhausted. But she took comfort in John's calmness as they discussed this new turn her diagnosis had taken. After two hours, the tow truck arrived, driven by a man in his fifties who looked haggard and told them he had poor eyesight. When he asked if he could smoke while driving, they felt they couldn't say no. In the darkness and falling snow, they crawled the remaining 112 miles to Missoula.

Hadley told me it was the scariest drive of her life.

SIXTEEN:
THE PATIENT WILL SEE YOU NOW

The Internet has ushered in a patient empowerment revolution that's had a tremendous impact on the doctor-patient relationship. The term "e-patient" was first coined by Dr. Tom Ferguson, visionary medical editor of *The Whole Earth Catalog* and author of the 1996 book *Health Online: How To Find Health Information, Support Groups, And Self Help Communities In Cyberspace*. After Ferguson's death, his work was advanced by others, including Dave deBronkart, a high-tech marketing executive who was diagnosed with stage four metastatic cancer in 2007 and given twenty-eight weeks to live. Using the Internet to explore treatments and clinical trials, deBronkart, known as "e-patient Dave," was able to beat his cancer and blogged about the experience. By 2009, he had become an international spokesperson for the e-patient movement and co-founded The Society of Participatory Medicine. The nonprofit describes itself as "a movement in which networked patients shift from being mere passengers to responsible drivers of their health, and in which providers encourage and value them as full partners." According to the Society for Participatory Medicine, 90% of patient health care takes place outside the doctor's office, much of it through Googling and interaction with online patient communities.

While there's plenty of bad information in cyberspace that can pique a patient's curiosity (and sometimes her paranoia), a discerning patient-detective can sift through sites and become educated about her illness. A patient's research can make appointments more complex for doctors than they used to be; patients like Hadley and I often arrive with a list of questions about new research and therapies. In her book, *In the Kingdom of the Sick: A Social History of Chronic Illness in America*, Laurie Edwards addresses this doctor-patient paradigm shift:

> (The model) used to be that physicians know everything; patients know nothing, and patients were lucky to even get time with their physician. Culture change is not easy, seamless, or immediate on either side, and simply barging into a physician's life with email or downloaded information is not an appropriate way to go about cultural change. The keys are engaging patients in shared decision making, providing them with credible, peer-reviewed health resources, and acknowledging that patients are doing right by getting informed. Not every patient who comes in with a stack of printouts is a cyberchondriac, and not every physician who gets frustrated with misinformation is unreceptive to patients...

Dr. Bright has always honored my curiosity by answering my questions respectfully but efficiently. When I see him twice a year, I'm eager to touch on the latest clinical trials and to parse the benefits and side effects of PD medications. Often, he seems measured in his responses, as if driving with one foot hovering over the brake pedal. I've wondered if this is his way of protecting me from both getting my hopes up and becoming discouraged. If so, for this patient at least, he's chosen an unnecessarily cautious way to drive; I've learned enough about Parkinson's that he should feel assured that I can handle whatever uncensored news he might have to share.

One example of how my online research and our Parkinson's Facebook group has spurred interactions with Dr. Bright that wouldn't have occurred in pre-Internet days was our conversation about the risks of levodopa when I first started taking it in 2010. Dr. Bright assured me that I had little to fear with levodopa, especially since I responded very well to it from the very beginning. I was highly motivated to believe in the safety of this medication, as I was dependent on it to be able to walk. However, a highly controversial topic in our young onset Facebook group at the time was when to begin levodopa therapy and when to increase the dose. (The answer to the latter question, I would discover, is that it is obvious when an increase is needed.) Those who were delaying starting levodopa therapy made persuasive arguments: the possibility of its being toxic long-term, disrupting other brain chemicals, losing its efficacy over time, or causing the involuntary movements of dyskinesia. Their vehemence set off alarm bells for some of us who were already reliant on levodopa. There are also plenty of Internet testimonials by health practitioners that have warned of levodopa's potential dangers. Movement Disorder Specialists frustrated that some patients are reluctant to accept their medication protocols, have recently started referring to this particular patient concern as "levodopa phobia."

Dr. Bright informed me of a 2014 study that has provided MDSs with research that supports their conviction that levodopa is still the "gold standard" medication for PD. More than 1,600 Parkinson's patients, some treated with levodopa and some with dopamine agonists and other PD meds, were followed for seven years. By the end of the study, the levodopa group demonstrated greater mobility and fewer side effects than the agonist group. This is great news for many people with Parkinson's and for doctors prescribing levodopa. But, the study's participants were all sixty or older. What about YOPD patients who are thirty or forty when they're diagnosed—will levodopa still be efficacious for them way down the road? No one will know until a decades-long levodopa study of people with YOPD has been done. Until then, it seems reasonable, even prudent, for YOPD patients to worry aloud about the long-term effects of levodopa or any other PD medication. The professionals taking care of us don't all agree. In a 2014 article about the levodopa study on the website of one of the nation's three largest Parkinson's foundations, I read:

> Patients and family members should also think twice about raising (their) concerns over levodopa during doctor visits. Bringing them up, especially at the start of an appointment, could take precious time away from health concerns that need to be addressed.

I was surprised that this bit of paternalism—the word used to describe a common doctor-patient dynamic—had crept into a message from a foundation whose mission is to be patient-centered. Alas, paternalism has persisted for centuries in the medical field. As recently as the early 1990's, doctors often wouldn't share with patients the details of treatments they were being given, and the patients were sometimes forbidden from looking at their own medical records.

In *The Decision Tree: How to Make Better Choices and Take Control of Your Health*, Thomas Goetz writes:

> It's not that doctors don't want the best for their patients; they do. But there's a persistent paternalism in the profession, a fretting over how capable ordinary people are of understanding medical info and acting on their own behalf. A 2007 survey of primary care physicians...found that most were unprepared for patient-driven medicine, and nearly all were skeptical of the health information patients receive from government or insurance company Web sites. Such opinions reflect the strong conservative tradition in medicine, one that puts faith in the physician above all else. In medicine, paternalism isn't a dirty word; it's the default mode.

Paternalism might have made sense in an era when patients didn't have access to medical information and relied on their physicians to be all-knowing. In the past, doctors had more time—and thus familiarity with their patients, which meant their directives were more informed. And paternalism suits some patients: For whatever reason, many are not eager to engage with their own health problems, let alone research them, and prefer to have someone else make their medical decisions. Perhaps also at play in the persistence of paternalism is that some doctors believe they need to maintain a facade of authority, no matter how uncertain they are, in order to gain and preserve their patients' confidence in them. However, when a doctor is reluctant to be forthcoming with her patient or is unreceptive to a patient's wish to be participatory in his own health care, an inequality is established that compromises the potential for a collaborative, professional relationship.

During my conversation with Dr. Bright, I didn't have the courage to directly express how dismissed Hadley felt by what felt to her like empty reassurances. I'm sure his intention, conscious or not, was to be protective rather than paternalistic. His decades-long experience with patients of all kinds probably has made it difficult for him to tailor his approach to meet the particular emotional and intellectual needs of each of his patients. I have no doubt that, as he wrote in his email to Hadley, he's had many patients who have needlessly suffered while imagining the worst about their illness. But by defaulting to this assumption about Hadley, he was not seeing her or her disease.

Both Dr. Bright and Dr. Youngman chose to deliver a confident diagnosis for Hadley rather than to appear to be in uncertain territory; Dr. Bright affirmed the original diagnosis, Parkinson's, and Dr. Youngman went so far as to embrace an entirely new disease, primary lateral sclerosis. Dr. Jerome Groopman discusses uncertainty in his book *How Doctors Think*:

> When a physician encounters conflicting or unusual symptoms, he becomes vulnerable to the uncertainty ... Physicians, like everyone else, display certain psychological characteristics when they act in the face of uncertainty ... Does acknowledging uncertainty undermine a patient's sense of hope and confidence in his physician and the proposed therapy? Paradoxically, taking

uncertainty into account can enhance a physician's therapeutic effectiveness because it demonstrates his honesty, his willingness to be more engaged with his patients, and his commitment to the reality of the situation rather than resorting to evasion, half-truths, and even lies.

By avoiding uncertainty, Dr. Bright and Dr. Youngman took Hadley even further from finding an answer. Their certainty, because it was unsupported by Hadley's experience with her illness, created not only more uncertainty for her but also nearly crippling self-doubt because, in the past, she'd so often been made to feel that her symptoms might not have a diagnosable cause.

There can be comfort in not knowing a diagnosis; while there's ambiguity, there's a flicker of hope that what's ailing you is not as serious as you've feared. But not knowing also means you're stuck. Even when you can't control the disease you've been diagnosed with, the diagnosis allows you to plan to focus on what you can control. What Hadley wanted from the specialists she consulted was an honest, thorough, and respectful appraisal, even if it meant they'd continue to bumble around in the shadows with her, looking for a light switch.

Instead, they stopped looking, leaving her alone in the dark.

SEVENTEEN:
BEHOLD THE MAYO

"**D**o you think you'd be able to manage such a large commission?"

In early November 2012, this was the question posed to Hadley about the Montana State Capitol Building mural project. Hadley was the only Montanan—the only Westerner, in fact among the three finalists. Her work was well known, but so was her Parkinson's diagnosis because of her organization, Summit for Parkinson's. Now, Hadley herself was wondering if it was reasonable for her to remain in the competition.

On the phone later that day, Hadley and I mulled this over. On the one hand, she was so tired and slow-moving that it was difficult for her to imagine physically executing the mural. On the other hand, she still didn't have a clear diagnosis, and the finalist selection was a year off; she could be fine by then, for all anyone knew. She decided to be optimistic and stay her course. If she were to win it, the mural commission would be the most exciting project of her career.

Hadley continued work on the Missoula Catholic Schools murals, grappling with her increasingly bothersome symptoms. Since all of her movements were slow and stiff, her dexterity was worse, climbing scaffolding to work on the large panels was becoming difficult, and she had trouble getting up from a squatting position without support. All it took for her to lose her balance was someone tapping her on the shoulder from behind. She fell several times, luckily without injury. In addition, she was struggling with focus and concentration, and her field of vision seemed to be narrowing.

Fortunately, Hadley's Missoula neurologist, Dr. Reid, was still very much in her corner. Dr. Bright's diagnosis of Parkinson's and Dr. Youngman's dismissal of both Parkinson's and MSA (and his embrace of upper motor neuron disease) still didn't make sense to Dr. Reid. She felt it was time to call in the big guns—The Mayo Clinic in Rochester, Minnesota.

The Mayo Clinic scheduled Hadley for a series of appointments during a ten-day period over Thanksgiving. Hadley wanted John to stay in Missoula during her first week at The Mayo Clinic so that Sarah could spend the holiday in the festive way she was used to. John would join Hadley the second week so that he could be with her at the important appointments summarizing the Clinic's findings. Jana had gone with Hadley to the Arizona Mayo Clinic but now needed to stay home to take care of Charlie. To break up the stretch of time, Hadley would be alone, I decided to fly to Rochester on the Saturday after Thanksgiving to be with her for a few days.

∞

On my first night with Hadley at The Mayo Clinic, we paid for our mojitos and hustled out of the bar into the slipstream of the crowded mall. The drinks hadn't been strong, but we must have appeared a little drunk anyway, with our awkward walks. For both of us, maneuvering through crowded spaces had become trickier. To make matters worse, for diagnostic purposes, Hadley had stopped taking levodopa for the duration of her time at The Mayo Clinic. I could tell she was concentrating hard on not running into the racks of scarves and hats and people swimming toward us in their fat coats and boots.

But at least, unlike me, she knew where we were going. Many times in the past six days, she'd traversed the underground arteries that branch from the mothership Mayo; they minimize a person's contact with Rochester's harsh winter temperatures. Fast food, fast souvenirs, fast art—in the mall, they're all available for the 35,000 people who work at The Mayo Clinic and the thousands of patients who are killing time between heart-pounding visits to the medical specialists who'll send them back to Riyadh or Rome, Marseille or Missoula with the most costly souvenir of all: a diagnosis that will change their lives.

The teeming tunnel spewed us into the lobby of The Mayo Clinic. I took a deep breath as the soaring glass curtain wall lifted the compression in my chest. The Gonda building was the newest in the 3.5 million-square-foot medical center and has the ambiance of a five-star hotel or corporate headquarters; a sea of beige marble, bronze statuary, and medusa-like glass Chihuly sculptures make it easy to believe that it is The Best Medical Center In The World. On Monday morning, Hadley and I would be back here at 9 a.m. for her appointment with the Movement Disorders Specialist. But now, we were just passing through to the garage, hoping to be on time for a movie we'd chosen to see.

I climbed into the driver's seat of a rented red Chevy Impala, and Hadley sat next to me, navigating with her iPhone. The Galaxy 14 Theater was five miles south on

Route 63, a road lined with warehouses and malls, devoid of landmarks—unless you counted Target, which I soon learned people there do.

Hadley was subdued. Finally, she asked, "Do you want to hear what that one doctor wrote in her report about me?"

I did. Hadley scrolled through her email. Mayo reports are sent to the patient within a couple of hours after each appointment. Hadley had told me that the first doctor she met with six days ago, a general neurologist, had given her a "probable" diagnosis of multiple system atrophy. But the next day, a physical medicine and rehabilitation specialist reported inconsistencies in Hadley's exam that might suggest she didn't have an organic disease at all. This was the report that was bothering Hadley.

"I felt like she was trying to trick me," Hadley said. "Listen to this: 'Though she has definite organic problems, she has inconsistencies on her examination. During handwriting, she wrote small but has excellent coordination and grasp/relax of the pen. While I was typing my notes, she was toying with the ring on her finger, moving her fingers in a normal and fairly rapid way without difficulty that seemed very different than her formal exam findings. She has a broad-based ataxic, stiff-legged gait with decreased arm swing and a very turgid trunk and pelvis. However, her gait as she left the examination room was at least 50% better than during the exam.'"

Hadley slapped her phone down on her lap. "In a half-mile, take a left turn," the phone instructed us. "You see what I mean? It's like she was looking to trip me up."

"Wait," I said. "Read it to me again. I think I know what you mean, but I need to hear it again."

When Hadley finished reading, I understood that the doctor had been looking for contradictions in Hadley's movements. I wondered why.

"That whole thing about me having a better gait when leaving the exam?" Hadley said. "Of course I did. She had me walking back and forth in this tiny room, every two steps having to turn, and turning is always hard for me. When the appointment was over, I got to walk straight out the door, which is a different thing." I knew this difficulty Hadley was talking about; changing directions when walking can often feel precarious to me. "And when she was watching me twirl my ring?" Hadley went on. "That's a small repetitive movement, a habit like a twitch almost, completely different from the bigger hand movements she'd asked me to do. Also, my decent coordination with the pen is because I've been working with an occupational therapist on my grip so I can keep painting." Hadley sighed. "But she believes all this is proof that it's all in my head. It's like she's saying, 'Gotcha! It's functional!'"

"Functional" was clearly the hot-button word for Hadley, but I wasn't familiar with it.

"It's a movement disorder brought on by psychological causes, not organic," Hadley explained. "Listen to this part—she's so evil! 'Alert, appropriate affect, excellent historian. Admits 'I am not the best patient.' Totally out of context!" Hadley says, before reading on: "'She was told she had Parkinson's disease and had been pretty comfortable with that until this summer when things changed. She has moments when she is very overwhelmed. She expresses a lot of self-doubt. Depression is likely. She may need further psychological evaluation and counseling relative to the functional overlay.'"

Hadley groaned. She was flushed and furious. She suspected this doctor's report had biased the Movement Disorders specialist she saw the next day, who wrote in his report:

Impression: Gait disorder and rigidity. The patient has a very unusual exam. This is not a classic disease of anything. I agree we need to consider things like stiff person syndrome and primary lateral sclerosis. I am not comfortable with the diagnosis of multiple system atrophy. I find the signs of her parkinsonism to be unusual, and I think a functional etiology needs to be in the differential diagnosis for her problem.

It seemed MSA and PD were no longer even on the table, having been blown off by the gust of a suggestion: functional movement disorder.

I found myself thinking again about Munchausen syndrome, in which a patient invents symptoms and travels from doctor to doctor, changing her medical story. Could this "functional" word suggest something like that? I didn't buy it. Once again, I felt indignant on Hadley's behalf. Despite the fact that no doctor in recent years had doubted she was afflicted with an organic disease, I could see her confidence was shattered, and she was in the grip of all the memories of doctors who hadn't taken her symptoms seriously.

Hadley's phone announced that we'd reached the Galaxy 14. We parked in the nearly empty parking lot, and the insides of my nose froze as we ambled toward the entrance. Inside the huge, red-carpeted lobby, there were only the ticket seller, popcorn scooper, soft drink dispenser, Hadley, and me. I ordered some popcorn for us, trying to cop some much-needed feeling of fun. I began to worry whether the movie would be okay for Hadley. Although there were fourteen theaters in this one building, we'd only considered two of the movies playing, deeming the others too stupid, too violent, or too sad. We'd finally nixed the Bond movie for potentially being too stimulating after Hadley's exhausting days at The Mayo Clinic. That left *The Sessions.* "Heartwarming," the reviews said, which to me sounded prescriptive.

There were three other people in the cavernous theater. Who would come to watch a movie about a man in an iron lung on a fourteen-degree Monday night? I wondered. Loneliness settled over me, and I knew Hadley felt it, too. She pulled out her phone, and it lit up her face like an old friend.

The Sessions is based on the true story of Mark O'Brien, a polio victim who spent most of his life in an iron lung. In his thirties, he hired a sex therapist with whom he could lose his virginity. The film was touching and poignant, but I wasn't watching it through my own eyes. I realized shortly into it that I was trying to see it through Hadley's. Could it be entertaining to watch someone else's cruel medical plight when you were seeking a diagnosis for your own?

Hadley leaned into me. "I'm worried that after all this, I'll leave The Mayo Clinic without knowing anything more," she whispered. "What do you think of what the rehab specialist wrote?"

How could I possibly have imagined, with everything on her mind that Hadley would be able to concentrate on a movie? In my head, I tried to rationalize the doctors' reports, reminding myself that this was The Mayo Clinic after all, and I should keep an open mind and let the professionals do their work. Besides, I hadn't yet had a chance to research what this "functional" diagnosis meant. But then my intuition blared: "Functional movement disorder" simply did not fit Hadley's case.

"Forget about that doctor," I whispered. "She just has something to prove. No one will pay attention to her report."

When Hadley laughed and said, "Right? Oh good," I knew I'd said the right thing.

Still, she barely touched the popcorn. Occasionally, she checked her phone. Then, for a while, she seemed to settle into the movie. Helen Hunt sweetly caressed her disabled client; witnessing the movie's intimate scenes in such an empty theater, I felt more like a voyeur than part of an audience. I wondered if Hadley was wondering, as I was, whether this man's horizontal life was better or worse than her life would be.

Each time the caged man laughed, it signaled a little victory for humankind—a testament to how, if only for a moment or two, we can rise above even the most challenging circumstances.

EIGHTEEN:
SEEKING THE TARGET

B ack in my room at the TownePlace Suites after seeing *The Sessions,* I grabbed my laptop and Googled "functional movement disorder." I wanted to avoid issuing her more uninformed assurances.

I discovered that FMD is not uncommon. About a third of all new neurological outpatient patients present symptoms that can be only somewhat or not at all explained by an organic disease. About 5% of those patients experience sensory symptoms, weakness, seizures, or a movement disorder, and they can become as disabled as patients with Parkinson's or other organic neurological diseases.

"All in your head" doesn't honor the reality and complexity of this mysterious disorder. The term "functional" describes a condition caused by a change in the functioning of the nervous system rather than by neurological damage or disease.

Although FMD was once labeled "psychiatric," and neurologists referred patients with the condition to a psychiatrist, now they know that FMD neurological symptoms are not invented; they originate in the neural pathways connecting the brain and the mind. Unlike Munchausen syndrome, the mental health of a patient with FMD might or might not play a role in causing FMD. FMD can alter the way the brain sends or receives messages to or from the body, resulting in disabling symptoms like dystonia, in which an extremity adopts an unnatural, painful position, uncontrollable tremors, twitches, spasms, and gait disturbance. All of these are also symptoms of Parkinson's, which can make diagnosis difficult.

One way to distinguish FMD from neurological diseases like Parkinson's is to think of it as a software problem as opposed to a hardware problem. An FMD patient's "software"—his thoughts, emotions, behavior, and sensations—has caused the nervous system to malfunction, so medications like levodopa that address the "hardware" damage are ineffective for FMD.

Unlike Parkinson's or MSA, FMD can be cured over time with physical therapy, a patient's determination, and strong emotional support. For this reason alone, I wanted to be persuaded that FMD was Hadley's diagnosis. But the more I read, the more convinced I was that the condition didn't mirror Hadley's; she had autonomic symptoms that couldn't be explained by FMD, and levodopa, at least for a while, had helped her.

Hadley's fear that she would leave The Mayo Clinic with no clear diagnosis or be challenged to prove she had an organic disease was understandable. This scenario not only would mean more appointments but also would impede her ability to get help managing her illness. There's a stigma attached to any condition like FMD that is believed to have a psychogenic rather than organic cause. The disability it causes can be perceived as less legitimate and therefore, less deserving of help or compassion. As an example of this kind of bias, people often line up for months to supply dinners for a friend recovering from a stroke or dealing with cancer. But for those with less understood illnesses like debilitating chronic fatigue syndrome, say, or a major depressive episode? Not so many casseroles for them. This bias not only cuts off a patient from critical support but can also feed a patient's fear that they are to blame for their illness.

In the morning, I awoke and inwardly shivered at the maroon-and-grey color scheme of the hotel room, a corporate decor that coordinated with the landscape outside the window: chalky warehouses, chain link, and patches of dead weeds rooted in asphalt under an overcast sky. The refrigerator motor ground away. I imagined how difficult it must have been for Hadley that week, being alone in this austere place. The night before, she'd told me how she'd spent her time when not at her Mayo Clinic appointments. Since our hotel was outside town on a highway, there was nowhere to go without a car. One night, she walked to Target to buy sushi, crossword books, and jigsaw puzzles. In the room at night, she had Hot Pockets and Gatorade, then sat in bed with a tray, putting together the puzzles. She spent hours on medical websites. On Thanksgiving, she had gone to the home of a friend, a dermatologist with six children. It was a warm and welcoming evening, she said, but it somehow made her feel even lonelier.

My phone chimed. "You won't believe what I discovered last night," Hadley texted. "I can't wait to tell you."

We met at the hotel elevator to make the drive for her appointment with the Movement Disorders Specialist. She'd arranged to have this particular meeting that day so that I could be with her, another set of ears. Outside, a light snow was falling, dusting the Chevy Impala. We marveled at the largest snowflakes I'd ever seen—their crystalline form was entirely visible; their clarity seemed like a good omen.

We'd asked the woman at the TownePlace Suites front desk where we could buy yogurt and good coffee, and she'd told us, "Starbucks. Inside the Target."

"That woman," Hadley said in the car, "when she's not working the desk here, she works in a medical lab." Her mood was noticeably brighter than the night before. "She talked to me about... Let's get some coffee in us before I tell you."

"The" Target on Route 62 was an overwhelming Main Street of merchandise and services, exacerbating my sense of being lost with Hadley on a vast plain without landmarks. It was a relief when we were back in our car clutching our same-everywhere brand of coffee, and I had a *Thelma and Louise* fantasy of driving forever—past the two other Targets on Route 62, past The Mayo Clinic, across the continent to outrun this villainous diagnosis chasing Hadley.

"So," Hadley said. She'd been up late, Googling. One of the diagnoses that The Mayo Clinic had on its list to look into was Wilson's disease, a disorder in which copper accumulates in the liver and brain, often causing Parkinson's-like neurological symptoms. Hadley's copper level was normal, she explained to me, but her nocturnal research uncovered that an abnormal ratio of copper to ceruloplasmin, a copper-carrying protein in the blood, is also a marker for Wilson's. Going over her blood tests, she discovered that her ratio was indeed abnormal. She took her findings to the receptionist/lab technician at the TownePlace Suites, who told her she thought the abnormal ratio was significant. Back in her room, Hadley called a lab technician friend in Montana, who agreed.

As always, I was in awe of Hadley's command of medical information; she seemed to be a walking, breathing Merck Manual. Her determination, rather than flagging after her six miserable days in Rochester, seemed to be intensifying. Of course, it was—she was fighting for a diagnosis, for her life.

"Wouldn't it be amazing if all this was just about too much copper?" Hadley said. Inspired also by the caffeine, I felt my spirits rise at the thought. "It would be the best thing ever!"

Hadley was silent for a while. Then she said, "But I don't want to bring this ceruloplasmin thing up to the MDS today because all my detective work will just make me look more like I'm nuts and have a functional movement disorder."

"How about I bring it up to him then?" I said.

The Mayo Clinic's 12th-floor waiting area was huge, plush, and comfortable. We chose a couple of upholstered chairs facing the floor-to-ceiling windows that looked out at the other Mayo buildings and an attractive plaza. I had always associated medical appointments with bland, artificially lit spaces that worsen white-coat anxiety—that sweaty, slightly queasy feeling. Now, I soaked in the natural light and the expansive space and views, hoping they'd soothe us. If I'm nervous, I thought, how must Hadley feel? She told me that her stomach had been very upset since arriving at The Mayo Clinic over a week ago.

As we followed the assistant down a narrow hallway to a tiny, windowless exam room, I realized the patients, not the doctors, were the real beneficiaries of The Mayo Clinic's luxury architecture. Hadley and I sat, both twisting our hands in our laps. I could tell that she was preparing for the Inquisition. "What if he decides it's functional?" she said. I told her he wouldn't.

The MDS came in and shook our hands. "She's my friend," Hadley explained to him.

"I have Parkinson's myself," I added as if to lend legitimacy to my presence.

The doctor smiled; his manner was gentle serious. He looked over the records on the desk in front of him.

"Hadley found some interesting information last night," I blurted. I explained the bit about the copper-ceruloplasmin ratio, and my cheeks flushed with heat; I suddenly felt like a student again, hoping my contribution wouldn't end up humiliating me.

"Huh," he said. "I haven't heard of that. I'm sure you don't have Wilson's, but I'm not opposed to checking your urine copper level. And we could also send you to the ophthalmologist to check your eyes for KF rings. We can certainly do that." KF rings, Hadley had told me earlier, are rings of copper visible in the eyes of Wilson's patients. The doctor's offer sounded concessionary. He wrote on his pad, briefly checked his computer, then swiveled his chair to look at Hadley.

"I can sure see how you fooled all your doctors," he said.

There was a slackness in the room then, like at the dinner table when guests have stayed too long. Hadley's face was chalky.

"I think Hadley's very worried," I said as neutrally as possible, "that she's going to return to Missoula without a solid explanation for her symptoms that are attributable to an organic disease process." Since I would be leaving the next day, this was my only shot at speaking up for Hadley at The Mayo Clinic. Knowing I had nothing to lose—he wasn't my doctor after all—I pressed on, enumerating Hadley's symptoms. "And the fact that she has had not great, but at least some response to levodopa?"

"This is just not a clear case," the doctor said. "But let's run these couple of other tests. And it looks like you'll be seeing the neuromuscular specialist next."

Two hours later, Hadley and I looked at the MDS's report online.

IMPRESSION/REPORT/PLAN

All of the patient's symptoms could be explained by a disorder of excessive muscle stiffness, including her speech, her skeletal muscles, and possibly the urodynamic findings. I am not seeing any convincing evidence for an organic parkinsonism at all. I think the chances of this being Wilson's disease is very low, but the patient is understandably concerned about that. We will get a 24-hour urine, and I will send her to Ophthalmology to look for Kayser-Fleischer rings, but I suspect they will be normal. I offered her blood tests for Wilson's disease gene testing, but that has to be approved by her insurance company first, so we will not get that now. She can always get that drawn at home. The patient will follow up on Thursday in the Neuromuscular Clinic for them to reassess whether they think she has primary lateral sclerosis to explain all this muscle stiffness. I think that is a reasonable possibility, but I think a functional etiology should also be considered. If no organic etiology can be found, the patient may benefit from our weeklong program in Physical Medicine, and Rehab called the BeST Program, which helps people with functional problems to help retrain the brain and move normally. Of course, organic causes need to be ruled out first.

DIAGNOSES

#1 Muscle stiffness

Muscle stiffness? With everything that was going on in Hadley's body, after all the time and physical and emotional energy she'd spent, she and I couldn't believe she would be going back to Montana with a diagnosis of muscle stiffness, functional problems, and a prescription for retraining her brain.

I looked at Hadley, who sat expressionless and limp. It occurred to me that throughout this whole ordeal, I'd never seen her cry. She had three more days of appointments at The Mayo Clinic. In that time, I hoped with all my heart that the doctors would solve her mystery and pull her off the rollercoaster.

Until that time, I was pretty sure tears would not dare to fall.

NINETEEN:
STRANDED

O n my last day in Rochester with Hadley, she had no appointments at the Clinic. Deciding she needed a break from the medical scene, we drove the red Impala an hour and a half to the Walker Art Center. We were excited—both of us are art enthusiasts and had never been to Minneapolis.

The museum was showing a retrospective of Cindy Sherman, whose work has been largely focused on the exploration of identity. Over thirty years, Sherman has been her own model, capturing herself in a huge range of guises and personas. The Walker's exhibition included 170 very large self-portraits, photographs for which she'd painstakingly transformed herself with clothing, makeup, wigs, and even prosthetics to become someone else: 1950s movie star, a figure from a Vermeer painting, society doyenne, clown, sexy provocateur, to name only a few. Hadley and I wandered through the rooms, amazed by how difficult it was to find the real Cindy Sherman in each of the bold portraits. They were fascinating and disturbing; I found myself somewhat relieved when, at the end of the exhibit, we watched a video of the artist discussing how she works—finally, the real Cindy Sherman.

The portraits stayed with me. On the plane back to San Francisco the next day, I couldn't help thinking about the challenge of presenting ourselves to the world in a way in which we can be truly seen. In Hadley's case, she had put herself on exhibit for doctors over and over again. Unlike Cindy Sherman, she wore no disguises and strove to paint the clearest possible self-portrait, which made it especially hard for her to swallow The Mayo Clinic's suggestion of a functional movement disorder. By trying to catch inconsistencies in Hadley's movements, it was almost as if the doctor who'd first reported FMD had been looking for the disguise Hadley might be wearing to fool the specialists. During her diagnostic journey, Hadley had been scrutinized, analyzed, drugged, twisted, tilted, poked, punctured, injected, shocked, X-rayed, scanned, and operated on. And still, doctors couldn't seem to see her.

Before all of their testing, what the doctors could see they recorded in their medical reports:

Hadley Ferguson is a 33-year-old, right-handed woman from Montana

Patient is a very pleasant 33-year-old artist who works from home. The Patient is a well-developed, well-nourished woman in no acute distress.

Patient was awake, alert, and oriented x 3. Attention span and concentration were normal.

There was no evidence of thought disorder. Affect and mood were unremarkable.

Verbal expression, comprehension, repetition, reading, and writing were intact; prosody was intact.

Hadley is a pleasant, alert, conversive, well-hydrated, well-nourished female in no acute distress.

Mrs. Ferguson is a pleasant 36-year-old woman

Alert, appropriate affect, excellent historian

Mental status was normal

She may need further psychological evaluation and counseling. Depression likely

The mighty Mayo machine spit Hadley back out into the oncoming winter with nothing certain to wrap around herself. The urine test for copper had been normal, and her eyes had revealed no K-F rings, so Wilson's disease was off the table. John flew out to be with her for her last days there, and she was discharged with the following report:

EMG showed poor activation of upper and lower extremity muscles, suggestive of an upper motor neuron process. There is no evidence of anterior horn cell involvement or any neuropathy. Our initial impression was a Parkinson plus syndrome with upper motor neuron findings. However, thorough evaluation did not demonstrate any Parkinsonism. There are inconsistencies in her examination, which points to a functional overlay. At this point, I think that she has an upper motor neuron syndrome of undetermined etiology with functional overlay.

She will benefit from PT. She is open to being evaluated by a behavioral psychologist close to her home to explore a psychological basis of functional overlay.

DIAGNOSES:

#1 Upper Motor Neuron syndrome of undetermined etiology

Hadley returned to Missoula depleted, confused, profoundly distressed, and wishing she'd never gone to Rochester. She was once again filled with self-doubt and wondered why, if she was seriously ill, so many doctors were conflicted about a diagnosis. Could she have made herself sick?

As the Montana winter deepened, she struggled with her painting projects. Dr. Reid agreed with her that she should go back on the levodopa because it was clearly of some benefit to her movement. On New Year's Eve, she was terrified when she experienced some cognitive confusion: Sitting in front of her dinner plate, she couldn't remember which hand to hold her knife and fork in and how to use them.

On the phone one day, Hadley said to me, "Well, whatever it is, they'll find out when they autopsy my brain, I guess." I realized she was at her lowest point yet. When she said she might start writing down her thoughts, I encouraged her.

> None of us knows our fate; I just happen to be in a place where people are trying to predict mine, and it's all over the map. It's terrifying. If my unknown disease had a name, I would have something to fight. I have to decide that Unknown Disease is my fight. This is hard.

I am not there or even close to that yet. My only hope is that someday, my experience will provide answers that will help doctors understand better this unknown disease so someone else will have a name for their disease. I have to believe there's a reason I'm going through this, that the reason is beyond myself and is a key to helping others.

Hadley wrote a letter to her MDS, Dr. Youngman. Even though she wouldn't send it, she found relief in the exercise.

I don't believe I have motor neuron disease. When you gave me that diagnosis, my instincts were jumping up and down, waving wildly, holding up signs that said STOP! WRONG WAY! I still believe I have a parkinsonism. I believe you were right about MSA or atypical Parkinson's and that someday you will have that confirmed. I think there is a lot in this world that relies on data and facts that may not be the same in every situation, and in those cases, we have to step out and consider things we can't see. I think you and I both lost some of our trust in ourselves in this process.

I wonder how things might have been different if you had given me some real thought that last day I saw you if you had talked with me about the reasons for the abrupt shift in diagnosis to motor neuron disease, or even just said, "I really don't know; motor neuron disease looks like what it could be, but let's keep an open mind over the next six months to a year." If you'd said that, I probably could have avoided the whole ordeal at The Mayo Clinic, which has only confused my situation further. Instead, shifting my diagnosis has derailed me from getting help, from feeling optimistic, from wanting to face things head on and make the most of life. It has taken everything away from me that was helpful. You left me stranded, and I had to fend for myself. It was sudden, without warning, and then you were done, gone.

On another day, Hadley wrote:

The financial burden of my health is hard to ignore. I feel a responsibility to take care of those burdens. It is because of my medical situation that we struggle every month to stay on top of our bills. We're working so hard, and at some point, there is only so much we can do.

In her journal entry, Hadley describes the quadruple whammy of her situation: feeling her body failing, being separated from the creative work she loves, letting her family and clients down, and racking up medical expenses. Because of her pre-existing condition from birth, pulmonary stenosis, her only choice for health insurance was a state plan with a very high deductible. In 2009, before she was diagnosed with Parkinson's, she and John together had earned plenty from her painting and his law practice and were easily able to meet all their expenses. But Hadley's productivity fell as her health worsened and bills piled up. On the last day of 2009, she had had an episode of incontinence that, considered together with her nerve pain, had indicated the need for two emergency MRIs. Because she hadn't yet met her health insurance deductible for the year 2009, by the beginning of 2010, she and John owed over $11,000. As the designated bill-payer in their household, Hadley became increasingly anxious about their financial situation. John was working as hard as he could, but in 2010, Hadley earned less than a quarter of what she'd earned the year before.

She tried to solve the money problem without worrying John by putting some of their expenses on credit cards and letting a few bills go. Occasionally, she would trade a painting for professional services, like therapy. In 2011, she had her most successful year yet, earning more than double her 2010 income, and it seemed as though they were getting back on track. But debts still dogged them, and Hadley started dreading the mail when it came. Finally, in 2012, while she was at The Mayo Clinic, John went through the mail and saw the many past due and collection notices. On his own, he decided to have their mail forwarded to a P.O. box so that Hadley would no longer have the stress of looking at the bills. Hadley appreciated that he never made her feel guilty about the debts, and from then on, they've worked together on their finances. But the question of how they would manage Hadley's medical expenses with her reduced income still plagued them. With partisan battles raging over Obamacare throughout 2012, Hadley held onto the hope that she would be one of those who would significantly benefit from the new insurance laws.

In late February 2012, Hadley was clearing out her medicine cabinet, perhaps as a way of uncluttering her mind. She ran across the levodopa that Dr. Youngman had prescribed at her appointment nearly a year ago, which she'd never taken. Levodopa medication is formulated with a combination of levodopa, the chemical that replenishes dopamine, and carbidopa, an agent that counteracts levodopa's side effect of nausea. The medication comes in many ratios of carbidopa/

levodopa, and most patients are sensitive to the differences. While Hadley had taken medication with ratios of 10/100 and 25/250 carbidopa/levodopa without much benefit and a lot of nausea, she hadn't taken the 25/100 formula that Dr. Youngman had prescribed. On a whim, she decided to try it. Within a few days, she felt a dramatic change.

"It's how I felt a year ago," she told me on the phone. "My energy's back. I can't believe it! I feel like I could make it up Mt. Sentinel. And camping sounds fun to me. Maybe I only have Parkinson's after all!"

I had just awakened and was still in bed; I sat up when I heard the excitement in her voice. "Maybe you do only have Parkinson's!" I said. "Wouldn't that be amazing?"

In my head, I quickly tried to rationalize why this particular ratio of carbidopa/levodopa would make a profound difference in how she felt. Could it be that the smaller proportion of carbidopa in the prescriptions she'd taken previously had made the side effects from the levodopa overwhelming for her body? The 25/100s she was now taking was the formulation I had been taking for three years with great results. Her general improvement seemed explainable by the change in meds, I reasoned, pushing back the doubts. But what about her autonomic problems, like urinary retention and orthostatic hypotension? I stayed quiet. I knew Hadley probably heard her own chorus of doubting voices. But she seized this shift with gusto. She posted the new development on our Parkinson's Facebook page, and our group responded joyfully and thoughtfully. "We are all unique," one person wrote. "I don't see how they can clinically lump us together for treatment. You are a great example of this."

Hope can burn so brightly it hurts, but it's hard to look away from. Hadley's reprieve was short-lived.

TWENTY:
SUBMITTING OUR STORIES... AGAIN

In the spring of 2012, before my fall trip to The Mayo Clinic to visit Hadley, I sent my revision of *Dream House* to an agent who had been reading the manuscript in 2011 when the "it just screams film!" agent made her preemptive grab for it. I liked what I'd heard and read about Nora and the books she'd represented. Unlike many agents who, if they acknowledge your query at all, send (or have an assistant send) a two-sentence rejection, Nora was a generous communicator, unafraid of leaving doors open—a quality I appreciated, at least in the beginning. Our email relationship began with an apology soon after she received my manuscript in March:

> Sorry to be slow. Have been deluged with reading; then, after I read, I carry the MS back and the day's work is intense so it prevents me from writing to the author. And then in the office, it is always incredibly busy, so days can pass.

A couple of weeks later:

I do have a lot of little post-its with notes. And some general notes I want to type out, but am racing the clock now. Let me see if I can type it out tomorrow and also send the pages with notes to you so you can see what was on my mind. I actually don't think it is impossible that we would see eye to eye! But I have to write, and I have to send, and I am out of here in ten minutes now, with another editorial letter to the client in the computer... so let me do what I can to relay my thoughts in a few days....

Double negative notwithstanding, my hopes velcroed themselves to the message that was buried in the middle of her hectic email: She wasn't saying no. As promised, the next day, she wrote:

I well remember this book from the last time I read it. I think the writing is fabulous. Your scenes are fabulous. You spin out amazing story material. And I am still a fan. My problem is that it does not yet totally fully resonate with me. And in this market, you need the agent to feel 150%.

Despite what came after—a foot-long explanation of what in my story worked and what didn't, her opening praise flooded me with optimism that I could revise the manuscript in a way that would take her to that magic 150% place. She closed by saying:

So, I am in this weird spot. I like this a lot, but the pieces of the puzzle obviously don't fit together for me just right yet. BUT you are a terrific writer, and this is a truly engaging world you create. I bet you are absolutely exhausted from editing and revising. BUT if you were to work more on this, I would happily read it again.

Warmth! I wanted Nora to be my agent. If she would "happily read again," I would most certainly, even ecstatically, revise again. From March to November, I worked on the manuscript feverishly and when my editor Jay and I felt I'd made the storyline as clear as possible without hammering the reader over the head, I sent the manuscript back to Nora. In December, one week after I returned from The Mayo Clinic, she wrote me another foot-long email outlining the ways in which she still felt uncertain about the story. Then she added:

> So, I could be your guy! But today, I am not all there. I am so sorry—this leaves you in a bad spot, but at least you have my thoughts, and maybe they will be helpful. You are TRULY a strong, beautiful writer. That is not the problem. The problem is that in this awful market, your agent needs to be 150%, and the editors are that much harder to convince. So I have become much tougher!!! BUT I so appreciate your patience and your letting me read this. Tell me what you think of all this when you can.

I was briefly tempted to hang my hat on. "I could be your guy!" But this time, I was perplexed by Nora's notes and questions. Some of her critiques made me wonder if she'd read the manuscript while preparing her taxes during a cocktail party (she confessed, for example, that she'd forgotten the name of the main character. I was forced to consider the possibility that it wasn't clarity she was missing but something else altogether, something that even she couldn't identify. I'd been working toward landing her for eight months. Where was I, percentage-wise, 85? 135? What were the chances that further revisions would get me to 150%?

I needed to move on. I thanked Nora for spending time on *Dream House* and retreated from the agent search. Here is where a younger writer or one without Parkinson's would have simply compiled a new list of agents to approach; in the tough world of publishing, I'd gotten only a small taste of rejection. Rejection I could handle. But I didn't have the stamina for the painfully slow pace and the needle-in-a-haystack nature of the submission process. Every day, my bradykinetic body reminded me that time was precious. Finally, in late April, I decided to give *Dream House* to the agent who'd wanted it in 2011. He was thrilled, and it felt great knowing he'd convey his unequivocal passion to publishers.

Meanwhile, Hadley was in a state of agonizing discombobulation, trying, like me, to make the pieces of her story fit so that it would be accepted and understood. Her miraculous-seeming response to the 25/100 formulation of levodopa remained consistent for a few months. Still, by May the medication was wearing off more quickly, and sometimes it seemed as if it hadn't kicked in at all. She wondered whether this might point back to an MSA diagnosis. Not wanting to alarm her family, she kept her worries to herself. But she continued to write about them.

June 14, 2013

I feel lost with my situation and where to go or what to do from here. I have so many commitments and projects to complete. How will I get everything done? How will I tell people that I won't be able to complete what I said I could do? I wish I could spend my days with Sarah and John and soak in every moment. I feel like I have to get these things done before I can do that, and what if it is too late? What if I work and when the projects are done, I have missed my opportunity and time with my family? What was I thinking to say yes to the projects on my plate?? I am digging myself into a deep hole and I am worried I won't get out of it.

Dr. Reid was supportive, and together they made decisions about Hadley's medication regimen, but neither of them knew what they were treating. Hadley turned to the large Parkinson's network she'd acquired through Summit for Parkinson's and our Facebook group. She collected the names of movement disorders specialists in Colorado, California, Washington, Pennsylvania, Texas, and Canada and began researching them. She called a friend who works with the Michael J. Fox Foundation and asked to have the MJFF's medical experts identify the top three. When she inquired about these doctors in our Facebook group, two of the members responded that they were seeing Dr. Truitt, a Movement Disorders Specialist in Houston, Texas.

They told Hadley that Dr. Truitt had been an MDS for thirty years and had "seen it all," so Hadley could count on getting a very frank assessment. Since our Facebook friend Lucy would be seeing Dr. Truitt in July, Hadley scheduled her appointment for the same day. Hadley and her mother, Jana, flew to Austin, where Lucy met them with a dinner-to-go, and the three of them drove the three hours to Houston together.

The next morning at Hadley's appointment, a resident spent an hour going over her health history and examining her. He then left the room for a long consultation with Dr. Truitt, during which time Hadley felt very anxious that she would be facing a rerun of her experience at The Mayo Clinic. Finally, Dr. Truitt entered the exam room and shook hands with Hadley and Jana. After a few questions for Hadley, he became somber and very focused.

"Have you ever heard of multiple system atrophy?" he asked.

When Hadley told him yes, Dr. Truitt expressed without hesitation that her symptoms and tests supported an MSA diagnosis. "I hope I'm wrong," he said. "But this is what I think it is, and now that we know, this is how we're going to treat it." He went on to explain that he treats MSA very aggressively with levodopa, and he bumped up Hadley's prescription from 300 to 1000 mg/day, three times the amount that I was taking for Parkinson's, almost seven years from diagnosis. This is how Dr. Truitt saw Hadley.

IMPRESSION:

This 36-year-old right-handed freelance painter/acrylic artist from Montana presents for evaluation of a 4-year history of progressive fatigue, global bradykinesia, gait instability, falls, and dysautonomias manifested chiefly by orthostatic lightheadedness, urinary retention, constipation and cold hands and cold feet sign. She has tried various medication regiments in the past, namely Azilect, Mirapex, levodopa, and Amantadine, with variable response as detailed above. The constellation of symptoms and signs suggests the diagnosis of multiple system atrophy (MSA-P). Her rigidity and bradykinesia are fairly symmetric. Her dysautonomia, including urinary retention, constipation, and history of orthostatic hypotension, are prominent and have occurred early in her disease course.

Moreover, the relatively rapid progression of her symptoms and her young age are atypical of Parkinson's disease. Her MRI brain and DaTscan were reviewed and would further corroborate a diagnosis of probable MSA. She has had an inconsistent response to levodopa in the past, which would further go against Parkinson's disease. In sum, the combination of adult onset, sporadic progressive onset with Parkinsonism, dysautonomia and inconsistent response to levodopa, abnormal imaging, and relatively rapid progressive course corroborate a clinical diagnosis of probable MSA-P.

The name—multiple system atrophy, chillingly describes this disease's course and inevitable, grim outcome: As nerve cells die and areas of the brain atrophy, multiple parts and functions of the body shut down until even breathing and eating are not possible. There are two types of MSA: MSA-P, in which parkinsonian symptoms like stiffness, slowness, gait disturbance, and balance problems present first, and cerebella type, or MSA-C, whose features include coordination, balance, and swallowing difficulties as well as slurred speech. Often, patients start out with the symptoms of one type of MSA and gradually develop symptoms of the other, but all patients eventually succumb to an autonomic nervous system failure. Whereas in Parkinson's, it is primarily the substantia nigra area of the brain that atrophies as its dopamine-producing neurons die off, in MSA, the substantia nigra, cerebellum, and brain stem all experience significant loss of nerve cells. The brain stem is the command center for the autonomic nervous system, regulating heart and respiratory rates, blood pressure, digestion, salivation, and urination, among other functions. A brain MRI can support a diagnosis of MSA by showing areas of atrophy, but not always. As with Parkinson's, it's believed that nerve cell death in MSA is attributable to an abnormal accumulation of the protein alpha-synuclein in the brain.

Multiple system atrophy is rare, annually affecting about three people per 100,000, predominantly over the age of fifty. It has no cure, and it progresses very fast compared to PD; a patient diagnosed after age forty has a maximum life expectancy of seven to ten years. In 2018, doctors recognized that people with young onset MSA (diagnosed before forty) had a longer life expectancy of up to eighteen years.

Treatment for MSA involves managing symptoms to make patients as comfortable as possible and to maintain their bodily functions. As in Hadley's case, levodopa can relieve parkinsonian symptoms like slowness, stiffness, and rigidity, but the drug typically loses its effectiveness over time, and not all those with MSA respond. Physical therapy is always recommended to help maintain strength and balance as long as possible, and speech pathologists help to improve speech and voice volume. Low blood pressure, which people with MSA experience when standing, is treated with steroid medication that helps the body retain salt and water; later, a pacemaker might be needed to regulate heart rate. Medications can help with urinary retention at early stages of the disease, but a catheter eventually becomes necessary. Late in the disease, both breathing and feeding tubes might be required.

Leaving Dr. Truitt's office with the MSA diagnosis, Hadley cried briefly and told her mother she was sorry. When Jana hugged her and asked her why, Hadley said she felt awful that Jana would have to endure her illness along with Charlie's Parkinson's. She called John and her father, and she texted me the news: "I know it's terrible, and I'm scared, but it's so good to know what it is and to have someone tell me they're going to help me with it." She sprinkled her message with emoticons that I knew were intended to reassure me she was handling it. But they only made this new reality more surreal.

A few days later, Hadley told me that all the noise in her head from years of trying to get a diagnosis had been sucked out, and she was experiencing a "huge silence." Finally, she could stop trying to explain herself to the world. Finally, she had been seen.

TWENTY-ONE:
THE PARALYSIS OF MISDIAGNOSIS

O ver the course of two years, Hadley was diagnosed with the following conditions in this sequence: Parkinson's disease, possible multiple system atrophy, Parkinson's disease, primary lateral sclerosis, probable multiple system atrophy, possible functional movement disorder, upper motor neuron syndrome of undetermined etiology, and multiple system atrophy. These diagnoses didn't comprise an aggregate of multiple illnesses; rather, each ruled out a previous one. Hadley's movement disorders specialist, Dr. Youngman, diagnosed her with Parkinson's, then possible MSA, and finally, denying Parkinsonism altogether, he settled on upper motor neuron disease. It's significant that the first doctor to see Hadley at The Mayo Clinic in Rochester was also the last because it demonstrates how the diagnostic process can become derailed. At their initial appointment, the doctor made the diagnosis of probable MSA but changed it to upper motor neuron syndrome after Hadley had been seen by the other Mayo specialists. Finally, in Houston, after studying the same health history and test results, Dr. Truitt diagnosed MSA.

For months at a time, Hadley had been stuck in a medical quagmire. How did this happen?

The National Academy of Medicine reported in 2015 that annually, about 5% of adults receive misdiagnoses that contribute to about 10% of patient deaths. Ideally, algorithms or statistics used in making a diagnosis are objective; when a doctor recognizes a familiar pattern of symptoms that can be supported by laboratory testing, a diagnosis can be made with confidence. However, when a patient's symptoms don't fit the usual pattern or tests are inconclusive, the reliance on data will often constrain a doctor's thinking. For example, one of the reasons Dr. Bright gave Hadley for not thinking she had MSA was that, to his knowledge, there had been no cases of MSA diagnosed before the age of forty.

Data is not a substitute for a careful examination of and dialogue with a patient. Many factors come into play when a doctor examines a patient and takes her history. For example, how a patient describes her symptoms is critical, but when stressed, she might overemphasize or underreport certain symptoms. Personal history, culture, and emotional state all play a role in how a patient communicates with her physician. Hadley has this insight about herself as a patient:

> I think my skill at adjusting to stressful situations and creating a facade that I am doing fine has sometimes kept me from being taken seriously by doctors. Even when I seek help, I put my best foot forward and minimize how I feel because it's embarrassing to make a big deal of something and then discover it isn't serious and I'm just being a wimp. I always assume first that I must be overreacting.

Equally influential in the diagnostic process are the doctor's own temperament, biases, and state of mind. Is he impatient to get an answer or, frustrated that he can't, in a rush, or over-confident? Does his bedside manner earn him the trust of his patient so that his questions will prompt a spontaneous and open dialogue? Is he biased by something he sees in the patient that might not have anything to do with her symptoms?

Pat Croskerry, a professor at Dalhousie University in Halifax, Nova Scotia, who was trained as an experimental psychologist and went on to become an emergency medicine physician, has written extensively about what he has labeled "cognitive errors" in doctors' thinking that lead to misdiagnosis. Cognitive errors stem from failures in perception, failed heuristics (problem-solving techniques), biases, and the emotions of the doctor who is diagnosing the patient. Hadley's journey to diagnosis illustrates some of the cognitive errors Dr. Croskerry names: attribution error, affective error, confirmation bias, and diagnosis momentum.

Attribution errors occur when a patient fits a positive or negative stereotype. For example, a young man wearing worn and dirty clothes who comes into the emergency room in a state of disorientation might be assumed to be on drugs when he's actually suffering a neurological event. A very thin, haggard twenty-year-old who comes in complaining that she vomits every time she eats might bear a powerful resemblance to one of the twenty million women in the US suffering from an eating disorder, but she might have a serious autoimmune disease. When Hadley, a healthy-looking, industrious, articulate, and delightful twentysomething, first complained of a variety of symptoms that didn't fit a clear pattern, doctors were inclined to believe that she wasn't seriously ill.

Doctors see a surprising number of patients—estimates run as high as 11.6%—who have somatic symptom disorder or who are unnecessarily anxious about their symptoms. Because of this common phenomenon, Hadley was unfairly told by both Dr. Bright and Dr. Youngman not to "obsess" and by doctors at The Mayo Clinic that she might have a functional, or psychogenic, movement disorder. These admonitions and misreadings betrayed the doctors' preconceptions and reliance on past "evidence" as well as their lack of understanding of the individual in front of them—Hadley.

Intrigued by the different labels Dr. Crosskerry has assigned to cognitive errors made in diagnoses, I couldn't resist trying them on to see how they might fit Hadley's case. Doctors make affective errors when they are biased in the direction of a positive outcome for the patient. In this case, the doctor will pay attention to the symptoms and information about a case that will confirm this positive outcome. Hadley's movement disorders specialist, Dr. Youngman, seems to have made this type of error when he set aside all the symptoms he originally noted that pointed to parkinsonism and abruptly changed her diagnosis from Parkinson's or MSA to upper motor neuron disease. He based his decision on two tests known to often be inconclusive, a DaTscan and a levodopa challenge test, as well as a test ordered by a neuromuscular specialist. Hadley was on a first-name basis with Dr. Youngman and considered him a friend. Did Dr. Youngman's feelings of friendship influence him to veer away from a drastic diagnosis and pass her on to another doctor?

When I suggested that Hadley see my Dr. Bright to confirm or rule out MSA, I might have unwittingly set up Dr. Bright to make an affective error. I admit to having had fantasies that he would swoop in on the proverbial white horse and rescue her from the terrible fate of MSA or Unknown Disease; he might have understood that to be my motivation in referring Hadley to him. When he met with Hadley and John, I'm sure he wanted to be able to give the vibrant young couple good news. He focused on all of Hadley's symptoms that are typical in Parkinson's, appearing to downplay the symptoms that most concerned her: rapid disease progression and an inconsistent response to levodopa, as well as orthostatic hypotension and other autonomic symptoms that are associated more with MSA. Such cherry-picking of data to support a diagnosis and minimizing information that contradicts it is called confirmation bias. I wondered: Could Dr. Bright have been cherry-picking?

Later, when Hadley pressed Dr. Bright in her email to explain what he saw that made him rule out MSA, he relied on statistical data and evidence from his own experience, citing the fairly common occurrence of young-onset Parkinson's and the fact that he'd never seen a case of MSA in someone under forty. (This second point was especially frustrating to Hadley because online, she'd found numerous cases of MSA in people under forty.) Dr. Bright's approach might have demonstrated another affective error when he told me that when it comes to diagnosing and treating his patents, he doesn't want to "perpetuate their irrational fears." It's easy to see why well-meaning, caring doctors might be susceptible to making affective errors; it must be very difficult to see a patient cut down in the prime of their life by a deadly disease. To err in this way is human. As Jane Austen wrote in her novel *Persuasion*, "We each begin probably with a little bias and upon that bias build every circumstance in favor of it."

Diagnosis momentum is another kind of cognitive error doctors make when they rely on previous diagnoses. In his book *How Doctors Think*, Jerome Groopman tells the story of a woman who, for fifteen years beginning when she was twenty, suffered severely from chronic abdominal pain, vomiting, and diarrhea. Doctors diagnosed her over and over again with anorexia, bulimia, and irritable bowel syndrome, even though she told them she was doing everything she could to gain weight. Finally, at thirty-five, when her bones had begun to decompose and her immune system was failing, she consulted a new specialist. The doctor set aside her enormous stack of medical records and asked her to tell him her story. He listened carefully. He then examined the patient with a thoroughness that no other doctor had. He ran a few tests that confirmed his suspicion: She was suffering from celiac disease, an autoimmune disorder in which the body can't digest gluten. For fifteen years, the cereal, bread, and pasta doctors had been recommending to the young woman for weight gain had been slowly killing her.

In Hadley's case, the misdiagnoses were not as "sticky" as that of the woman with celiac disease but sticky enough that the diagnosis of one doctor seemed to unduly influence that of the next, creating something more like "diagnosis diversion" than diagnosis momentum. It was Dr. Youngman who first suggested MSA to Hadley. Still, when Dr. Bright ruled it out, Dr. Youngman, after running a few tests that didn't support an MSA diagnosis as well as one that could suggest upper motor neuron disease, abandoned the possibility of MSA. Hadley was unconvinced of the upper motor neuron disease diagnosis and traveled to The Mayo Clinic in Rochester to sort out whether she had Parkinson's or MSA. On her second day there, although no specialist had ever suggested a functional movement disorder, a doctor planted this new possibility in her records. In the absence of another clear explanation for Hadley's myriad symptoms, the functional diagnosis gained traction, appearing to cloud the diagnostic process for The Mayo Clinic doctors who saw Hadley later in the week.

"It's a truism in medicine that difficult diagnoses are most likely to be made by the most or least experienced doctors,"

Dr. Lisa Sanders writes in her book *Every Patient Tells a Story: Medical Mysteries and the Art of Diagnosis*. Without preconceptions and experienced-based biases that can build up over years of practice, a novice might be able to see a patient in a fresher light. Doctors with the most years of experience, on the other hand, have in their mental libraries a vast number of cases from which to draw when making a difficult diagnosis. It's not surprising that Dr. Truitt was able to diagnose Hadley with MSA at her first visit; he has been examining people with Parkinson's and MSA for decades. Hadley and I could be considered the novices in her case since we knew nothing about MSA when we started talking to each other about how its symptoms mirrored hers. We knew that people with the disease were often first diagnosed with Parkinson's. We were focused on how her experience diverged from typical PD. We paid no attention to statistics regarding MSA's rarity, typical age of onset, or the reliability of certain tests for it. Nor did we know about other illnesses that it could resemble, like functional movement disorder and upper motor neuron disease. With our limited knowledge, it was easy for us to remain focused on the evidence that supported a diagnosis of MSA.

To be fair, it is well known that distinguishing MSA from Parkinson's is tough. Because of the diseases' many overlapping symptoms, most doctors rely on time to clarify whether a patient has PD or MSA: if, within just a few years, a patient who's been diagnosed with PD has become incontinent or has profound orthostatic hypotension, for example, MSA is more likely to be the cause.

A different patient—less focused, curious, skeptical, or perhaps more fearful—might have resisted digging for bad news. But Hadley didn't want to wait until she was falling down every day to get her diagnosis, and she felt very alone with her feelings of urgency. Most published diagnosis stories describe heart-pounding dramas in which a patient's life hangs in the balance in the emergency room, or death is otherwise imminent because a diagnosis can't be made. When every second counts, doctors worry about a misdiagnosis that can hurt or kill their patient. However, when a patient is very ill, but her life is not in immediate danger, there can be a slackening in a provider's drive to find an answer. Fortunately, Hadley's Dr. Reid in Missoula remained steadfastly intent on helping find a diagnosis because they'd developed a strong doctor-patient bond. But in cases like Hadley's, when the patient is passed among specialists with whom they don't have an ongoing relationship, doctors can be less invested in the outcome. One specialist Hadley saw wrote in his report:

> Complex individual has a plethora of complaints associated with meager findings.

This doctor was expressing a phenomenon that Dr. Croskerry calls "yin-yang out." When a patient has been "worked up the yin-yang," doctors begin to feel that every avenue has been explored and that they've hit a dead end.

Another factor in the confusion surrounding Hadley's case: Because there is no treatment that will slow or alter MSA's progression, some of the doctors she consulted might have assumed there was no reason to rush into naming such a dire diagnosis. But without a diagnosis, she was forced into a preoccupation with her health that took an enormous emotional and financial toll on her and her family. She lost days and weeks of being with her family and of working on her art, as well as hours of sleep and the kind of rest a seriously ill person requires. Misdiagnoses that were made, especially of functional movement disorder, caused her nearly paralyzing psychological trauma. In this terrible limbo, Hadley was unable to see her future. How should she take care of herself, and who would help her? How could she soothe the fears of those closest to her when she herself was living with such uncertainty?

Although death was not imminent for Hadley the way it might be for someone in the ER, her lack of diagnosis was undeniably life-threatening. She was an artist in acute distress.

In *How Doctors Think*, Jerome Groopman suggests that to help avoid a prolonged or murky diagnostic process, patients should encourage their doctors to think outside the box by asking them, "What's the worst thing this can be?" He adds, "That question is not a sign of neurosis or hypochondria." His reassuring statement, of course, acknowledges that many doctors do find this question neurotic and hypochondriacal, which is why we laugh dismissively at ourselves when we wonder aloud to our physician whether the tightness in our chest could be heart disease or if the new speck on our arm might be skin cancer. When I was scared about my symptoms of yet-to-be-diagnosed Parkinson's, my doctor told me there was nothing physically wrong with me; I was just "very anxious." And when Hadley asked Dr. Youngman and Dr. Bright whether she might have the "worst thing," MSA, they warned her not to "obsess."

Maybe doctors, not their patients, should ask themselves unprompted, "What's the worst thing this could be?" I say "maybe" because there are plenty of patients who would rather not know the worst-case scenario, especially if it's unlikely. Another way to handle a situation in which a diagnosis is unclear would be for the doctor to ask the patient, "What are you most worried about?" The question signals that the doctor takes their patient's symptoms and any associated fears seriously and will investigate their case thoroughly, with appropriate urgency.

TWENTY-TWO:
LOSING GROUND, GAINING ALTITUDE

I n the weeks following her MSA diagnosis in July of 2013, Hadley hustled to meet the design proposal deadline for the Montana Women's Mural competition. The mural, which would hang permanently on the third-floor wall flanking the Montana State Capitol's grand staircase, would be a dream commission for any artist. The work was to commemorate the 100th anniversary of women's suffrage in Montana by depicting women's contributions as community builders throughout the state's history. Noting that of the forty existing art pieces in the Capitol's permanent collection, only seven included an image of a woman; two women legislators had initiated the Senate bill for the commissioning of the mural. The guidelines stipulated that the work not depict any one recognizable woman but rather represent Montana's "unsung heroines" in their diverse roles: on ranches, in their tribes, in government and business, and as founders of schools, theaters, libraries, and hospitals.

As a strong community contributor, feminist, and the mother of a daughter, Hadley was deeply inspired by the project's objectives; ideas and images for a narrative about women's roles in Montana's history came to her fast and furiously. But the day before she planned to drive her design proposal from Missoula to Helena, the mural project's administrator called Hadley and the other finalist to tell them that budget constraints had forced them to put the project on hold indefinitely. Hadley had mixed feelings about this development. On the one hand, she'd put almost everything else aside to complete a design she was excited about; on the other, she was exhausted and had been worrying about how she would execute the mural if she were given the commission. Maybe it would be a blessing in disguise if the project was canceled.

But losing the mural commission and its substantial fee would mean a bigger financial burden for Hadley and John in the coming year, so she got busy researching grants for artists. Again and again, I was amazed by her resourcefulness and perseverance. Anyone else confronting her physical, financial, and professional challenges might have been deterred, even if temporarily. But Hadley had found her way to a place of equanimity. Because Hadley had never talked about writing, I was surprised when she told me she'd been inspired to write about all she'd been feeling.

COME BE WITH ME

I am entering a very peaceful place. There has been so much noise and distraction through this medical process, most of it with a lot of negativity attached, and as I further accept my diagnosis, I am slowly leaving behind chunks and pieces of the past year/years. My body feels so light and free. I feel like I have almost let go of all of the weight I have been hauling along with me. All the noise was pulling me further from myself, isolating me. With the release of it, I feel centered in a way I have never experienced. I feel open. I feel so calm. I feel happy.

I am not afraid of the road ahead. It is inviting and comforting. It is bringing me closer to people I love and allowing me to be with them. I feel like the wall I started building when I was young is starting to come down, and what I see on the other side is beautiful. I am not only seeing what is on the other side, but for the first time I am bringing it down for others to come be with me.

This centering is bringing me to a new place that I have never been before, a place I have always wanted to be but I didn't know how to get to... It is amazing. I finally see myself, and everything in my life is so clear. It is as if I have been hovering someplace outside myself, and my shell has been maneuvering through life. I'm suddenly struck by the feeling of being back in my body and feeling what it is to live again.

As I move forward, I hope to bring people closer to me. It is hard for me to feel their sadness, and I want to bring them with me to this place of peace. I want to be with them, support them, to love them. I want them to come be with me.

Would I be able to go with Hadley to "this place of peace"? On many days, it seemed impossible not to become preoccupied with the painful inevitability, as I aged, of losing people in my life. Just months before Hadley's MSA diagnosis, one of my closest friends was diagnosed with metastatic cancer. Like Hadley, Sylvia was a very informed patient, dogged in her medical research. She'd survived breast cancer ten years earlier, but now four major hospitals were unable to agree on what kind of cancer she had, making a treatment plan unclear. Throughout the summer, Sylvia endured rounds of chemotherapy with good humor, sending me photos of her new hair from the wig shop and planning outings for her weeks off from the poison. Every time I saw her laugh, I wanted to cry: How much longer would I get to see her blue eyes dancing as she delivered her incisive analysis of the news? One day, she told me, "I always thought I'd be around to take care of you when your Parkinson's got bad." Her telescoping punched me in the gut.

Hadley's and Sylvia's courage was an important reality check when my mood slumped because my agent hadn't been able to sell *Dream House*. A couple of the thirty or so that passed on it explained they could only take books that would be "big." One of them lamented that publishing was at its "lowest point in my long career." The rejections were generous, at least, and it seemed that, in some cases, I was in the right place at the wrong time.

> Armsden does a marvelous job of (blah-blah-blah) ... I was really impressed by (blah-blah-blah) ... But as much as I admire the book, I confess I'm not sure I see the best way to really break this one out. It seems that this otherwise wonderful business becomes harder and harder, the market being what it is. So, with admiration, I should pass.

When July was gone without a publisher in sight, I decided it would be unhealthy to remain in waiting mode.

I opened the file for the other novel I'd been sporadically writing for five years. Working around commitments to family and friends, a house full of dust raised by contractors who were six months into our remodel, and my symptoms, I made myself sit at my laptop and type words that would push my story along. For two weeks, everything I wrote was slow and sticky, as if my fingers were connected to a donut, not my brain. The donut was dense, full of fat, and static.

Finally, I realized that my real life was outshouting the voice of my fiction. Every time I spoke with Hadley, I felt an urgency to listen and rehash details, to wonder aloud with her, to dissect the characters and dialogue in her life that stood out so vividly. I recognized this urgency as the thrust that often launches a new writing project.

The troubled teens in my novel could wait! I wanted to tell Hadley's story.

Hadley seemed pleased yet somehow reserved about the idea. She thought her experience would resonate with others trying to get diagnoses and raise awareness about neurological diseases. Braiding together our two stories was a way for me to be with her and to process my experience with Parkinson's. I'd witnessed the empowerment fellow Parkies gained from throwing themselves into PD advocacy, education, and fundraising, and I had a feeling that through writing, I, too could put Parkinson's on a leash, instead of the other way around.

That October, I was acutely aware of how hard Hadley and Sylvia were working to make the most of each sick day, honoring their bodies' limitations and struggling to remain equanimous in the face of terminal illness. On a drive with Lewis one day, I told him that it felt unfair that I was losing friends at such a young age. He replied, "Catherine, I know what you're saying, but I'm just not there with you. I don't feel that death is around me the way you do."

A couple of weeks later, Lewis flaunted his disregard for his mortality by taking his hands off his bicycle handlebars going downhill at thirty miles per hour. After hitting a bump in the road, he flew off his bike, breaking three ribs and his collarbone and mangling his left hand so gruesomely that it took three hours of surgery and subsequent skin grafts to return it to 85% functionality.

I would like to say that the first emotion I felt—after fear and then profound relief that Lewis was alive without head injury or internal bleeding, was compassion. But it was anger. At that moment in my life, just being human seemed harrowing enough; I had no patience for dangerous sport. "What were you thinking, taking your hands off the handlebars?" I asked him a few days after the accident. "You have a big life, a family, and twenty-five employees who depend on you." Lewis confessed he frequently rode for short stretches with no hands and had a "speed problem." Since he was a boy, he'd loved going fast. This latter fact I knew from being his passenger in our car; another tip off was the four vintage motorcycles in our garage that he occasionally raced. What alarmed me was what he said next: "Even though I know cyclists have accidents all the time, I have never once imagined it happening to me. It's like I lack an inner warning system that would tell me I'm being too risky." It was a revelation for both of us, and I was grateful for his insight and honesty, albeit arrived at the hard way.

Human bodies are miraculously designed, but we are not cars that come with different safety ratings. Yet even though we are all constructed of flesh and bone, vulnerable to the same injuries and illnesses, and even though we all will die, each of us has our own special relationship with mortality. Illness or accident will bring most people face-to-face with the specter of death; some survivors will make the consequences of human vulnerability into a cause. Among the unaffected, however, are those who curiously lack an inner sense of what threatens their survival or might block such threats from their consciousness. It is as if the mere thought of them might be a harbinger of death.

There is certainly an exhilarating freedom in living life as if you're immortal. But confronting one's mortality can bring about a different kind of unburdening, one that comes with a heightened appreciation for life. In 2015, upon learning he had terminal cancer, the renowned neurologist and author Oliver Sacks wrote:

> Over the last few days, I have been able to see my life... with a deepening sense of the connection of all its parts... My predominant feeling is one of gratitude. I have loved and been loved; I have been given much, and I have given something in return; I have read and traveled and thought and written... Above all, I have been a sentient being, a thinking animal, on this beautiful planet, and that in itself has been an enormous privilege and adventure.

Dr. Sacks wrote his essay just a few weeks after being diagnosed and six months before his death. Hadley's piece, "Come Be With Me," describes a very similar shift in life view even though she still had years to live. Practitioners of mindfulness know the rewards of feeling grateful and present in the moment, but what if all of us, even without facing terminal illness, could attain this gratitude for life, could seize on it right now as if at any moment our bodies that provide us the power of sentience could be broken?

The passion, vigor, and attitude in Sacks' and Hadley's words prove that we can find thrill right where we are. Even riding carefully, hands firmly on the handlebars, we can let go, and we can soar.

TWENTY-THREE:
GIRLS' WEEKEND, NEURO STYLE

Hadley's stepfather, Charlie, died from complications of Parkinson's on October 10, 2013, only four years after being diagnosed. He was seventy-three. Hadley had been close to Charlie, and I knew she was going to miss him tremendously. I wondered how it had been for her to witness his precipitous decline only a few months after learning her own illness was terminal.

When I asked her about this, she told me, "Watching how this all went with Charlie made me think about how I might do some things differently." I wanted to know more but sensed Hadley wasn't ready to elaborate.

I was sad for Hadley and her mother, Jana, and Charlie's death rattled me in another way. Charlie wasn't old; why had his disease progressed so fast? I wondered. Could he have had Parkinson's for many years before he was diagnosed? Why were medications not working for him? When you have a disease, it's hard not to feel afraid when that disease whisks someone away.

For the next couple of weeks, Hadley helped Jana with the transition, completing paperwork, planning a memorial, and going through Charlie's things. When I spoke with her in late October, I was struck by how weak and hoarse she sounded. "I finally hit the wall," she said. "You can probably hear it in my voice."

Hadley told me she'd started LSVT LOUD, Lee Silverman Voice Training, a protocol developed to specifically address the vocal impairment that can be caused by Parkinson's and MSA. With both diseases, inadequate muscle movement in the larynx, respiratory system, and mouth can compromise vocal loudness, breath, and articulation. Conventional speech therapy has been unsuccessful at treating this condition, in part because PD patients sometimes have a deficit in sensory processing that makes them unable to perceive the softening of their voice. LSVT addresses all aspects of vocal function through a series of exercises that are focused on the goal of speaking loudly. Rather than training people to shout, LSVT brings the voice to a healthy volume without strain by stimulating the motor speech system. Sensory awareness training also helps the patient learn to recognize the volume level of their voice.

"Oh, guess what else?" Hadley said. "I had a swallow test. I know this sounds silly, but I'm feeling pretty good because my chewing and initiating a swallow were normal, but there was a delay when the food got farther down my throat."

She paused, and I tried hard to grasp where the good news was in this.

"You have no control over that part of swallowing farther down," she explained. "It's part of the autonomic system. You can't cause that dysfunction just by being anxious."

Once again, I was reminded of how deeply traumatizing it had been for Hadley that people didn't believe she had a real, organic disease. She was still struggling to shake the self-doubt their dismissiveness had seeded.

Hadley had scheduled a November follow-up with Dr. Truitt in Houston, which she again arranged for the same day as our YOPD Facebook friend Lucy's appointment. I decided to meet the two of them there. It had been a year since I'd spent time with Hadley at The Mayo Clinic, and writing about her made me miss being with her in person. I was also curious to hear what Dr. Truitt would say about Hadley's MSA four months after he'd diagnosed her. And I was excited to meet Lucy, who never failed to make me laugh with her wickedly irreverent Facebook posts.

From the lobby of the Houston Hilton, I watched Lucy and Hadley emerge from Lucy's white Audi station wagon. Hadley—slim, demure-looking with her long hair and glasses, jeans, and cardigan, too covered for the eighty-three-degree day, moved slowly toward the car trunk. Lucy sprang from the driver's seat, all tan and tank top, Lycra and platform sandals, big hoop earrings, and a hip, don't-mess-with-me short haircut. She lurched to the trunk and yanked out their suitcases with enough force to propel them across the street.

We exchanged warm embraces, and from that moment I became aware of every detail. My sojourn with Hadley and Lucy would provide a rare opportunity to observe members of my tribe; if I paid close attention, they would have things to teach me about myself. As we headed to the elevators towing our suitcases, Lucy took the lead at top speed, carving wide arcs across the lobby. "Once I get moving, I have to move!" she called back to us. Lucy had had PD for ten years since finishing her medical residency in pediatrics. Before taking levodopa, she'd had severe difficulty walking and needed a scooter to get around. Levodopa restored her ability to walk, but she was among the unlucky ones who almost immediately develop dyskinesia after starting the medication. It looked exhausting to be in her perpetual-motion body, and I knew she occasionally hurt herself when an errant arm or leg made a sudden move. Immediately, I felt an even deeper admiration for her energy, sense of humor, and proud style.

The three of us were all fumbling hands, trying to operate the elevator. We blamed ourselves when we couldn't get the slot in the panel to accept our room cards. We were hopeless! At least that's how it felt until three other women got into the elevator and couldn't make their cards work, either. We laughed: The cards were the problem.

I was taken aback that the hotel room I'd reserved was as unfriendly as the Rochester TownePlace Suites had been, decorated with the same maroon and gray color scheme. The large windows didn't open. Twelve stories below us, in the toaster-like slot of space between the modern building slabs of Baylor Hospital, lay a rectangle of turquoise—a pool without a single soul in or around it. We couldn't escape the room fast enough. Lucy had lived in Houston and knew where we could grab some comfort and good vibes to normalize this strange interlude. We indulged in the best Mexican food I've ever eaten—a scrumptious concoction involving pomegranate, walnuts, and poblano chilis. Lucy and I ordered margaritas, and Hadley had her usual, a mojito. We took a few selfies. We giggled. We could've been friends on a girls' night out, like the ones at the next table. We were. Girlfriends, more or less.

In the morning, I wondered aloud to Hadley and Lucy if we should avoid parking problems by walking to Dr. Truitt's office. When Lucy said, "It's almost half a mile," I was embarrassed; for Hadley, half a mile would have felt like three. When we arrived at the medical building's parking garage, it was full. We were directed to a valet area another block away, and when we got out of the car, we walked down a series of corridors for what seemed like a half mile to the neurology clinic. Lucy zoomed ahead. It was already 10 a.m., her appointment time and the faster she moved, the more her body careened. Dyskinesia, I had learned, is always worse when you're late.

As we approached the check-in desk, Dr. Truitt's receptionist took us in: a dazed variety pack of wacky-walking women. Only two other patients sat in the waiting room—so different from Dr. Bright's waiting area in San Francisco, where people come from all over northern California to be seen by neurology specialists. Sometimes, whole families fill that space. The forty-seat room always provides me with a reality check on how lucky I am that Parkinson's is my only hardship. I'm often the only one there without a caregiver. The children in Dr. Bright's waiting room especially break my heart—babies in arms, children in wheelchairs, as do their weary-looking parents. The white-coated doctors come out to cheerfully greet their patients, sometimes humoring them as if they're children. Let's face it: When you're neurologically impaired, you are, in some ways like a child, losing basic abilities that you worked so hard to master as a youngster. By the time Dr. Bright comes to fetch me for my appointment, I'm often sweaty and filled with mixed emotions: relief that I am as well as I am and that my children are healthy, and profound fear of what's ahead.

Dr. Truitt's empty waiting room triggered the heebie-jeebies in me, even though I was not the one with the appointment. Lucy was jiggly in her chair; after dinner the night before, she'd stayed out late with a friend from medical school. She knew I was going to accompany Hadley to see Dr. Truitt. "I'm totaled," she told us now. "I wouldn't mind having another pair of ears at my appointment."

Delighted I could be helpful, I told Lucy I'd be those ears.

While we waited, Hadley was silent. I knew she'd barely slept because every time I'd turned over, she was under her covers reading *Brain On Fire,* a memoir by a young woman who nearly died of encephalitis after being misdiagnosed with psychosis. Hadley didn't eat or drink when she got up, either. I wondered if her expectations about her meeting with Dr. Truitt were raised, especially since she'd flown from Missoula to Salt Lake City, endured a two-hour layover, flown to Austin, and then driven three hours to Houston. But what did "raised expectations" mean in the context of her MSA diagnosis? It didn't mean good news because there was no good news yet about MSA. It didn't mean new information because Hadley had done her research. In the absence of news or information, I imagined what she hoped for was to establish a bond with Dr. Truitt, the doctor who'd finally seen her and her rare disease. Perhaps this was unreasonable thinking on my part since Hadley was only one among hundreds of patients in his care. But our specialist is the person in our life who best understands our disease. It seems natural that we would regard him or her as a kind of guardian of our new, permanently altered selves and would seek a degree of protectiveness and empathy from them.

Finally, Dr. Truitt ushered Lucy and me into his exam room. "How are you?" he asked Lucy as we sat down.

When a doctor throws out this question at the start of an appointment, I never know if it's rhetorical or how to answer. "I'm fine, thank you," is never exactly truthful, so I usually end up saying, "All things considered, I'm doing well," which is itself a throwaway. So maybe "I'm fine, thank you" would suffice after all.

In the chair, Lucy's legs and arms were shifting like branches in a blustery wind. I imagined her thinking: How do you think I am? "I'm having a lot of dyskinesia," she said.

"Let me see you walk."

Lucy stood and walked the two feet toward the closed door, then turned around.

"Actually, you look pretty good."

I was shocked. Dr. Truitt couldn't possibly assess Lucy's dyskinesia from that tiny maneuver. "You need to take her out in the hall and watch her walk," I said.

He did. I got out my notebook and started taking notes. When they returned to the room, Lucy pulled out her phone. "Here's a video Hadley took of me yesterday while I was folding laundry."

Dr. Truitt leaned in to watch. "Whoa," he said. "You really get going. I can see that." He questioned her closely about her dyskinesia and her medication schedule. "I think you need to be taking a lower dose of levodopa more frequently. That might help with the dyskinesia. You're getting too much levodopa all at once. But also, I think you should get evaluated for DBS surgery. You're a perfect candidate."

Lucy groaned. As a doctor and a Parkinson's patient, she'd seen this coming for at least a year. She was taking less levodopa than I was, but as her disease progressed and she needed more, the uncontrolled movements the medication was causing would only get worse. Deep brain stimulation (DBS) surgery more often is becoming the intervention for this, even in younger patients, as it can reduce the need for levodopa for many years.

"What's your concern?" Dr. Truitt asked.

"It's brain surgery. I have two little kids. I worry about the risk of cognitive decline caused by the surgery. I mean, isn't there anything we can try that's less invasive?"

She knew the answer was no. Later, Lucy and I would talk about the Michael J. Fox Foundation study that had just begun that was testing a new drug for the treatment of levodopa-induced dyskinesia. The research was promising. But how long would it take for the FDA to approve it, and could Lucy afford to wait?

"The risk of cognitive decline from DBS is pretty low," Dr. Truitt told Lucy. "We don't want to miss the window for your having the surgery." Lucy nodded, but I didn't know what the doctor meant by "the window," so I asked. Dr. Truitt explained: "We won't do DBS on patients who already exhibit cognitive decline. It's too risky."

He was recommending the surgery to Lucy because, cognitively, she was still in great shape. I understood her conflicted feelings—I couldn't imagine being the mother of two young children facing this decision. It would be one thing if she were unable to walk, drive, or play with her children, and brain surgery would give those things back to her. But she could do all that and was making her life work in her own dancing way.

Dr. Truitt typed on his computer, then looked at Lucy. "So, are you still practicing?" he asked.

"You mean medicine? Oh no, I haven't done... I was licensed in Arizona, but when we moved to Texas, I had this ...thing going on, and I never got around to getting licensed. And with two kids..."

"You're not seeing patients anymore?"

I winced as I scribbled down their conversation. Did Dr. Truitt think Lucy could treat patients and take care of her own kids with the dyskinesia she had? Also, how could he not know that his question would be a total downer for Lucy?

Lucy's hands were busy now, touching her face her hair; her feet were wagging and twisting. "No, no. Not for a long time. It didn't seem like a good idea. And my three-year-old's kicking my ass."

"So you can't practice, but could you do something else? They're always looking for doctors to review records."

"Oh, sure," Lucy said. She sounded far away. "I mean, I'm always thinking of things I could be doing, like there's this organization that teaches science to girls. I'd think about doing something like that at some point."

Lucy wriggled as if trying to work her way out of a tight space. I had a fantasy that her unruly foot would make contact with Dr. Truitt's shin, and she'd say, "So, should I have the brain surgery before or after I restart my medical career?"

But Dr. Truitt only nodded. He told Lucy to stop by the appointment desk on her way out to schedule an evaluation for DBS.

"God," Lucy whispered when we were in the hallway. "Why does he always ask me that? Every time I see him, I tell him I'm no longer practicing. It makes me feel so bad about myself."

"He probably wanted to relate to you doctor-to-doctor," I said. "I bet he won't ask Hadley about her work." Lucy rolled her eyes.

Hadley's appointment followed on the heels of Lucy's, and Dr. Truitt got right down to business by asking how she was, this time in a productive way: "How are you doing relative to when I saw you in July?"

As Hadley began to speak, he typed on his computer. By 2013, about 50% of doctors had switched from paper to electronic records, which meant that they were, and still are, often typing while talking to their patients. Dr. Truitt was not watching Hadley as she reported she was stiffer, her balance was worse, and she had to keep herself from falling every day. "I stay pretty close to walls and furniture so I can catch myself." She told him she couldn't urinate all day sometimes and that she was working with a urologist. "Have you used a catheter?" Dr. Truitt asked, still looking at his screen. Yes, a couple of times, Hadley told him. She mentioned that she had drenching sweats for no apparent reason and that she was often hot and cold at the same time.

"People with your condition have trouble regulating body temperature," Dr. Truitt said. "How about breathing?"

"Sometimes I have a hard time breathing out." "Do you have to sigh to get the breath out?" "Yes." "Is the levodopa helping you?" "It takes the edge off." "We should increase your dose. You're taking a very small dose."

"Really? A thousand milligrams a day?" Hadley said. I was surprised, too; that was more than three times the amount I was taking.

Dr. Truitt put Hadley through the neurologist's drill, as he had with Lucy—foot tapping, finger pinching, following his finger with her eyes. Then he asked, "Are you able to function relatively independently? If you had to live by yourself, could you manage?"

Hadley was taken aback by this question, and so was I. She'd just gotten herself from Montana to Texas, and why would she have to live by herself?

"Yes," Hadley said. "I can take care of myself." She turned to me and laughed. "What do you think, Catherine?"

"You can definitely take care of yourself! And you juggle a lot of other things, too," I said.

If Dr. Truitt had asked Hadley what she was juggling or working on, her response might have been very helpful with his assessment of how she was faring with her disease. Of course, it also would have humanized their interaction. He asked nothing further and scrolled on his screen. "Your brain MRI from this morning looks remarkably unremarkable. It's really good. Essentially normal unless the radiologist sees something I don't see."

"That's good," Hadley said, though she and I knew she had mixed feelings, since, in the past, normal tests had been responsible for delaying her diagnosis.

In July, when Dr. Truitt diagnosed Hadley with MSA, she'd been relieved to finally have a name for her disease. Now I could tell we were in the home stretch of the appointment, and I found myself wondering why MSA hadn't been mentioned by name; maybe after all these months, I needed to hear it, too. "Can people with MSA have normal MRIs?" I asked.

"Initially, yes, especially when they're very young, like Hadley." He didn't name it, but his answer was a confirmation of sorts.

Hadley asked, "What do you think about the prognosis—from here, looking out?"

Eyes on his screen, Dr. Truitt said, "I'm encouraged by your minimal change since July, and you do have some response to levodopa. And a good MRI. Can I see you back in about six months?"

Hadley wasn't going to get a prognosis from him, and maybe that was okay; who could say? As we left Dr. Truitt's room with him, I glanced at my watch. Hadley's appointment had been eighteen minutes long. In the corridor, it became clear why he'd moved through Hadley's and Lucy's exams with the efficiency of a mechanic: I could see patients waiting for him in other rooms. "How are you?" I heard him say as he slipped into one and closed the door.

On our way out of the clinic, Hadley didn't stop at the desk to schedule a follow-up appointment.

The next day, as Hadley and I were wheeling our suitcases from the hotel to Lucy's car so she could drive us to the airport, I glanced back at Hadley and caught something in her face I'd never seen before. Her eyes were saucer-like, her mouth pulled into a grimace—it was a look of terror, as if she were witnessing a grisly murder right there in the serene, jasmine-filled courtyard. When she caught my eye, she smiled, and her expression turned soft again. I thought: *MSA is the monster only she can see.*

TWENTY-FOUR:
CHASING EMPATHY

Hadley's eighteen-minute appointment with Dr. Truitt in Houston had taken her twelve hours to get to and about the same amount of time to get home from. When she was back in Missoula, she told me the trip unexpectedly had triggered painful memories of her time at The Mayo Clinic the year before. I imagined that the combination of her diagnosis sinking in, the hours and hours of traveling alone and to unknown places, and the impersonal medical and hotel environments had made her feel even more isolated. Probably most significant was the quality of her appointment with Dr. Truitt, which had seemed more like an auto maintenance check than the beginning of an important collaboration. I asked her if she would schedule a follow-up with Dr. Truitt in six months, and she said no; it wasn't worth the financial and energy expenditure or the emotional one. She hoped her Missoula neurologist, Dr. Reid, could manage her care by checking in with Dr. Truitt as necessary.

By now, Hadley was no stranger to feeling alienated by doctors. Dr. Truitt hadn't insulted or actively dismissed her as some others had. But there was nothing about their meeting that motivated her to seek in-person care from him. Their lack of connection can, in part, be blamed on a built-in imbalance in the doctor-patient relationship. Hadley has one body and a couple of doctors to guide her through her illness; a specialist like Dr. Truitt sees hundreds or even thousands of patients a year. Dr. Truitt was pressed for time that morning, with patients waiting. But this is just an excuse. With a bit more eye contact or a couple of key questions, he might have been able to communicate an understanding of Hadley as a complex individual saddled with a deadly disease, rather than an engine to be monitored as it sputtered and failed. Empathy doesn't take more time to convey than indifference.

But first, a doctor has to feel it. During the last two decades, researchers have sought to understand the causes and remedies for the widely acknowledged dearth of empathy—what has informally been filed under the heading "bedside manner", in the medical profession. Until fairly recently, medical students were trained to respond with "detached concern," an approach that would guard them from becoming emotionally affected by a patient's struggle. The rationale for detached concern was that resonating too deeply with a patient would cloud the doctor's ability to diagnose and treat him with clinical objectivity. Psychiatrist-ethicist Jodi Halpern, author of *From Detached Concern to Empathy: Humanising Medical Practice,* is one of many medical professionals who have debunked the benefits of detached concern. They assert that emotional empathy not only improves doctor-patient relationships and patient outcomes but is also correlated with higher job satisfaction among medical practitioners.

Once it was determined that emotional empathy is a win-win, scientists got to work on why it's lacking and how to inject more of it into clinical settings. To that end, they discovered something interesting: Medical students show more empathy at the start of their training, suggesting that over time, their empathy gets ratcheted down. This trend is attributed to many aspects of the medical school experience, including mistreatment by supervisors, burnout, and lack of emotional support, as well as the objectification of patients. A doctor's hard-wiring and background, too, factor into how able they are to empathize. Given these variables, the question educators have been left to tackle is: Can empathy be taught?

It turns out it can be. There is, of course, nothing that better teaches us how another person feels than sharing the same experience; this is why some patients are more emotionally reliant on their health support groups than their doctors day-to-day. Since the coincidence of a doctor sharing her patient's illness is not common, another way to step into the shoes of a patient is to experience a simulation of their symptoms. An inventive example of this is a project undertaken in 2014 by Analogue, a UK theater company, in conjunction with a neuroscientist and other researchers. The group designed a wearable technology that creates symptoms of Parkinson's disease; when connected to the device, a person can be subjected to the myriad wonders of PD: tremor, dizziness, and speech problems, to name a few. Liam Jarvis, co-director of Analogue, explains the project's goals: "Our principal interest is to work out how we can improve and facilitate communication and empathy by using simple technologies to immerse participants in the remote embodied experiences of others."

In March 2016, I participated in a similar empathy-building experiment implemented by Smart Patients, a UK online health community. Smart Patients matched professionals who were interested in understanding the Parkinson's experience with patients for the study, which they called #Parkinsons1day. I was partnered with Eli Pollard, Executive Director of the World Parkinson Coalition; for one day, I would be her "teacher," and she would be my "learner." Eli, like many of the "learners" participating in #Parkinsons1day, has devoted her career to the Parkinson's cause but is not a doctor. Her desire to participate in #Parkinsons1day is, in itself, an indication that she is already a very empathetic person.

Smart Patients furnished Eli with an "empathy kit" containing a pair of oversized dishwashing gloves— guaranteed to make any task requiring dexterity miserable, and ankle weights to simulate the bradykinesia that makes me feel as if I'm trudging through deep snow. After a phone conversation in which I shared my habits, schedule, and symptoms, Eli rose in the morning, donned her weights and gloves, and headed to work in Manhattan. She and I communicated throughout the day by text. I reported to her all of my Parkinson's related sensations ("Dystonia!" Accompanied by a photo of my toes curled up), frustrations ("Meds wearing off! Scattered, can't figure out how to wrap up this paragraph and my mouse is moving too slow"), and activities that included my daily three-mile walk and a trip to Walgreens to pick up five refills. In turn, Eli shared with me the challenges of being encumbered with this simulated Parkinson's:

> Okay, so I woke up this morning, and waited in bed for a bit after taking my vitamin. Had my iPad, and read some news, waiting for "the meds" to kick in. I took my shower last night, using my weaker hand fully and trying not to use my dominant hand much. It was slow and annoying. Curling my hair this morning was, well, slow. I didn't burn myself, but did

use my left hand, and it was all very slow and deliberate.

Later in the day, she wrote:

> I am wearing the ankle weights, and every time I stand up, I realize that I've forgotten I have them on, and it's like walking through quicksand. It hits me quickly. I remember that happening sometimes when I was pregnant; I'd actually forget until I tried to stand up or roll over.

Suiting up for a Freaky Friday in order to understand a patient's plight is interesting and educational but impractical for training more than a narrow swath of the medical profession.

The complicated challenge of producing doctors who are more empathetic has come into focus for medical schools during the last few decades. Understanding that empathy must be part of the equation in the selection of future doctors, schools have begun to look for applicants with a wide range of interests and experience rather than only those who've maintained a stricter diet of pre-med science. The expectation is that broader life exposure encourages greater emotional growth. In addition, while the selection of candidates for medical school historically has relied on cognitive test scores and grades, applicants now might also be required to take tests that measure their emotional intelligence. Once students are admitted to a program, they will take courses that aim to teach them how to be good listeners and caring practitioners. Sometimes actors who are trained to simulate a patient with a particular set of symptoms are used to rate a medical student's skills at taking the patient's history, giving a physical exam, and communicating. At the end of the simulation, the actor reports on the doctor-in-training's ability to make them feel listened to, respected, and understood.

Further training in empathy is offered to medical residents and fellows as well as established doctors who are interested in a refresher course on bedside manners. In 2011, Dr. Helen Riess founded the Empathy and Relational Science Program in the psychiatry department at Massachusetts General Hospital, with the mission of improving interpersonal relationships in healthcare. The program is the first of its kind offered by a hospital in the U.S. and has been so popular that in 2013, Riess started Empathetics, an online course that trains health care professionals globally.

As a writer, I found the most intriguing research on empathy to be that of Dr. Rita Charon, founder of the Program in Narrative Medicine at Columbia University. Dr. Charon was a pioneer of the movement to steer medical students away from "detached concern" and toward "engaged concern." Her prescription? The inclusion of literature and narrative writing in Columbia's medical program in order to strengthen reflection, awareness, and compassion. In her 2001 paper, "Narrative Medicine: A Model for Empathy, Reflection, Profession and Trust," Dr. Charon wrote:

> Like narrative, medical practice requires the engagement of one person with another and realizes that authentic engagement is transformative for all participants... Unlike its complement, logico-scientific knowledge, through which a detached and replaceable observer generates or comprehends replicable and generalizable notices, narrative knowledge leads to local and particular understandings

about one situation by one participant
or observer. Logico-scientific knowledge
attempts to illuminate the universally true
by transcending the particular; narrative
knowledge attempts to illuminate the
universally true by revealing the particular...
The narratively skilled reader... understands
that the reading of a text arises from the
ground between the writer and the reader...
With narrative competence, multiple sources
of local—and possibly contradicting—
authority replace master authorities; instead
of being monolithic and hierarchically given,
meaning is apprehended collaboratively by the
reader and the writer, the observer and the
observed, the physician and the patient.

In 2011, a decade after the publication of Dr. Charon's
paper on narrative medicine, a study published in the Annual
Review of Psychology corroborated her premise, revealing
that reading fiction made people perform better on tests
that measured empathy, social perception, and emotional
intelligence. Scientists have known for some time that
reading activates the brain in much the same way as real-life
experiences. Brain imaging has shown that when a person
reads, both the language-processing area of the brain and the
sensory regions are activated; for example, reading the word
"lavender" stimulates the region of the brain responsive to
smell. Similarly, words in a story describing action stimulate
responses from the motor cortex area of the brain that are
even differentiated according to which part of the body
is activated. Further research by Canadian psychologists
Raymond Mar and Keith Oatley, published in 2006/2009,
revealed a large overlap in the brain networks used to

process stories and those used to navigate interactions with other people. MRIs showed that reading stories and socially engaging with another person elicit similar responses in the amygdala, the brain's center for emotions. Fiction's rich, imaginative details and language, when combined with complex characters who face serious challenges, offer a transportive experience for a reader, as we are invited to fully enter characters' thoughts and feelings in a way often not possible in real life. In short, reading stories significantly strengthens our brain's capacity to understand each other. Interestingly, another study published in 2013 found that not just any fiction will do when it comes to increasing empathy; while literary fiction engages important psychological processes, more commercial fiction genres such as thrillers and romance do not have the same impact.

From the beginning of time, humans have sought out stories, proving we are insatiably curious about what makes us tick (or sick!), and what causes us joy or suffering. The story, not the outcome, is why we enjoy literature. When we read a novel about a brilliant astrophysicist who turns to alcohol and winds up homeless, we don't think, yes, he is a drinker; inevitably, he has become a homeless drunk. Because we have walked with him on his journey, confronting the obstacles and conflicts the author has created for him— that controversial, impassioned choice he made at twenty, the betrayal of trust at forty, the boat accident at fifty, we still hold him in our minds as the upstanding, albeit all too human, scientist he was when we met him. We might root for him or judge him along the way. He might enrage us or draw our sympathy. Whatever our feelings, if the story is well crafted, we understand him and learn something about ourselves, too. Because while we were reading, a part of us became him.

We've always known that emotionally empathizing with other people, whether real or fictional, is enlightening and satisfying in some primal way; now, we also know it's good for our health as well as our healthcare system. Pauline Chen, a physician who took the online Empathetics course, wrote:

> I decided to try out what I had learned... The next day at the hospital, I took extra care to sit down facing my patients and not a computer screen to observe the changing expressions on their faces and to take note of the subtle gestures and voice modulations covered in the course. While I found it challenging at first to incorporate the additional information when my mind was already juggling possible diagnoses and treatment plans, eventually, it became fun, a return to the kind of focused one-on-one interaction that drew me to medicine in the first place. Just before leaving, one of the patients pulled me aside. "Thanks, Doc," he said. "I have never felt so listened to before."

Dr. Chen's story reminds us how dependent we are on each other for feeling rewarded and honored in life. When we are one-on-one, the simplest kind gestures or words exchanged between patient and doctor convey what we humans might need to know most in order to carry on: We matter.

TWENTY-FIVE:
WHY?

When trying to make a diagnosis, a doctor is presented with the outcome of a story—the patient's condition. They must bushwhack backward through that patient's health history, focusing on elements that might be relevant in order to most expediently arrive at the "what" of an illness—and a treatment plan. The "why" of it is a critical but not urgent piece of the narrative that is chased down by scientists or the curious patient.

It's impossible for me to think about my friends' and my own illnesses without wondering what details of our personal histories might point to causes. And, aside from the particulars of each case, I see our diseases as part of a larger narrative about the health of our generation. Or, more precisely, the ill health of our generation. My robust father, who died at ninety-one, two months before my Parkinson's diagnosis, often commented on the difficulty of growing old and watching friends die. I understood the pain he must have felt, watching the lights go out around him as the shadow of his own inevitable death moved closer. My equally vigorous father-in-law, Lew, said to me, "You have Parkinson's, and here I am, ninety-six years old, with nothing ailing me." He shook his head because it didn't seem fair to him and because my disease made him sad. It makes me sad, too. But my sadness has an edge to it because too many of my generation have been stricken with serious illnesses. My friends and family have dealt with five different kinds of cancer, not including two rare blood disorders that became cancer, heart disease, ALS, stroke, Alzheimer's, diabetes, fibromyalgia, lupus, psoriatic arthritis, and a host of other debilitating autoimmune diseases, all long before the age of sixty.

Yet, journalists continue to optimistically present evidence of our longevity: "The median age of cancer death is seventy-two. We live long enough for it to get us" and "Cancer mortality is decreasing." Statements about cancer's biologic inevitability seem especially heartless considering that many cancer patients won't live nearly long enough to experience "inevitable."

Similarly misleading is the spin that's often put on the increasing prevalence of Parkinson's disease, that more people have Parkinson's because we are living longer and we're better at diagnosing it. My primary care doctor doesn't buy this. She's concerned about the increasing number of PD patients she is seeing, many of whom are under fifty. Historically, PD has been considered a rare disease, but between 1990 and 2015, the number of people with the disease doubled to over six million. In eight years, that number has grown to seven million; by 2040, the number is projected to be over twelve million. In their 2018 book, *Ending Parkinson's Disease*, four international experts in Parkinson's disease, Ray Dorsey, Michael Okun, Bas Bloem, and Todd Sherer, declared that we are experiencing a Parkinson's pandemic. Although PD is non-infectious, it meets other criteria for being labeled a pandemic, including its exponential growth within every major region of the world. For many decades it

was considered a rare disease; now the lifetime risk of PD is
1 in 15.

As we boomers age, TV ads depicting retired folks
wallowing in freedom, adventure, and Viagra seem less
and less relevant. Most of us are spending a lot of our free
time caring for not only elderly parents but also our very
ill partners, friends, children, or ourselves. Can we bear to
ponder why? Maybe not so much. Occasionally, when I sing
this solemn note, someone will exhale a commiserating,
"I know!" But often, people will give me that "Well hello,
sunshine!" look.

Along with rejoicing in our greater longevity, people
of my generation often wax nostalgic about the freedoms
we had as kids that our own "overprotected" kids haven't
enjoyed. Indeed, my childhood on the coast of Maine was full
of delicious risk-taking. Before I was even ten, my friends and
I would skate unsupervised on literal thin ice, get caught in
powerful tidal currents in sailboats, and lose our way in the
woods. There were incidents and accidents galore, but they
were considered part of life's big adventure. Even the story
my parents often recounted about my running down the hill
when I was two and launching myself off our dock into the
cove always elicited light-hearted laughter. "That's why we
called her 'fleet-foot,'" my mother would say. (My grandfather,
dressed in a wool tweed suit, had been in the yard and ran
down the hill and jumped in to retrieve me.)

We were awash in freedom. Freedom to run wild through
our neighborhoods or ride alone on a public bus, to row a
boat without a lifejacket, to bike without a helmet, to wrestle
and sprawl, unbelted, in the back of the cigarette smoke-
choked family station wagon. Freedom to eat Twinkies,
Velveeta, Froot Loops, a smorgasbord of canned and frozen
foods miraculously preserved by new chemicals. And that
yummy school paste! Blissfully unaware of pollution, we

were allowed to wade into anything liquid, bake ourselves jerky-brown on the beach, and chase the DDT truck as it spread its cool fog through our fields. We were the aerosol generation and anything that could be sprayed would be sprayed: hair products, deodorant, mosquito repellant, paint... The inexpendable air and endless ocean could surely carry away our insults. The earth's generous crops fed us well, thanks to powerful pesticides developed after World War Two. Compared to the era of our parents' childhoods, wedged between two world wars and chastened by The Great Depression, ours was a lucky time to be a kid.

But then, a few good earth stewards crashed our reckless party. In 1962, Rachel Carson, in her book *The Silent Spring*, laid out the impact on the earth and its creatures of the widespread use of DDT and other chemicals, kicking off the environmental movement that would lead to the ban a decade later of DDT for agricultural use. President Nixon created the Environmental Protection Agency in 1970, which wrote and enforced measures passed by Congress designed to protect the environment from human activity. But enforcement came too late for those of us who'd grown up with "better living through chemistry."

Rarely, members of my Parkinson's Facebook group will muse about possible causes of their PD. Some point to prolonged exposure to certain chemicals in their workplaces. Others mention drinking well water at their childhood homes that were next door to farms where pesticides were used. The brains of PD patients post-mortem have been found to contain higher levels of pesticides than brains from control subjects.

Other chemicals—solvents like trichloroethylene (TCE) and certain precious metals are linked to Parkinson's, but pesticides (a term that includes insecticides and herbicides) appear to be the biggest troublemaker. Since the ban of the insecticide DDT, two herbicides, Agent Orange, a defoliant used during the Vietnam War, and paraquat have been linked to Parkinson's. Agent Orange was banned worldwide in 1971. Paraquat is considered the most toxic herbicide to be marketed in the last sixty years. Several studies since 2009 have revealed that agricultural workers with long-term exposure to paraquat have a two and a half times the increased risk of developing PD. Perhaps more shocking is the discovery that people who lived within 1,600 feet of agricultural sites where paraquat was used were 75% more likely to develop Parkinson's. Since these studies, paraquat has been banned in at least thirty-two countries, including China (which, shamefully, owns the company that manufactures it) and Switzerland (where, also shamefully, the company is headquartered). Joining these two NIMBY but-we'll-take-your-money-for-our-poison, is the UK, which also has banned paraquat, but sells it to developing countries. And then there's the US, where paraquat has not been banned and is manufactured by Chevron USA, Inc., and at least 8 other companies. Its use has doubled since the discovery of its unambiguous role in causing Parkinson's.

One of my most troubling discoveries soon after my diagnosis in 2009 was that at least some of the organic fruits and vegetables I'd been seeking out for my family for many years were likely to have been treated with an insecticide shown to cause Parkinson's in animal models. Because Rotenone is derived from the roots and seeds of tropical plants, it was considered "natural" and has been used ubiquitously in organic farming as well as in flea powder and lice treatment for humans. In 2004, following up on research linking it to PD, the EPA ordered a study to test inhalation neurotoxicity. Rather than submitting to the study, the makers of Rotenone opted to discontinue its use in food growing; in the U.S., it is now used only for piscicide—to kill fish. However, because the EPA has not banned Rotenone, organic produce treated with it in other countries can be imported by the U.S. and labeled organic.

When it comes to hunting down the causes of Parkinson's, there is more in play than exposure to toxins in the environment. Most people who've had even long-term exposure to pesticides won't develop the disease. Rather, a combination of nature and nurture makes a person susceptible to PD. Scientists put it this way: "PD is a case in which genetics loads the gun and the environment pulls the trigger." PD is heritable; people who have a family member with the disease have a 4-10% higher risk of developing it themselves if they carry at least one of several gene mutations associated with PD. LRRK2 is the most common mutation known to cause familial PD and occurs in 1–2% of all people with Parkinson's. Some with PD carry variants of the gene ABCB1, which restricts ABCB1's role in helping the brain to flush out toxicants. Studies have shown that the relationship between exposure to pesticides like DDT and Parkinson's disease is 3.5 times stronger in those carrying the ABCB1 gene variants than in non-carriers.

For the approximately 90% of people with Parkinson's who, like me, don't have the gene variants associated with PD, scientists believe there has been more than one cause for the death of dopamine-producing neurons. For example, in a literal case of adding insult to injury, the risk of Parkinson's doubles when someone exposed to certain pesticides has previously sustained even a moderate head injury. A blow to the head interrupts the blood-brain barrier that protects the brain, allowing toxins to chronically seep in, setting in motion the death of dopaminergic neurons. Head trauma also produces an increase in alpha-synuclein, the protein heavily implicated in neuronal death (More to come in

Chapter 26). Add to the mix LRRK2 or other gene mutations implicated in Parkinson's, and the risk is even higher.

Before learning about the one-two-punch etiology of PD, I had hypothesized that the monstrous mosquito population in Maine and the prophylactic spraying of our family's favorite repellent, OFF!, were to blame for my PD. But then I discovered what might be another clue. At the recommendation of a friend, I went to see an osteopath for a nerve irritation in my lumbar spine. After gently manipulating my skeleton from my knees to my skull, the osteopath said, "I'm going to easily get a handle on the problem in your back, but what concerns me is your head. Have you been in a bad accident?"

I was taken aback. I told him about two serious car accidents I'd been in as an adult, neither of which had caused me harm enough to warrant a doctor's visit.

"Anything else? A bad fall?" he persisted.

I thought about this. "Well," I said. "I did fall eighteen feet from a tree when I was about ten."

"Aha!" he said. "How badly were you hurt? Did you hit your head?"

I pictured the messy grove of sumac trees that grew on the steep dirt slope next to our house in Maine. My parents had planted them to hide the neighbors' new concrete ranch house across the cove. They were tall and spindly, their trunks no more than three or four inches across, their narrow branches brittle. I was a monkey, forever pushing my luck, scrambling from limb to limb. One day, when I was high in the trees, the limb I was sitting on broke. The fall was long enough—eighteen feet, we measured later— that I remember reaching out for branches I passed, hoping to interrupt my descent. I landed on my side, winded and stunned. My mother, who was enjoying iced tea in a lawn chair right next to the sumacs, heard the crack and the thud.

I don't remember anything about the time after the fall—my sister thinks she remembers I was knocked out for a bit, but I must have seen a doctor because I recall having to wear some kind of neck collar for a couple of weeks.

The osteopath explained to me that the head and spine are designed for constant movement; in a healthy adult, there's an inherent motion in the central nervous system and the cerebral spinal fluid that is reflected in the subtle motion of the cranial bones and dura mater, a membrane that encloses the brain and spinal cord. He felt that my cranium, and therefore my dura mater, had been immobilized—a condition he would typically find in a patient who'd experienced serious head trauma. My cranial rigidity, combined with hypercontracted spinal muscles caused by long hours at the computer and aggravated by Parkinson's, he said, could be restricting the flow of blood, lymph, and cerebral spinal fluids. By mobilizing my cranial sutures and applying gentle pressure to surrounding tissue, he felt he could release restrictions and restore more normal function.

The osteopath stopped short of suggesting that his finding could be a clue to my PD, and I had read nothing in the Parkinson's literature that implicated a restricted flow of fluids to and from the brain in the development of the disease. However, the connection made a lot of sense to me. My brain cells have been dying at an abnormal rate; couldn't this be at least in part because they've been insufficiently supported by my body's circulatory system? I thought about Hadley, too: Could her pulmonary stenosis at birth and her lifetime of extremely low blood pressure have impaired the bloodstream's transport of oxygen and other nutrients to her brain cells, making them vulnerable to toxicants like the epoxy resin she used while sculpting?

In 2015, after my first visit to the osteopath, a major discovery was made of a network of lymph vessels in the membrane surrounding the brain and spinal cord that connects the brain to the body's immune system. Until this finding, scientists believed the human body had been thoroughly mapped and that the brain's and body's immune systems were separate. It was assumed that the blood-brain barrier largely protected the brain from the full assault of pathogens on the body as well as the immune response they triggered. The discovery that the central nervous system and immune system are connected not only provides new clues about neurological diseases like multiple sclerosis (MS) that are known to have an immune component but also suggests that immune cells might also play a role in Parkinson's. In PD, incorrectly formed alpha-synuclein proteins collect in the brain and become pathogenic, driving neuronal death. Two studies published in 2021 showed that people with PD have altered glymphatic drainage systems that are unable to properly dispose of the neurotoxic proteins.

In 2014, it was discovered that chronic activation of the immune system is the cause of many symptoms of neurodegenerative disease. Initially, our immune system gears up to protect our body from infections, toxins, and injury, but if activation is prolonged, it can cause a heightened inflammatory response. In PD, this suggests that hyperactivation of the immune system can cause the death of dopamine-producing neurons that help control the body's movements. Learning this was a revelation. In Chapter six, I discussed how my integrative medicine doctor had explained my illness in my early forties as being caused by an overactive immune system, a diagnosis my primary care physician at the time had a good chuckle over. Looking at the research, it seems more and more likely that he was on target and that the immune activation could have hastened the onset of Parkinson's. Now, the unearthing of vessels connecting the central nervous system to the immune system will shed light on exactly how the body's immune response impacts the brain. This carries enormous implications for the future of PD treatment.

Understandably, some might wonder what the point is of looking backward at the causes for our disease. It might feel more productive to pour our resources into finding treatments and a cure. However, as we learn more about factors that might contribute to the development of neurological conditions, we patients can broaden our approach to living with disease, and healthy people can take more preventative steps. We know now that our precious brain, once considered "immunologically privileged," is connected directly to the body's immune system and that a stressed immune system creates excess inflammation that can precipitate neuronal death. Perhaps knowing this will make us more vigilant about keeping our bodies healthy and treating anxiety and depression, which affect our immunity. The growing publicity about the potentially dire, delayed consequences of head trauma might make us more willing to don a helmet when skiing or riding a bike and less eager to encourage our children to play contact sports.

Our bodies, our brains—they are our houses for life. When they start to fall apart, we don't get to rip them down and start over. But if we ask enough questions, we can get to know them and care better for them, room by messy room.

But we also need to get out of our own houses, because there is more we should be doing! With so many of us struggling with Alzheimer's and Parkinson's—in the U.S. alone, six million and over one million, respectively, it's time to consider that we didn't simply get dealt a bad (or shaky) hand and wind up with a devastating, brain disease. It's time for all of us who are affected by neurological disease to become pro-active about the continued use of pesticides, TCE, and other chemicals linked to Parkinson's that have not been banned in the U.S. A Google search for "paraquat + Parkinson's" tells us all we need to know about the refusal of corporations to take responsibility for their role in creating the Parkinson's pandemic.

TWENTY-SIX:
ALPHA-SYNUCLEIN,
THE MENTAL MARAUDER

W hen Robin Williams, one of the funniest people on the planet, took his life in August 2014, the tragedy rocked us all. The night after it was revealed he had Parkinson's, I dreamed I watched a man jump from a high window of the building across the street from me. I couldn't see where he landed and was afraid to move closer to my window. Finally, I walked to the window and saw his crumpled body on the sidewalk. I'd been a huge fan of Williams since his first appearances on *Mork and Mindy* in the '70s; his death, only twelve miles from where I live, also hit close to home emotionally.

At the time of Williams' suicide, Parkinson's organizations and my fellow Parkies used the news to raise awareness about depression, one of PD's non-motor symptoms. To me, it seemed too simple to blame his death on the depression that can be caused by PD. Despite telling NPR's Terry Gross in 2006 that he had "gotten a lot out of psychotherapy," Williams went on to claim that he didn't have clinical depression. Yet for decades, he'd struggled with cocaine and alcohol addiction, and later, we learned he'd been bipolar, a disorder that no doubt enhanced his warp-speed swings from deepest dark to hilarious during performances. As he said, "A comic feels all things—he has to." Whatever his mental health diagnosis, I believed it was his intense scrutiny of what it means to be human—and what it meant to be Robin Williams, that made his future with Parkinson's seem unendurable. His identity depended on his rubber-face animation, quicksilver gestures, and hyperkinetic tongue, his thoughts turning on a dime. These happen to be precisely the things that Parkinson's takes away from a person. "Who will I be without them?" I imagined him thinking. For someone with such a passion for performance, I reasoned, Parkinson's might just be the worst possible disease.

But it wasn't the worst. Three months later, an autopsy revealed Williams had Lewy body dementia. LBD is the second most common type of dementia after Alzheimer's and is as common as Parkinson's, affecting 1.3 million people in the U.S. Because LBD, like Parkinson's, involves the death of dopamine-secreting neurons in the brain, causing motor symptoms, someone with LBD might first be diagnosed with PD, as was the case with Williams. But unlike PD, the non-motor symptoms of LBD develop rapidly. Patients usually experience a steep decline in cognitive abilities as well as heightened emotional states like fear, anger, and depression. Hallucinations and paranoia are also common in LBD.

When all we knew from the press was that Williams had Parkinson's, it seemed tragic to me that he'd been unable to find fulfillment in everything he'd already given to the world or make peace with a possible future of "just" being a father, a husband, a friend—albeit a slower, quieter one. However learning he had LBD radically altered my understanding of his desire to end his life. He wasn't just shaking, slowing down, and losing his edge; he was already imagining terrifying things and hiding watches in a sock. How would any of us feel knowing we would be living with such demons until death? This is one of the key questions spurring refinements to Medical Aid in Dying laws that will hopefully allow humane alternatives to suicide in cases of severe or late-stage dementia.

When people ask what scares me most about Parkinson's disease, I tell them it's the possibility of cognitive decline. I can hardly bring myself to say the word "dementia."

Until fairly recently, Parkinson's was described as a movement disorder that affects the motor circuits of the brain. But now we know that as the disease progresses, other circuits are also impacted, causing symptoms like depression, anxiety, sleep disturbances, and cognitive issues. Unlike in Alzheimer's, which is associated with increasingly severe memory problems, cognitive decline in Parkinson's is mainly manifested by an impaired ability to focus, multitask, and efficiently process and communicate information. People with PD might also have difficulty processing visual information and find themselves disoriented when, for example, navigating a busy supermarket. Scientists estimate that in 20-80% of people with Parkinson's, mild cognitive impairment (MCI) will develop into dementia. This squishy statistic means that on a good day, I focus on the 20%. On a bad day, I feel doomed to become part of the 80%.

Dementia is what most scares my friends who don't have Parkinson's since now that we're in our sixties and seventies, all of us seem to have had at least one parent or sibling who's struggled with Alzheimer's or other dementia. Sometimes I look at it this way: We're all aging, some of us faster than others because our cells are misbehaving. Apparently, until we're around fifty-five, our bodies are pretty good at repairing DNA damage. However studies have shown that around age thirty, our major organs are already going into decline. There's plenty of debate, but some studies indicate that cognitive abilities are at their peak between the age of thirty to forty and begin to diminish in our fifties.

The difference between having a disease that can cause cognitive impairment and not is that I'm always in the lookout tower, scanning my brain for mental marauders. When a friend can't remember the name of a movie she saw last week, she slaps her forehead and says, "I hate getting old!" When I can't remember the name of the movie I saw, I think, "Oh no, it's happening!" Then there are the disappearing words: More and more, when orally describing something, I've been having trouble retrieving a word that I know would precisely fit what I'm trying to convey. Can I blame nervousness, fatigue, or natural aging? Or is it Parkinson's? My word-fishing has irritated me to the point that instead of moving on and settling for a more imprecise word ("thing" is a tempting stand-in), I sometimes stop and wallow in my frustration, even soliciting the help of my listener. "Impeccable?" he will suggest. "Meticulous?" "No, no, that's not quite it," I'll say, and then realize that any further deliberation will surely confirm that I am indeed becoming demented. Too, there are all the facts that I forget. I'm quick to Google, yet sometimes I will resist, forcing myself to dredge up an elusive fact from my deepest storage lockers just to prove to myself that I can. It's like digging for clams, though, because I don't know if the fact is actually still down there in the muck.

More than nine million Americans over sixty-five are expected to develop some kind of dementia by 2030; I am four to six times more likely to do so than my arm-swinging (non-PD) friends.

A story about Parkinson's disease would be incomplete without mention of alpha-synuclein—sort of like *Star Wars* without Darth Vader. Alpha-synuclein is a protein found throughout the body but most abundantly in the brain. It is essential for communication between nerve cells and for normal inflammatory and immune response to viral and bacterial infection. Like the villains in many stories, alpha-synuclein makes an important contribution to our health and well-being until it's corrupted by bad influences. Once this happens, the protein forms gangs that become intent on ruining the brain, one neighborhood at a time.

What happens with alpha-synuclein in people with Parkinson's, multiple system atrophy (MSA), and Lewy body dementia (LBD) is that it mutates, creating a toxic version of itself. (Alzheimer's involves a similar scenario but with a different protein, beta-amyloid.) Normal proteins are in a folded "stack" unless something causes them to change shape or misfold. The causes of the protein misfolding are still not completely understood, but scientists know that some misfolding is attributable to a heritable gene mutation associated with PD, such as LRRK2. Once it has misfolded, alpha-synuclein then clumps, forming aggregates called Lewy bodies that infect other brain cells, causing them to die. Infectious proteins that spread disease within the body in this way are known as prions. Not only do people with PD, MSA, and LBD generate too much misfolded alpha-synuclein, but their brains also become unable to properly dispose of the toxic and dead cells, so they build up and continue to do damage.

Since the living brain is relatively inaccessible, researchers have been investigating other areas of the body where alpha-synuclein occurs, trying to determine, among other things, what species of it forms the toxic aggregates found in neurological disease. In 2003, a husband-and-wife team of scientists presented a hypothesis that Parkinson's starts in the gastrointestinal tract rather than the brain. They proposed that a pathogen (a virus or bacteria) could enter the body through the mouth or nose and travel to the digestive tract, where it could cause alpha-synuclein to misfold. From there, misfolded alpha-synuclein could begin its path of destruction as it makes its way to the brain along the vagus nerve, an important nerve that connects the enteric nervous system (aka the "gut's brain") to the brain, as well as the lungs and the heart. This scenario is supported by the fact that alpha-synuclein is found in both the intestines and the nose, and often, the earliest symptoms of PD are constipation and loss of smell. This also makes sense when considering that motor symptoms like tremor and bradykinesia show up many years later after the misfolded alpha-synuclein has infected about 80% of dopamine-producing neurons in the substantia nigra area of the brain.

When I first learned about this hypothesis in 2014, I found it compelling, so I brought it up with the gastroenterologist who was about to perform my routine colonoscopy. Lying on the gurney while the doctor, a man in his fifties, and his three young assistants bustled around me preparing for my procedure, I said, "I have a question: If you find a polyp, or have to take tissue samples for any other reason, could you test it for alpha-synuclein?" I didn't expect him to agree to do this, of course; I just wanted to hear his take on the research. (Also, I was showing off.)

The doctor whirled around to look at me, amused and clearly stumped. I went on to explain. "Really?" he said. "I haven't heard about that."

One of the assistants said, "Wow, that's interesting."

"You guys," I said. "You need to keep up on this stuff." I laughed so they'd know I was teasing.

"Hey," the doctor said, "I'm a gastroenterologist, not a Parkinson's doctor."

I was struck by his remark, not just because he was unfamiliar with the research but also because he seemed to be saying that it was irrelevant to his practice. But the G.I. tract is his territory, the place he goes to work every day, and we're talking about how it might hold a major key to understanding devastating neurological diseases. The gut is connected to the brain! How cool is that!

It seems inevitable that in the near future, gastroenterologists will be mining more than polyps. Nearly every scientist working in Parkinson's research has taken on the challenge of alpha-synuclein, exploring how they might bust up Lewy body gangs or keep them from forming in the first place. Other strategies might involve increasing the brain's capacity for disposing of toxic cells or somehow inhibiting the production of alpha-synuclein. A vaccine that activates the immune system to produce antibodies against the protein is moving forward. But scientists first need to determine the amount of alpha-synuclein the body needs to function normally.

To summarize what I've written about the possible causes of Parkinson's disease: Head injury that interrupts the blood-brain barrier, making the brain more permeable and therefore vulnerable to neurotoxins; the impact of head injury, which in itself can trigger the misfolding of alpha synuclein; gene mutations that are inherited; chronic exposure through air and water to environmental pollution and toxins, especially pesticides; and a gastrointestinal infection caused by a virus, or bacteria.

To summarize this summary: It's very, very complicated!

TWENTY-SEVEN:
MOUNTAINS TO MURALS

On December 5, 2013, five months after she was diagnosed with multiple system atrophy, Hadley received the thrilling news that she had been selected to be the artist for the Montana State Capitol Women's Mural. She signed a memorandum of understanding a few days later and eagerly awaited the contract that, once signed, would provide a deposit for her work. The timing was critical, as Hadley and John were burdened with several large medical bills.

There was more good news: In November, Hadley had applied for a grant from The Stephen King Haven Foundation, which supports artists whose careers have been threatened by illness or accident, and was given $7,000. Also, she finally managed to secure affordable healthcare for her family. For days, she'd been trying to sign up on healthcare. gov, but the website had been jammed; awake one morning at 3:30, she finally got through. The new insurance plan was significantly more affordable—they'd been paying $1,100 per month with their old insurance, and their new fee would be $780. With their old plan, her family's individual deductibles added up to $26,000 and didn't include prescriptions; the new plan offered a family deductible of $2,500, and prescriptions would be free. These financial gains were an enormous relief for Hadley and John.

In addition to her talent and experience with painting history-themed murals, two other factors had made Hadley's proposal especially appealing to the selection committee. The request for proposals had asked for a single mural on the east wall under the barrel vault of the Capitol's third floor, but Hadley felt a second mural on the west wall would create a more balanced composition for the space. In effect, she was offering them two murals for the price of one. One panel would depict the lives of Montanan women, both settlers and Native Americans, during the mid-to-late 1880s, pre-railroad; the second would illustrate women in roles of leadership, entrepreneurship, social activism, and service following the arrival of the railroad and the 20th century. Another strong selling point was that she stressed her interest in approaching the project collaboratively in all phases. Part of her proposal read:

> The best and most important part of any project is the collaborative work that goes into design and painting elements... Details about clothing, choice of women illustrated in the mural, subject matter, colors, final presentation, and all aspects of design are elements that become even richer when thought out as a team.

When Hadley received the contract for the Montana Women's Mural one week before Christmas, she was excited and terrified. From small things said and unsaid, she gleaned that she'd nearly lost the commission to one of the other finalists who pulled out of the process because of scheduling conflicts. In light of this, the committee's repeated praise for Hadley's spirit of collaboration temporarily shook her confidence, making her wonder if they doubted her artistic abilities. At night, she lay awake worrying. There was, of course, the expected nervousness any artist would have about whether they had the skills to meet expectations for this major public project. But also, what if she became too sick to follow through on the mural—would it be possible to get help with it? Once the project was underway, would she be able to be honest about her health, or would she have to put extra energy into hiding it?

The schedule for the mural project would be tight. Hadley would need to complete a design by mid-March and deliver the two finished panels to Helena by mid-October 2014. In November, they would be unveiled in honor of the 100-year celebration of the women's suffrage movement in Montana.

With the Women's Mural Project looming, the pressure was also on for Hadley to finish the murals for the Missoula Catholic Schools. Also in progress was work for the University of Montana Department of Forestry and Conservation. In the 1930s and 1950s, the department had commissioned an artist to paint scenes of logging. Now, they wished to complement these with illustrations of post-1950s conservation work: the restoration of rivers and streams, controlled burns, and protection of wilderness areas. In the mornings, Hadley scaled a stepladder at the Loyola Sacred Heart School to work on finishing the twelve-foot-tall murals there; in the afternoons, she'd work on laying out the designs on a trio of five-foot-tall Forestry murals for the University. Her pattern was to work intensely when she had the energy and then crash for a day or two. "I need to keep going while I can because I feel like I'm at the bottom of a huge mountain, and if I stop, I'll never be able to get going again," she told me.

Standing for long periods of time was exhausting and often made Hadley dizzy. Her hands cramped up, and big movements with her paintbrush were difficult enough that she worried the paint would dry faster than she could keep up with it. And her balance had deteriorated to the point that she had to be ever-vigilant to avoid falling.

Late at night, getting ready for bed, she'd look in the mirror and wonder about the stranger looking back at her. Her face was losing its animation and softness, no longer expressing the spark she felt inside. She told me there was some relief in knowing that at least the finished murals wouldn't reveal her struggle to create them, "working from the cage" around her body.

Hadley had another critical task to attend to before the start of the Montana Women's Mural—creating a large enough work area in their home to execute the two five by ten-foot panels. Her painting studio was in a large room upstairs in her house, but she would need to expand into an office area that was crammed with files and paperwork generated by thirteen years of her artist's practice. She dug in, dismayed to discover that mice had taken up residence in the piles of old contracts, drawings, and research. Most of the files had to be discarded, and the rest sanitized. It was a physically exhausting ordeal, and emotionally trying to go through the business of her past. She couldn't help wondering: Will I be around in another thirteen years?

Several weeks after signing the contract for the Montana Women's Mural, Hadley drove to Helena to meet with the mural committee members. She felt honored to be working with such accomplished women, a collaboration that exemplified the murals' theme of "women as community builders." As they discussed the issues they had with her original design and brainstormed solutions, she was invigorated by the conversation. But at times, she realized they were veering away from the subject of "women as community builders." After the meeting, she kicked herself for not having had the presence of mind to pull the conversation back on course. As an excellent listener and conceptualizer with a great memory for details, she'd always felt on top of things at meetings; if the discussion digressed, she would be the one to rein it in so that everyone would leave with a strong sense of direction.

This time, Hadley came away from the meeting muddled and realized she was very likely experiencing mild cognitive impairment, a symptom of her disease. During a follow-up conference call, she didn't contribute much but listened hard to her collaborators' ideas and questions while they tried to nail down the mural's content. Her mind churned— how would she convey all the ideas discussed on the two canvases? She'd determined that each painting would be grouped into several sections: a large center image within an oval surrounded by four small corner images. Scenes from Montana women's history would fill the two ovals; one would depict Native American women trading goods with European American women, perhaps medicine and food for cloth. To contrast with this rural image, the women discussed creating an urban scene for the other mural's oval. Hadley wanted to make the scene more poignant than a simple depiction of life in town, and the committee exchanged ideas about images that would reinforce the community-builders theme. They settled on an illustration of the women's suffrage movement. The four corner pieces bracketing the two ovals would add supporting images: women digging bitterroots, women sewing or beading, teaching, nursing, canning, women with children, as aviators, and cowgirls.

Hadley felt more settled after the conference call but was still not satisfied that the ideas for the mural were gelling. In the meantime, Montana, like other areas of the country that winter of 2014, was experiencing a "polar vortex" in which daily temperatures plunged to the negative digits, worsening her stiffness. Missoula was plagued by storms that would break a 1939 snowfall record. An avalanche slid down Missoula's Mount Jumbo, burying the house of Hadley's friends, a couple in their sixties; the man was pulled from the snow and survived, but tragically, his wife died from her injuries.

The week before her big mural meeting, Hadley had planned to do research at the library, but when Sarah came down with a virus, she didn't leave the house for four days. If she'd felt confident in her vision for the project, such a delay wouldn't have thrown her, but the disruption came at a sensitive point in the process. Her spirits sank with her energy. She told me her mind felt like a huge messy pile she had to sift through every time she needed to find something, mirroring the actual experience of sorting through her collection of images and her own paintings to pull visual elements for the murals. Sometimes, she would forget what she was searching for. Other times, she'd lose track of what she'd found and what she was going to do with it. An added frustration was that it was taking her longer to complete tasks that in the past would've been simple for her—a drawing that might have taken several hours to complete just a couple of years ago was taking her several days.

Hadley rallied. The following week, on February 20, she would have a meeting with the committee in Helena, and she scolded herself: "Get your act together." At least the four days at home with Sarah had allowed her necessary rest, and her body felt stronger. She pulled out her computer and organized the documents and notes from her design discussions, made

a list of all the ideas that had come forward, and spent the next three days researching images that would illustrate those ideas. One of her most exciting finds was a photograph of three women hanging posters on a building during the suffrage movement; this was a perfect jumping-off point for the urban scene she would paint. As the images piled up, she began to see an opening into her vision. There was hope!

For the meeting, the committee wanted to see Hadley's design projected in situ to satisfy their concerns about scale and proportion. With paper, she created a five by ten-foot mockup divided into the five sections onto which they'd be able to project images. On the day of the meeting, she loaded her car with the mock-up, her pile of images, and eight new drawings. She felt almost like the old Hadley, productive and prepared to impress. Still, she would remain cautious until she could read the reactions of the committee.

The roads to Helena were a mess from snowstorms. The usual ninety-minute drive took her nearly twice that long, and it was white-knuckle all the way. By the time Hadley arrived, she was so stiff she could hardly get out of the car; this was one of the few times she knew there would be no hiding her condition. After hauling all her materials up to the third floor of the Capitol building, she had to recruit the committee to help her hang the paper mock-up. They were supportive and happy to help.

Hadley held her breath as she walked away to view the mock-up from across the stairwell. She turned and knew immediately that the mural was going to be everything she'd hoped for. When the others saw the layout with scenes projected on it, they were as excited as she was. Together, they went through the images Hadley had culled, and the conceptual and visual pieces began to form a coherent and compelling vision of women as community builders. Hadley was elated to get the green light to move forward.

At home in her upstairs studio, Hadley prepped the two huge powder-coated aluminum mural panels, sanding and then brushing them with two layers of gesso to create a more textured, uneven surface. Then, she drew the borders that defined the center ovals, triangular corners, and outside edges of each panel. She used a computer-generated template for these so the dimensions and curves would be accurate; for their design, she borrowed the details of the building's interior moldings. She made transparencies of the detailed pencil drawings she'd created for each mural so that she could project the images at a larger size onto the panels. Then she began the long process of drawing, stopping as she went along to correct proportions that were inevitably sometimes off.

Because she populates her murals with many figures, Hadley often uses live models and a camera. In spring, when the Missoula skies had cleared, Julie Cajune, a Native American member of the mural committee, took Hadley to the Flathead Reservation, home to the Confederated Salish and Kootenai tribes. Julie had arranged for friends to pose for Hadley so that she could photograph them in authentic Native American clothing and accessories. One wore a buckskin dress and braids decorated with traditional "otter wraps," one carried a cradleboard, and another rode a horse. Hadley positioned her models for a scene in which two women would be trading blankets and another that would illustrate the granting of Native American citizenship rights by the Indian Citizen Act of 1924. In addition to establishing historical authenticity, the photographs helped Hadley to accurately represent natural head angles, gestures, and the drape of fabric. On one of her favorite days during the mural project, Julie took Hadley and Sarah digging for bitterroots so they would experience this piece of history that would be included in the mural.

When Hadley transferred the drawings to the panels, the larger scale created empty spaces she needed to fill. She researched artwork and objects to decorate walls and tables, making sure every detail of a room, including lamps, rugs, and curtains, was historically accurate. Often, she referred to old Sears and Roebuck catalogs for furnishings. She studied hairstyles and obtained swatches of material from every decade from a historian of fabrics in Bozeman so that clothing would be appropriate. In outdoor scenes, she was careful to be seasonally accurate when choosing flowers in bloom and produce being harvested or sold in the marketplace.

The Women's Mural Project committee made a studio visit. Many ideas were tossed around, but at the end of two days of discussion that generated a few changes and some compromises, everyone was satisfied. The project had hit a major turning point. Finally, Hadley could dive in with her paintbrush and bring the colorful history of Montana's women to life.

TWENTY-EIGHT:
THE SUN COMES UP

few days after my Parkinson's diagnosis in 2009, I
scanned my shelves for a book to take on a family
road trip to Los Angeles and randomly plucked one
a friend had given me several years earlier. By some eerie
coincidence, I chose Sue Miller's novel, *The Distinguished
Guest*, about a writer, Lily Maynard, who has written a best-
selling memoir in her seventies. Halfway to LA, I learned that
Lily had Parkinson's disease. In the book, a journalist who's
interviewing the late-blooming writer for a magazine piece
struggles with how to frame her story:

> What happens to the writer when the writer
> is done? ...those who have taken heart by
> her appearance on the literary scene at age
> seventy-two, from the fine work she's done in
> her memoir and her fiction since then, may also
> take a kind of courage from her example at this
> juncture in her career when that chapter seems
> to be closing. Lily Maynard has Parkinson's
> disease, and its slow progress seems finally to
> have brought an end to her life as a writer. But

not an end to her life. Because Lily Maynard's story is nothing if not the account of a woman triumphing repeatedly over defeat, and it's with that same indomitable force and energy she has confronted this painful fact.

Indomitable. It's a word that appears often in narratives about people working hard to rise above adversity. When I read this passage in Miller's novel that day in 2009, I felt a resonant pulse of courage. But then I braced myself. As a writer, Miller is a masterful manufacturer of psychological complexity. I suspected that "indomitable" and "triumphing" would be demonstrated by her heroine, Lily, but not in the expected ways.

Wherever there's illness, there's talk about optimism, keeping a positive attitude, and my personal favorite: "Your illness is a gift." The first time I heard this line, I recoiled. It sounded a lot like a religion being thrust on sick people. A gift, I thought, is either something you're born with—like an ear for music or an eye for artistic composition, or something someone gives you, usually tied up with a ribbon. Illness is not a talent, so if it's the other kind of gift, there must be a giver, right? But who would give someone the gift of illness, and why?

I'm being annoyingly literal to make the point that this particular pronouncement, often trotted out as enlightenment, is, for many people, irrelevant and not always benign. It's true that illness, like accidents and other traumatic experiences, can sometimes jolt us awake from a slumber of denial, improve our perspective, clarify priorities, and open us up to others. Even losing everything in a fire or financial crisis can stimulate healthy renewal. But here's the thing: A calamity is only beneficial if you can recover enough

to live without enormous burdens. Illness can teach us valuable lessons and redirect us in good ways if we have the physical wherewithal and resources to make lemonade from the lemon. But many sick people don't have the strength or tools to even squeeze the lemon. For those who are housebound, poor, or alone, illness is a curse, and for the rest of us to talk about disease as a gift can be insensitive to their suffering. Despite all the good people and meaningful activity Parkinson's has put me in touch with, I can't imagine telling my husband and kids it's a gift. To do so would dismiss the pain and worry my condition will increasingly cause them.

What people must mean when they say their illness is a gift is that it has, in some way, changed them for the better. Perhaps before their illness, they worked too hard at a job they didn't like and came home every day cranky and self-absorbed; perhaps when ill health made them quit, they discovered a new appreciation for their partner and children or a new avocation. Maybe they were always in a hurry, and now, in their slower, less capable bodies, they've become more attuned to the beauty in the world and are smelling those roses, literally and figuratively. Some, through their suffering, might have gained access to a more compassionate part of themselves that makes them more giving.

Because Parkinson's can progress slowly and often people live with it for decades, it has given many in our Facebook group the opportunity to adopt new, compelling missions: fundraising for research, creating resources for patients, and becoming PD advocates. They are determined and dedicated and have inspirational role models, among them Michael J. Fox, who was diagnosed at twenty-nine. In his 2009 book, *Always Looking Up: The Adventures of an Incurable Optimist*, Fox wrote, "For everything [Parkinson's] has taken, something with greater value has been given—sometimes just a marker that points me in a new direction that I might not otherwise

have traveled." Since the sixty-one-year-old Fox is still delightful, articulate, and hard-working despite setbacks in the last few years due to many broken bones from falls, his optimism provides us with life-affirming sustenance. "What will we do if Michael loses hope?" I've asked my friends with PD. In his case, Parkinson's is a gift—not to him, but to all of us with the disease. In his enormously generous outreach to the PD community, unmatched support of research, and ability to motivate others, he is a superhero.

Fox is also merely human, a man whose life and body have been radically altered by disease. We, his fans and flock of Parkies may never witness him in his private moments of discouragement and defeat. Our feel-good culture has an unspoken rule: A revered public figure must put his best face forward and consistently offer hope and optimism. In 2023, Fox told an interviewer, "With gratitude, optimism is sustainable."

Americans especially have viewed positive thinking and optimism as tools to attract everything from love to happiness, and fortune. For decades, we read that positive attitudes might ensure better health in general and better outcomes if we were sick. Cancer patients were especially inundated by advice to think positively. The theory was that since stress is known to tax the immune system, shifting from a mode of worrying or feeling hopeless about one's illness to accepting it would, along with healthful changes to diet and other habits, help the body's immune system fight the cancer. It seems like sound science—a patient who's positive enough to be proactive about taking good care of himself could have a better outcome. But here's where the proposal is less reasonable: Cancer patients were often coached that a positive attitude might shrink their tumors. Gravely ill patients, already concerned about the impact of their illness on family and friends, were made to feel that if they let their fear, grief, or anger surface—even in the privacy of their own minds, they could hasten their own demise. (Barbara Ehrenreich has written a thoughtful book on this subject, *Bright-Sided—How Positive Thinking is Undermining America*.) Moreover, if they did adhere diligently to their positive meditations and their tumors grew instead of shrinking, they felt they'd failed in some way.

When positive thinking is imposed on someone who's struggling, it can isolate that person, leaving him alone with his deepest fears and pain. Sometimes, we so badly want a good outcome for someone that we carelessly put a positive spin on his or her situation. At the supermarket, an acquaintance and I discussed someone we knew who had been sick for three years with metastatic cancer. The cancer, which would kill her eight months later, had moved from her breasts to her hip, then to her leg and her spine. It was devastating to think about, especially because she had two children still at home. I expressed my sadness. "But she looks fantastic!" this woman responded brightly. I was shocked by her attempt to brush aside the gravity of the situation. Unable to let it go, I said, "But she's going to die." I remember feeling as if I'd uttered something horribly improper, obscene even, and I don't recall where the conversation went after that. I'm pretty sure I killed it with my "negative thinking."

Why do optimism and hoping for something that might be unrealistic comfort some people and make others feel more vulnerable? Is acknowledging vulnerability "negative thinking"? It turns out our brains are hardwired to focus on our vulnerability and bad experiences, an adaptation that helped to ensure early man's survival. When their safety was threatened by negative events, the primal machinery of the brain was activated, stimulating the production of chemicals that helped them to react or flee from danger. Because adverse events were often a matter of life and death for our earliest ancestors, it was imperative that they remember them so they wouldn't happen again. So, negative experiences were and still are quickly filed in the brain's deep storage.

Curiously, there is no equivalent transfer of positive experiences into the brain's deep storage, so we remember them less readily. Mindfulness practitioners have tackled the question of how to make our positive experiences more dominant and enduring, suggesting that we first deliberately create positive experiences or take in the good around us, enrich those experiences through duration or intensity, and then focus on absorbing them into the body. In other words, we need to "marinate" ourselves in the positive. It's not a turning away from our grief and fear, then, but a focused effort to balance them with feelings of comfort, safety, and happiness.

When we can achieve such balance, positive thinking allows room for what is hard and true and makes it possible for us to cope with difficulties and work toward solutions. Optimism, on the other hand, can cause us to hang our hopes on the idea that things will always turn out okay. At its most extreme, this can involve potentially harmful denial. While Hadley and I were trying to get a diagnosis, our doctors' optimism cost us years of anxiety, time, and money. They simply couldn't or wouldn't believe that two seemingly high-spirited people could be developing a devastating disease. They explicitly made us feel we were preoccupied with negative thoughts and, in Hadley's case, possibly making herself sick. As another example, years ago, a perennially sunny and vigorous childhood friend told me she felt certain she would never get cancer because "I'm such an optimist." Fortunately, she was not so optimistic that she skipped her annual mammograms; twice in the next six years, she had not just one type of cancer but two, which she ably survived. But she felt blind-sided by her diagnoses because, as an optimist, she hadn't prepared herself for the possibility that she would ever have cancer. For her, discovering that terrible diseases don't prey only on worrywarts and the weak was a life-changing revelation.

The Parkinson's community wrestles with the potential pitfalls of optimistic forecasting. Patients and researchers alike have been talking about "the cure" for a very long time, although it still is not within reach. For me, keeping up my hopes for a cure would feel like trying to hold a heavy object in the air for a long time: Would the object come crashing down on me before a cure is found? I'm optimistic enough about future breakthroughs to be micro-monitoring Parkinson's research and donating my body and money to the PD cause. But I'm more comfortable rejoicing in the encouraging gains being made in understanding the etiology of PD and in developing better treatments than hoping for a cure. What seems most important, though, is not to passively wait for the next big thing but to learn all I can about how to optimally manage my disease and remain focused on what I'm still able to enjoy and accomplish each day. This is realistic, productive, and positive thinking.

For all of us with illness, the ability to think positively is as variable as the weather. I've heard that some support groups make members feel uncomfortable posting messages that express dark feelings about their disease or their medical care. I think often of the crowing of the movement disorders specialist who diagnosed me: "We have no self-pitiers in the Parkinson's Princesses!" I think our Parkinson's Facebook group would agree that a positive attitude includes being honest about how we're feeling without catastrophizing about our disease. Sometimes, a member will end a post with "Sorry to complain," to which someone will quickly respond, "Complain away—we all need to sometimes!" In our group, we know that along with our high-pitched announcements about running marathons or climbing mountains, lower notes will be played, will be heard, and will bring out the best of what our PD community can offer: information, advice, or comfort with an open mind and heart. And then there are the messages intended simply to raise our spirits. Our member Maria posts photographs she takes of the sun coming up over the lake where she lives. The images don't vary much visually, but therein lies their power: They wordlessly remind me of my gratitude for the reliability of sunrises and the chance to live another day on our magnificent planet.

In *The Distinguished Guest*, when Lily Maynard realizes that she's too diminished by Parkinson's to want to carry on, she secretly schemes to die, and not in a nursing home, as others have planned for her. I carried the weight of her story around Los Angeles for several days as I strolled with my family through museums and along the beach in Santa Monica. I didn't tell them what the book was about and how it had affected me because I knew they'd press me: "Why didn't you stop reading the book when you realized she had Parkinson's?" The answer would have been that I wasn't afraid to confront my sadness about having PD. But I was afraid of my fear, and Lily's story allowed me to live inside her for a week and face that fear. She became a kind of secret mentor. In a season when all of us try especially hard to put our pain aside and raise toasts to all that is merry and bright, Lily helped me not only to imagine being a late-blooming author but also to privately mourn the healthy old age I won't have.

Lily was indomitable, but not in the way the journalist interviewing her had supposed. She triumphed because she was her own captain to the end. She knew when to pull out of a battle that had finally stolen from her even the joy of a sunrise; she knew when to choose peace. At the time, so recently diagnosed, I was unsettled by her meticulously planned, nonviolent suicide. But now, fourteen years later, her story—neither pessimistic nor optimistic but real and irrefutably positive—echoes in my mind, a gentle and compassionate whisper when the voices of "indomitable" become too shrill and demanding.

TWENTY-NINE:
ON AND OFF, UP AND DOWN

People in the Parkinson's community often talk about a "honeymoon period"—generally the first few years following diagnosis, when symptoms are still mild and medications are working well. It's hard to fathom why anyone would come up with such an expression. For one thing, drawing a parallel between the course of a disease and a marriage proposes a cynical view of married life—as if it's all downhill after the honeymoon. Whoever decided to use the phrase with regard to PD either didn't have Parkinson's or had had it for decades and was looking back nostalgically on how relatively vigorous he'd been at the beginning of his illness. Gosh, what a shame that so many newly diagnosed people don't realize they're on a honeymoon!

I will say that when I was finally diagnosed with PD, the cheer I felt knowing that I wouldn't be subjected to more dismissive doctors was not unlike the relief I experienced when I married and could finally stop dating. Even more exciting was to discover I wasn't dying of a neurological disease worse than PD. I thought, "OK, everyone has their thing to deal with; this is mine." (Sparing you the marriage metaphor here.) And I felt good, not sick; so what if I walked a little like Frankenstein's monster? Just as the early years of blissful wedlock can create the illusion of a protective bubble, getting a big diagnosis made me feel exempt from all the other diseases that can affect people my age. This, of course, was ridiculous. Within seven years and after a few funerals for people my age, I'd lurched out of my honeymoon denial and realized that one bad marriage to an illness wouldn't protect me from another. Diseases are often polygamous.

In the previous chapter, I discussed how people with PD think about our disease in the big picture and how we strive to be positive and proactive. But there are many days when we aren't striving for anything more than getting through the day, picking off challenges hour-by-hour and, sometimes, minute-by-minute.

Everyone's Parkinson's is different, and of course, since it's a progressive disease, it can change in a matter of months. Seven years ago, in 2016, when I was first working on this book, I described a typical day with PD like this:

Days are often like a piano piece in which the right hand is playing a rich and lively melody while the left is playing an insistent dirge. Tuning out my left hand is easier on some days and during some hours than others. The low dose of antidepressant I've been taking for many years—predating my diagnosis, has helped enormously with insomnia, usually keeping me asleep through those particularly haunted hours between 2 and 5 a.m. Getting enough sleep is essential for anyone's emotional well-being, and with PD, it's hard to achieve. I wake up every time I have to shake out an excruciating leg or foot cramp or roll over, which is difficult for Parkies to do. Since I'm frequently visited by nightmares, in the morning, I wake up thinking, "Thank goodness that was only a dream." My second thought is, "Oh yeah—I have

Parkinson's." I'm groggy and thickheaded; it's been too many years to count since I last woke up feeling refreshed.

This is where I start my day: in a hollow that I must find a way to climb out of. Feeling low is one of the major non-motor symptoms of Parkinson's; about 50% of people with the disease experience depression, and 40% have anxiety at some time. The percentage is higher among those with a family history of these disorders. Depression and anxiety are attributable to neurochemical changes that occur as part of the disease process: Neural pathways in the brain that transmit dopamine and are affected by PD also transmit the neurotransmitter serotonin, known to regulate mood. In PET scans, changes show up in the same areas of the brain in people with PD and those with depression and anxiety.

Antidepressants have been found to be very helpful for people with PD, but about two-thirds of those suffering from depression aren't being treated for it. This might be partly because it can be difficult with a degenerative disease to find depression's root causes, which lie in not only neurochemical changes and our daily struggles but also living with the grim prospect of an ever-roughening road ahead. With other chronic illnesses that aren't always progressive, hope can be generated by unpredictability and variability—one could go into remission or even fully recover. Until there's a medical breakthrough, there will be no remission or recovery from PD. Those with younger onset Parkinson's are guaranteed to have the life of an old person before being old in years. The medications I take to sleep, my low-dopamine state and my restless nights are all in play on my melancholy mornings. Still, I will venture that the biggest killjoy is the simple knowledge that despite how well I take care of myself, I will be measurably more disabled with every passing year.

It's slow work to get my body out of bed and make the stiff trip to the bathroom, toes on both feet painfully curled from the dystonia of PD. Then, I return to bed with my laptop and reading materials. As much as I can, I structure my day so that I don't have to leave the house or be physically active first thing in the morning. This way, I can delay taking my first dose of levodopa because the later I start medicating, the fewer doses I'll need to get through the day. I spend the first few hours I'm awake perusing the *New York Times*, reading a novel, or working on my laptop, connecting with the people in my life and the world of information and ideas. I check in with Facebook to see what provocations, hilarity, and activism my friends have cooked up during the night. A little after 8 o'clock, I take my levodopa, which will kick in forty-five minutes later. I sign a couple of petitions and post an opinion or two. I allow the planet's woes to trouble me enough to diminish my personal plight but not so much that they sink me. Gradually, the isolation I felt upon waking recedes, and I feel I belong to the world. I have not yet left my bed, but I am participating, therefore, I am.

And now, flush with dopamine, I can move comfortably, so I can also do. By 9:30, I am further rejuvenated by my delicious breakfast—yogurt and berries mounded atop my homemade granola and coffee. Then it's off to the shower. Showers are scary places for people with Parkinson's, especially if you get caught in one when you're "off"—when the effect of levodopa has waned, which for me is about two to three hours after it kicked in. If I find myself "off" in that small, hard rectangle of space, I have to find a way to wash my hair with my eyes open because if I close them, I'll lose my balance. I struggle to make my sluggish arms perform the back-and-forth motion required to apply shampoo. Toweling off is laborious, combing out wet hair tedious and slow. I rarely let myself get caught in the shower when I'm "off." It doesn't seem safe and can also be an intensely disheartening confrontation with my impaired body.

Showered, "on," and ready, I sit at my desk, where I lose myself in thought and the arrangement of words, happily leaving my body behind. But it's not for long—just a couple of hours after I felt my first relief from levodopa, my thoughts begin to scatter. I'm squirmy in my chair. My energy flags, and then my mood slumps into "everything I'm writing is crap, so what am I doing this for anyway?" My hand is slow with the mouse, and my typing, which already is a barely respectable hunt-and-peck, is pathetic. When selecting, cutting, and pasting make me want to scream with frustration, I lift my 100-year-old body out of the chair and take a second dose of levodopa.

Forty-five minutes later, I'm medicated, and it's lunchtime. The combo infusion of food and dopamine turns back the clock, and I am sixty again, maybe even younger. All things seem possible. Lunch must be carefully timed and considered, however; too much protein will block the effects of my third dose, taken around 3:30 p.m. Eating a hard-boiled egg or chicken breast, for example, almost always guarantees that a walk, even two hours later, will feel like a trudge through three feet of snow.

My couple of hours of "on" time right after lunch are generally when I schedule meetings, social activities, or errands—anything requiring physical or social activity. One chore that must be squeezed into the hours when I'm fully "on" is food shopping. A busy market is probably one of a Parkie's biggest nightmares because it requires so much of what we are deficient in: motor control, dexterity, proprioception, and focus. A supermarket that's over-stimulating and crowded with impatient people is tricky to navigate with a cart, and it also requires that you pry open those uncooperative plastic bags to stuff in, say, a huge bunch of kale. Bagging groceries at the checkout is also very awkward, especially because I use unstructured cloth bags.

Something about the sequence of moves—reaching into the bag with an item, positioning it in the bottom, and retracting my hand, all the while trying to keep the bag from collapsing, taxes my dwindling motor neurons. Another everyday task that becomes especially difficult with PD is cooking. Like brushing hair and teeth, chopping, slicing, and stirring are sometimes impossible when the medication has worn off. Until recently, unless I had plans in the evening, I was taking three doses of levodopa per day, which gave me six hours of "on" time. When I realized I was making dinner in slower and slower slow-mo, I added a fourth dose on most days. The added medication has made it possible for me to revive one of my favorite dishes, risotto, with its forty-ish minutes of continuous stirring. I fantasize that I'll not only be able to hand-whip cream but also have a whole new life after dinner—time now spent talking, reading, writing, or watching movies—that could include who knows what? Dancing, perhaps?

Most everyone with Parkinson's rides the daily rollercoaster effects of levodopa. I'm lucky that my PD is relatively mild, and levodopa is still as effective as it was when I started it five years ago. What has changed is that when it wears off between doses, I'm more debilitated than I once was because my Parkinson's is progressing. The trough created by "off" periods gets deeper and tougher to pull oneself out of physically and emotionally. So, taking enough medication to minimize "off" time during the course of the day is critical for mitigating depression and anxiety. There are downsides to taking levodopa more frequently to get more "on" time, however. It's tricky to schedule meals so they don't interfere with its absorption, and more frequent dosing can cause dyskinesia or involuntary movement. One alternative to taking levodopa by mouth is Duopa, a drug delivery system approved for use in the US in 2015. Duopa uses a pump worn around the waist to deliver a gel form of levodopa directly into the intestines through a surgically implanted tube. While the Duopa system allows more continuous administration of medication, it has not been widely used in the U.S. due to complications of infection and intestinal blockages.

While brilliant scientists whack away in their labs at better treatments for Parkinson's, those living with the disease must develop everyday strategies for not letting our condition get the better of us. For some, that means carefully managing medications. Psychotherapy can help by providing a place to unpack fears and complaints to which we don't want to subject our families and friends. And one of the best tools we have is exercise. I know, I know—we've all been nagged relentlessly about the importance of exercise. And I confess, while I love being active outdoors, I've pretty much resented exercise for exercise's sake. Since my diagnosis, though, I've made sure to schedule it into every single day, typically taking a three-mile walk in the afternoon. In San Francisco, a walk has the added benefit of lending beauty to my day with extraordinary hilltop views and sunsets that paint the clouds behind the Golden Gate Bridge. I do Pilates once a week, and on days I don't walk, I hop on an elliptical or exercise bike. Maybe not "hop," exactly, because I still resist. It took some very persuasive science to lure me from my quiet hours of writing into the dreaded sweat zone.

We've known for a while that exercise can improve cardiovascular health, reduce osteoporosis, alleviate depression and anxiety, and have an anti-inflammatory effect. Now, there's increasing evidence that aerobic exercise might be neuroprotective. Several studies in the last few years have demonstrated that vigorous exercise can reduce PD symptoms like tremor; it has also been shown to improve cognition in people with PD and Alzheimer's. "Vigorous" is loosely defined as aerobic activity that raises a person's heart rate and need for oxygen for a sustained period—at least twenty to thirty minutes, ideally five days a week. The goal of such a regimen is to stimulate the production of BDNF (brain-derived neurotrophic factor), a protein found throughout the brain that promotes growth, survival, and plasticity of neurons. BDNF is powerful stuff; when it's applied to dopamine-producing neurons in a test tube, the neurons are protected not only from spontaneous death but also from specific, known neurotoxins. Since BDNF is significantly diminished in the brains of people with PD, the discovery that exercise can double or triple the release of BDNF in the brain is very exciting.

If you know someone recently diagnosed with Parkinson's who suddenly wants to ride their bicycle across Iowa or climb Mt. Whitney, it's because they know BDNF increases in proportion to the intensity of a workout. Recently, I decided that if I wanted to make an impact on my disease progression, I needed to step up my game and do a morning workout in addition to my afternoon walk. The exercise bike and elliptical, torture masters that they are, have become my new investment counselors. Every morning that I don't get on one of them and keep up my heart rate, I picture the stores in my brain going out of business.

Where there's a strong incentive, there's productivity and its reward: the feeling—even if only intermittently—that you're winning. But maybe it's not so much about winning as it is about feeling like you're not losing. Just as levodopa addresses the ebb of dopamine that makes people with PD feel greatly diminished, so too can exercise and staying engaged with the world help to prevent fear and depression from sapping our vitality.

Of course, this strategy is relevant for all of us as we age. Everyone, healthy or not, harbors fear about what the last decades of their life will bring. Sometimes, this comes out in indirect ways. A few years ago, an older friend, eighty-six at the time and in excellent health, visited his friend who was dying. "He's incredible," my friend told me. "He's had terrible cancer for three years, and he's never made any of us feel bad about it. He's a great example of going out gracefully." His words revealed his wish for how his own death would go: not messy with emotion, not scary or demanding of others. My friend didn't fight in a war and even at eighty-six, had had little exposure to the intimate details of illness and dying. His own parents' deaths were sudden and without warning: His father died in a plane crash, and his mother slipped away at ninety-four, napping in her own bed after balancing her checkbook and eating a grilled cheese sandwich and a Haagen Dazs ice cream bar.

We are drawn to death's neatness in such scenarios. When we find ourselves making gloomy predictions about our health, someone will often throw out, "Or, we could get hit by a bus tomorrow." It's a violent suggestion, but we must find it soothing both because it reminds us we can't fully control what will ultimately kill us and because a fatal accident would relieve us from a more likely descent into decrepitude involving such indignities as memory loss, bodily functions gone awry, and hospital gowns that gap in the back.

Most of us will avoid getting hit by a bus, and unless we're living with a progressive disease, we can imagine that death by grilled cheese and Haagen Dazs at age ninety-four is possible. Anyone with the good health to entertain this fantasy should never, ever take it for granted. The rest of us will be working hard not to imagine a life too truncated— walking, running, cycling, swimming, dancing, and boxing our fear into the margins of our stories.

THIRTY:
BLANK AND FULL OF EXPECTATION

In the year following Hadley's November 2013 multiple system atrophy diagnosis, I often contemplated the nature of our friendship. During the previous two years, we'd bonded over our weird neurological symptoms and had been collaborators with the clear mission to find her a diagnosis. We enjoyed a dynamic partnership in which we analyzed the research Hadley had uncovered and the details of her medical appointments. When uncertainty chilled us, we stood together and pulled a virtual blanket over our shoulders the way friends do.

Now that her medical mission was complete, Hadley was eager to stop being a full-time patient and get back to being an artist. Even if she'd wanted to take time to reflect on her new health status, her mural commissions made that impossible. She'd moved directly from a marathon to get a diagnosis to a marathon to create the Montana Women's Mural.

Once an active texter, Hadley pulled back from her phone and email. I was reluctant to contact her too often, as I knew that with her workload, every minute and each pulse of energy counted. Since I was writing about her, I also worried that probing questions about her symptoms might feel like research rather than genuine concern. During our infrequent phone calls, I tried to discern from the strength and tone of her voice how she was feeling physically as she talked about the challenges of the mural project.

Hadley's insecurity about whether she'd been a reluctant choice for the mural commission continued to haunt her throughout the winter and spring of 2014. While she had strong support from several of its members, a few off-hand comments by others had hinted there was some concern about her skills, especially when it came to painting people. Encumbered by her wavering confidence, she labored through the mural's design phase into the spring. She knew when she showed the committee her design drawings at the end of May, she would assure them that when the images were enlarged, details would appear much more refined. But the truth was, she was noticing changes, including a decline in her ability to organize material, process information, and work with her usual speed and efficiency, which made her question her own assurances. These are all manifestations of brain changes typical in MSA. Up to 49% of MSA patients experience executive dysfunction due to the atrophy of many different areas of the brain, as well as difficulties with problem-solving, flexibility in thinking, attention, and working memory.

"Not knowing if I can pull this off is eating away at me," Hadley told me. "This will be my last big project, and the thought that I might somehow feel shame about it is pretty terrifying."

I felt anxious for her, worried she'd lose the courage and energy to follow through on the Women's Mural Project. Maybe it was too easy to project on her my own disease weariness and discouragement about my agent's inability to sell my novel. I should've known better; Hadley exemplifies the proverb: "When the going gets tough, the tough get going." She's full of surprises; the last thing I expected was what happened next. "My friend invited me to have a two-person exhibition of our paintings in June," she told me one day in May. In my head, I jumped to the conclusion that she'd be showing paintings she'd done previously, but she added, "I'm having fun making all this new work for it." I gasped. How could she possibly take on another project? I think my words to her were, "Are you crazy?" She laughed, which seemed like further proof that she was losing it.

When I began writing about Hadley in 2013, I hoped the process would help keep us close. But you risk losing something when telling someone's life story. You have to stand at a distance, far enough away to see that person clearly. What I wanted was to sit across a table from Hadley, to talk over coffee and poke our conversation into all the little crevices we didn't access on the phone. Not a day went by that I didn't think or write about her, but I was missing my friend.

In June, I flew to Missoula. On my first day there, Hadley gave me a tour of her light-filled house and spacious studio tucked under the steeply pitched roof. A thrill rippled through me, looking at the almost entirely empty Women's Mural Project panels that I knew, within months, would be filled with life and hang prominently in the Montana State House. Then, I headed out in the car with Hadley, her husband John, and her daughter Sarah for a tour of Hadley's murals in downtown Missoula.

Surrounded on all sides by mountains, Missoula has all the best qualities of a small city: economic stability; an authentic main street that hasn't been cheapened by the tourist industry; a university that infuses it with youthful energy and at least a little diversity; charming, tree-filled residential neighborhoods. The city has ready access to wilderness and a wide river that runs through it—always a five-star feature. After one of the coldest and snowiest winters on record, Missoula was buzzing with activity on this postcard-perfect, seventy-five-degree day.

Driving to the murals' various locations, parking, and re-parking could've been a problem, but I noticed somewhat woefully that swinging from Hadley's mirror was a disabled person's parking placard. We climbed out of the car, and I immediately saw the "cage" in which Hadley had described being trapped: Her knees didn't naturally bend when she walked, so she lumbered, stiffly rocking from side to side. Her shoulders and neck were also rigid, and all of her movements were small and slow. My medication had kicked in, and I was "on," my gait smooth, but Hadley is never "on," so we ambled down the sidewalk at the pace she set. I was reminded of the walks I took with my father late in his life, except this time, I wasn't feeling like the patient daughter. Instead, I silently railed against the disease that was taking away my young friend's ability to put one foot in front of the other. Tailgating that anger, of course, was my fear about my own walking future.

At the corner of Higgins and Broadway, we stopped so I could gaze at Hadley's seven-panel Heart of Missoula Murals, which cover 2,400 square feet of the Allegra Print and Imaging building's exterior. The murals depict the development of Missoula's railroad, the founding of the University of Montana, and the city's industrial beginnings in the early 1900s.

Completed when Hadley was just twenty-eight, the murals were one of her first public projects. I was amazed by how much she'd packed into them—much more than anyone could take in just walking by. As I stood admiring them, a car honked boisterously. "Check out those awesome murals!" someone yelled, and I turned to see a woman leaning out the window of a station wagon. Hadley laughed—the woman was a friend. I realized Hadley is one of Missoula's treasures; she would be well taken care of.

We ducked into a bar, a bookstore, and a juice bar to check out Hadley's other murals. Each of them fulfilled the vision of the shops' proprietors, showcasing the breadth of her capabilities.

But the main event for me would be the murals she'd been creating for the Missoula Catholic School Heritage Project inside Loyola Sacred Heart School. A 2010 photograph of them on our Parkinson's Facebook page had been my introduction to Hadley, and I couldn't wait to see them.

Since it was Saturday, the school was closed, and we had the whole auditorium—once a church nave—to ourselves. Sarah had spent so many hours there with her mother that I imagined she'd memorized the murals; now, she careened around the voluminous space, shaking off excess energy. Three of Hadley's twelve-foot-tall murals hung on the east wall of the high-ceilinged but otherwise architecturally unremarkable room, lending it tremendous warmth. I couldn't help thinking about the long history of Catholic arts patronage as well as the glorious, stained windows that have for centuries brought life to many a somber house of worship.

Hadley's murals, populated by priests, nuns, missionaries, children, chickens, and horses, painted against a backdrop of Montana's glorious mountains and big sky, chronicle the work of the Jesuits in establishing in Missoula a "Catholic Block" consisting of three schools, a church, and a hospital. Hadley had collaborated with the Missoula Catholic Schools historian, who'd researched the schools for almost a decade.

The more I looked at the panels, the more awed I was by both the dizzying amount of work and the high degree of skill they represented. Hadley's compositions are carefully balanced to form an architecture that pleases the eye, yet they're never static or predictable. She's crammed a Wikipedia's worth of history into the scenes but has made them appear uncontrived.

The murals' animated figures are full of life and character; you can almost hear their deep conversations, their music, chatter, and laughter. Tonally, the paintings are quiet and have an earthy quality achieved by the use of an underlayer of sepia, which Hadley uses to ground and integrate the many colors she layers on top.

A fourth panel that hung on the west wall was in the "sepia stage," waiting its turn in Hadley's queue of commissioned work. Fortunately, the Catholic Schools mural committee had kindly agreed to put work on its murals on hold until the Women's Murals for the State Capitol were finished. "Is this the last panel you have to do?" I asked Hadley. She groaned. "No. Follow me."

We walked to the foot of the auditorium's stage, where the curtain was drawn shut. She lifted the corner of the velvet, revealing a tall scaffold on the stage. Behind it stood two more twelve-foot-high panels, both totally white—huge, blank, and full of expectation, possibility, and uncertainty. They were unfinished business in a life that would be unfinished.

I looked at Hadley. Her face had begun to take on the blankness of the panels, a hallmark of our diseases.

"I know," she said. "Don't even say it."

Hadley's art show opened the next night as part of Missoula's monthly "First Friday," when galleries in town are open late. Incredibly, in two weeks' time, she'd completed fifteen new paintings, most of them quite small, for the show. I helped her deliver the paintings—some still wet, to the gallery space, where she finished framing some of them. It was clear she'd had a lot of late nights. I couldn't imagine how she was going to hold up for the three-hour opening that evening.

She didn't just hold up; she held court with spunk and grace. Many friends, colleagues, her mother, and her doctor were there to admire her often pastoral, sometimes dramatically lit landscapes of Montana, Nebraska, Czechoslovakia, and the Oregon coast. Quite a few of the paintings demonstrated Hadley's interest in exploring the sky's limitless possibilities for shape and color.

By the end of the night, Hadley had sold twelve of the fifteen paintings. She was in high spirits, and although I assured her I would understand if she craved sleep, she wanted to go out and celebrate. So we did. She ordered her usual mojito. We didn't exchange one word about illness.

I'd thought Hadley was crazy to add the art show to her gigantic to-do list, but it was easy to see the magic the event had worked on her. For a few blissful weeks, she'd painted whatever she wanted—more like play than work. The show was an opportunity to make some much-needed money, but even better, it had bolstered her confidence at a time when it was flagging.

Hadley related the art show experience to the physical therapy she'd been having. "Do what makes you feel successful," her PT had told her when she was having trouble with one of the exercises. The therapist modified the exercises, so Hadley could do them without feeling frustrated. Similarly, Hadley's doubts about the looming, unfinished murals were offset by the pleasure and sense of accomplishment she gained by completing a new body of work. Looking ahead at the next five months, she told me with a big smile, "The energy and spirit that went into the show gave me a huge boost. I want to try to keep that with me." That spirit, I knew then, was what I'd come to Missoula to witness. There would be ups and downs for sure, but Hadley would ride them out.

I had no doubt she was on her way to pulling off something spectacular.

THIRTY-ONE:
IN THE CLENCH OF CRITICS

M y novel was not going to get published.

I'm sorry to have taken so long to read Catherine Armsden's fine and singular first novel, especially since I won't be making an offer for it. Her approach to the experience of going home after a long absence is utterly original, thanks to her training as an architect, but I'm afraid the novel as a whole was a bit too traditional for my somewhat peculiar tastes.

I very much enjoyed Ms. Armsden's deep and complex portrait of a middle-aged woman coping with familial loss, her living relatives, and the smaller everyday struggles of life. The relationships witnessed in the narrative felt fluid and natural, especially in the revealing of the past through Gina's journey back to Maine. I especially loved how the house itself was treated as a separate character with a personality of its own. Yet, despite its merits in capturing authentic familial situations and the visions of our pasts that remain imprinted in our minds and memories, I'm afraid I felt my traction with the emotional side of the narrative begin to slip a bit as I read on. While there were many heart-moving aspects to the novel, I'm afraid I just never lost myself over the whole so completely and totally that I would be able to give it the push it needs to succeed in such a tough marketplace.

It had been more than a year since my agent had sent *Dream House* out to publishers. The mini-reviews and "I'm afraids" somehow made the rejection worse. (Look what a good job she did! She almost had me!) I was standing metaphorically naked and cold at their gates, and they weren't going to let me in because they were, apparently, afraid. Every pessimistically leaning cell in my body was telling me that a traditionally published novel was not in my future.

In an unguarded moment, I indulged in some self-pity with my friend Sylvia. "Things could be a lot worse, Catherine," she told me crisply. I was duly chastened. Every optimistically leaning cell in her body was still fighting cancer. Chemo had been remarkably successful, and she was feeling pretty well. It was July, and the next week, she'd be having a biopsy and high-frequency ablation that would hopefully get rid of a small lesion on her liver. I was thrilled that come September, she and her husband would be moving into a place just a few blocks from me.

By July, the Montana Women's Mural Project panels were prepped, awaiting paint. Hadley's drawings captured the activities of Montana women as community builders during two time periods in the state's history. Panel one, titled "Women Build Montana: Culture," is set in 1898 and depicts ways in which Native American, Euro-American, and Mexican-American women and children contributed to the state's culture and economy through their paid and unpaid labor and social engagement. Panel two, titled "Women Build Montana: Community," is set in 1924, the tenth anniversary of Montana women's suffrage and the year the right to vote was extended to Native American women. The mural illustrates European American, Native, African American, and Asian American women at work in civic and volunteer activities, business, politics, homemaking, and education.

Four months: the time Hadley had to pour this rich, pictorial history onto the two five-by-ten-foot canvases in her upstairs studio. She hunkered down with her brushes. To begin, she chose the top left corner of panel one because it was a section she felt wouldn't need design adjustments. She had pleasant feelings about the scene—a Native American digging bitterroot, because of her memories of the day mural committee member Julie Cajun had taken her and Sarah to dig bitterroot on the Flathead Native American reservation. While they dug, Hadley and Sarah had delighted in Julie's stories about harvesting the root with her mother and the experience of discovering a ripe bitterroot and peeling away its bark.

Now Hadley's paintbrush was poised above the canvas, ready to bring definition to the first of thirty-three characters that populate the two murals. As soon as the bristles touched the surface, though, she froze: What if this is the brushstroke that makes this figure look all wrong? she wondered. Can I do this at all?

After a week of painting nothing but the Native American woman's face and a very, very precise braid, Hadley was dismayed by her lack of progress and low morale. It had taken her days to complete work that in the past would've taken just hours. "What I've produced is pretty pitiful," she told me. "I feel paralyzed, and I'm second-guessing each stroke I put on the canvas. This insecurity is so unlike me."

It wasn't so much her physical condition that was impeding her progress, Hadley realized, but rather the festering anxiety that the mural committee was unsure about her capabilities. It would sabotage both the project and her well-being if she couldn't recover the self-confidence that had lifted her after her June show.

Hadley knew she couldn't afford to wait for reassurance to come from an outside source; it had to come from her. One day, she hung a sign over the mural that said, "Just Do It!" Somehow, the sign was exactly what she needed to shut out the chorus of critics in her head. When she'd completed the woman digging bitterroot, she moved to the panel's upper-right corner, where two Mexican-American children were harvesting sugar beets. Finally, at the end of July, she described a shift in her outlook:

> After working on the children, I had several days of photographing friends who posed for the next set of mural images. In one scene, I wanted to create the sense of a light breeze, so I set up fans in a gymnasium that blew their skirts in a way that looked natural.
>
> We also spent a lot of time collecting images for several of the vignettes. In one corner of the mural, women are sewing a Montana flag, so we gathered all kinds of vintage sewing items, and I set them up as a still life and took photos for reference. We shared fun laughs while hearing the stories behind our collected items. The positive energy generated by working with my friends on these photo

shoots began to override my feelings of doubt. Working on the sewing corner of the mural after the photo shoots, I realized after a few hours that I was actually enjoying painting. This was a new feeling for me since starting the mural. I relished the slow pace and seeing each object come to life. When I painted the people, I felt their personalities come through, and instead of worrying about what a line might or might not do for a particular portrait, I just let it happen. The new pleasure I was feeling was very powerful. And here's the most powerful part: this week, as each person has emerged on my canvas, I've felt like I have one more person in this with me. The scary white canvas isn't scary or lonely anymore. It's filled with life. The women I've painted have become friendly souls who surround and encourage me. The children smile at me, and the women are laughing and talking together. This is an entirely new experience. I've never had this happen with any other painting. I can't believe that it happened with this particular project that has been such a struggle to get through. It feels like the ultimate mental and emotional achievement to move from such a desperate place to this place of enjoyment and security.

Along with her extraordinary bonding with the life in the murals, Hadley became more accepting of her physical limitations. She told me there were days when she pushed herself much too hard, and she would simply stop, rest, and hope the next day would bring her better energy. She was stiff and achy in her hands, neck, and back. But she experienced a new self-compassion, especially when she noticed that her very slow pace allowed a keener attention to detail. Happily, the quality of the work was exceeding her expectations.

September marked two months until the murals were scheduled to be installed at the State Capitol Building in Helena to celebrate the 100th anniversary of the Montana suffrage movement. Two months after that, on January 7, 2015, a formal dedication would take place. Hadley painted twelve hours a day, setting a timer for forty-five-minute intervals so she could rotate between the School of Forestry murals and the Women's Mural Project. She hoped that dividing the time this way would help to keep up her energy. But she was panicked and fairly certain she wouldn't be able to meet the November deadline, despite working as hard as she could and sleeping in her studio from midnight to 4 a.m. She wrote to me:

> My brain feels tired. I have such a hard time thinking, seeing the big picture, staying on task, and focusing. Incredibly, the paintings don't show this. The images are looking strong. But the big clue that I'm struggling with is that the amount of canvas that's covered is still minimal. I'm embarrassed to send you photos because I don't feel like I have enough new work done to warrant them.

On top of the mounting pressure she was feeling, a frightening new development nearly plunged Hadley into despair. Driving around town to pick up Sarah at school or do errands, she began misjudging distances and not noticing things in her peripheral vision, hitting curbs and nearly sideswiping parked cars. At intersections, she found she was having trouble processing all that was happening:

traffic lights, cars turning in front of her, and pedestrians in the crosswalk. Her reactions were too slow. At first, she attributed her bad driving to fatigue and stress. But the near misses began to add up, and she worried that she was experiencing more cognitive symptoms of MSA. One day, she was horrified when she nearly hit a mother and child while taking Sarah to school. John and her mother, Jana, told her somberly they thought she shouldn't be driving anymore, and Hadley agreed, though she hadn't prepared herself for this possibility. With her extreme rigidity and slowness, walking more than a block or two was not an option, and driving had given her the freedom her disease was taking away. She was devastated about the independence she would lose. "I never cry," she told me. "But this hit me hard, and I've cried about it every night."

The following week, Hadley braced herself to tell the mural committee that she couldn't have the murals done by November. To her enormous relief, the committee, though disappointed, was understanding. They conceded that because they'd delayed the artist selection and held up the project during the first few months, the November ceremony probably had been wishful thinking. They were content to focus on the January 2015 unveiling.

The reprieve made Hadley momentarily lighter. Then, stepping back from the murals to assess the amount of white surface and color she still had to fill in, she was caught in January's blinding headlights, speeding toward her.

THIRTY-TWO:
FINISHED!

In the days leading up to the January 7, 2015, unveiling of the Montana Women's Murals at the Montana State House, Hadley racked up some serious numbers. She painted eighteen hours every day. There were eighteen layers of paint on the murals' elaborate borders, for which she'd recruited help from friends and Sarah; the borders themselves took 245 hours to complete. Hadley wore out thirty-eight small brushes articulating the paintings' finest details.

When she wasn't painting, Hadley slept on a mattress she'd moved upstairs to her studio so she wouldn't disturb John. Her eyes burned and blurred, her body throbbed, and her mind numbed as she applied every ounce of focus to the canvas in front of her.

On the afternoon of January 5, she texted me: "I am f##ing finished!!!!"

Then she shepherded the two five by ten-foot murals to Rick's Auto Body, where they were powder coated, a protective treatment that would eliminate the need for plexiglass once the panels were mounted at the Montana State House.

I didn't have to twist my friend Cary's arm to fly to Helena with me for the mural unveiling. An artist herself, she was very excited to meet Hadley and to document the event with her camera. On the second leg of our flight, I noticed the man in the seat across the aisle from me had a hand tremor. Other afflictions cause tremors, but after a couple more furtive glances, I noted he was wearing a rubber bracelet imprinted with the words "whatever it takes to beat PD." He was young to have PD and was flying to Helena; he had to be a friend of Hadley's, I reasoned. I touched his arm lightly and asked if he was headed to the unveiling. He laughed and said he was making the trip from Portland. Thanks to social media, the world of people with YOPD is not that big.

Temperatures were in the teens in Helena, and for the first time in more than thirty years, I drove on roads packed solid with snow and ice. The landscape shone like satiny white frosting. Navigating our hotel's ice-paved parking lot in our smooth-soled city boots, Cary and I must have looked ridiculous, barely keeping our feet under us.

The next day before the unveiling ceremony, we met Hadley at the Victorian bed-and-breakfast where she was staying with John and Sarah, her mother, Jana, and her uncles and aunts from Texas and Nebraska. She appeared calm and serene—a heroic demonstration considering the heavy strain she'd been under and the important public performance she had ahead of her.

It wasn't until Cary and I arrived at the imposing Montana State Capitol—domed, Neoclassical, built at the turn of the 20th century, like so many others of its kind—that I felt the full significance of the contribution Hadley would be making. The muscular building's sandstone and granite merged with the grey wash of winter sky, smeared now with sunset pink. Inside, all pretense of solemn restraint dropped away, and we found ourselves in an enormous rotunda whose classical details were painted like a children's carousel: red, gold, green, yellow, teal. I welcomed the space's vibrancy and warmth on the bleak, frigid day. Historic paintings adorning the rotunda reminded me of the reason women legislators had determinedly lobbied for the Montana Women's Mural. Four circular paintings on the dome illustrate a Native American Chief, an explorer and fur trapper, a gold miner, and a cowboy. Other paintings in the space depict Lewis and Clark and President Ulysses Grant wielding a sledgehammer to drive the "golden spike" that announced the arrival of the Northern Pacific Railroad. Women were conspicuously missing from the narratives on display despite their influential roles in America's history. Montana boasts the first woman to serve in the U.S. Congress, Jeannette Rankin, who won her seat in 1916 and helped to pass the 19th Amendment, giving voting rights to women.

My legs were shaky as Cary and I climbed the grand staircase rising inside the barrel-vaulted hall. We were there early to claim our standing spot against the stair balustrade on the third floor. There, we'd have a good view of the program's speakers and both murals, now covered with blue cloth, that hung on facing walls on either side of the open stair. We people-watched until Hadley arrived with her family. Finally, Hadley came up the stairs, holding the rail and taking each step very slowly, greeting people she passed.

By the time the dedication ceremony began, more than 250 people had jammed the stair and the space that wrapped around it. Montana's first lady, Lisa Bullock, was the first to speak, calling the mural unveiling a "monumental moment." Julie Cajune, who had been especially helpful to Hadley with her research on Native Americans, spoke from the heart about both the murals and Hadley.

"Not only is Montana the only state to recognize American Indians in its constitution," she said, "but now our state capitol recognizes that women have been the sinew to keep body and soul, community and spirit together... Women have not just been homemakers. They've been healers, pharmacologists, teachers, spiritual people, and warriors. Women have done everything."

When she spoke about Hadley, Julie audibly fought back tears. She told the crowd that she and Hadley had worked "soul to soul." "I want to tell you what a fine artist she is," she said, "but also what a fine human being she is." She expressed appreciation for Hadley's genuine desire to explore the customs of Native Americans in order to paint their story. "Thank you," she said to Hadley. She spoke a few words in Salish, her tribe's language, then presented Hadley with a handmade quilt that she wrapped around her shoulders. By that point, I was the one blinking back tears.

Hadley stepped to the microphone with Sarah by her side. "It's truly an honor to have you all here," she said, thanking the crowd. She spoke of how meaningful the project was for her as an artist, a lifelong Montanan, and a collaborator with the many who made the murals possible. She read her artist's statement:

> The generations of women in my family have set examples and carved paths for my mom, daughter, and me to have the life and experiences we live today. That is what this project is about. This piece is about the generations of women in Montana who built families and contributed to their communities, the economy, and politics by working together to build strong communities for generations to come. It is not about one single important

woman but about all women. It is a broader
picture of women. Hopefully, any woman can
look at these images and see a piece of herself
in them.

There was a lot of pomp and circumstance—it was a
government affair, after all, but knowing the monumental
effort that had gone into the murals, no ceremony would've
seemed too grand. The murals waited behind their blue
shrouds; the suspense in the hall was palpable. When the
curtains were finally pulled away, the crowd erupted in
applause and exclamations. The Montana Women's Chorus
sang: "A woman's voice raised up in the silence can be heard
a long way / Revolution starts in a circle rising up from the
ground. / We believe in the power of women to turn this
world around."

Cary sprang into high gear with her Nikon, turning it on
the crowd and the murals with the rigor of a professional
journalist. I couldn't take my eyes off the paintings. From a
distance, they radiated warmth and liveliness and seemed
perfectly at home, as though they'd always hung on those
walls. Hadley had told me she'd made sure that her colors
would complement those of the building's architectural
features, including the enormous stained-glass skylight of the
barrel vault. This had been masterfully accomplished. Close
up, I marveled at the abundance and variety of activities
taking place in the murals' scenes and the precision and
sumptuousness of the details.

Women's History Matters, a website created as part of
a commemoration of the 100th anniversary of women's
suffrage in Montana, explains the history brought to life by
the two murals:

Stitching the Montana flag

Panel one, titled "Women Build Montana: Culture," is set in the spring of the late 19th century. It depicts Native women having come to a homestead to trade for goods. In keeping with the theme of Montana women as community builders, the scene portrays a meeting ground in which women acted as traders and cultural brokers. Montana women, Natives, and newcomers often lived quite near each other, trading knowledge and offering support as well as goods. The four corner vignettes depict women and children engaged in the paid and unpaid labor that helped build Montana... Women are digging bitterroot, an important food source for Native peoples and the plant that would become the Montana state flower. The two Euro-American women stitching a Montana flag, inspired by a historical account, represent the mixing of domestic arts and formal politics. Children harvesting sugar beets represent the Mexican-American families who contributed to the economy and community of eastern Montana. The Native mother and daughter beading and preparing a hide illustrate the teaching and learning of traditional arts across generations.

The central scene of the second panel, which is titled "Women Build Montana: Community," is set in the fall of 1924 in an eastern Montana town. While women won the right to vote in Montana in 1914, that right was not extended to Native women until 1924 with the passage of the Indian Citizenship Act. The scene marks the tenth anniversary of Montana women's suffrage and acknowledges the year in which Native women gained citizenship and the right to participate in formal state politics... The vignette of a woman canning fruits references not only the work of homemakers but also the important role of home extension agents. The telephone operators personify Montana cities' and towns' clerical workers and women as labor union members: the first union of telephone workers in America was organized in Montana. Thousands of Montana women joined voluntary associations that supported women's education, here represented by members of the Montana Federation of Colored Women's Clubs giving out a college scholarship. Education is also depicted in the vignette of a Native woman teaching botany. Botany was one of the few sciences that welcomed women, and Native women's knowledge of the medicinal and nutritional uses of Montana plants was and continues to be, important to both Native and newcomer communities.

After the ceremony, Hadley was quickly swarmed by reporters, TV cameras, friends, and family. She never sat down. I figured adrenalin was propping her up, keeping her from collapsing or even fainting—her specialty. I inched toward her through the crowd and caught her mother's attention; she had tears in her eyes. When Hadley's father, a history professor emeritus, embraced his daughter, he did too. "Just imagine," he said. "They'll have a Hadley Ferguson file in the state archives."

I finally got close enough to give Hadley a congratulatory hug. When we made contact, I felt as if the seams keeping me together might split. "I can't believe you pulled this off—they're... you're amazing!" I burbled over her shoulder. With her usual modesty, Hadley said, "I can't believe it either. They turned out the way I wanted them to. I'm just so happy."

The seams gave way; I cried. Not "Oh, I'm so happy for you" tears, though I was thrilled for her. They were the kind of tears that surge from your innards when you or someone you care about has just survived a near-death experience. Tears full of knee-wobbling relief and joy mingled with the pain of everything I knew Hadley had been through and what she still had ahead of her. Creating the murals had been a yearlong marathon, both depleting and sustaining, during which Hadley had courageously kept her illness, multiple system atrophy, outside her door. It had banged hard on that door, but she had another calling. And she emerged victorious, unveiling a gift to Montana and women everywhere that's nothing short of astonishing.

The real miracle? Not the masterpiece revealed but rather the complicated, veiled minutes of its making.

THIRTY-THREE:
THE BIRTH OF A BOOK

After the thrill of seeing Hadley's murals on the walls of the Montana State Capitol, coming home to my novel that was growing roots in a file on my laptop was hard. The disappointment I felt in myself was directly proportional to the admiration I felt for Hadley. It was impossible not to compare our trajectories. Hadley, plagued as she'd been with serious health issues all her life, had turned out many notable projects in her thirty-eight years, culminating in a historic, grand-scale commission. Here I was, on the verge of sixty, and I hadn't managed to get *Dream House*, the project that most mattered to me, out into the world. I'd witnessed Hadley's deep satisfaction in unveiling the strongest and most celebrated work of her life. I wanted that!

The week following my trip to Montana, I attended a rousing orchestral performance. I found myself imagining being a violinist, playing alone in her room. We don't think of writing as a performing art. But like musicians, writers work assiduously to craft an affecting expression of their ideas and stories to touch an audience with their words. Writers, I glumly mused as the orchestra played on, can write for years without having their work read.

Away with doom and gloom! I couldn't let my discouragement quash my determination. I began making inquiries about self-publishing. I had no well-considered bias against this route; I just didn't feel I had the stamina to make it happen. No sooner had I begun my research than an email popped up that made my heart gallop. Jay, my *Dream House* editor, had a colleague who was interested in publishing the book.

It was tempting to get carried away by the excitement of this news. But I didn't share it even with Lewis, because the only thing worse than riding the rollercoaster of publication hopefulness that had begun four years earlier was taking those closest to me along for the ride. Two weeks after Hadley's mural unveiling, in a state of suspended belief, I drove downtown to meet with Lisa McGuinness, publisher at Yellow Pear Press. We hit it off and, right then and there, nailed down details and deadlines to meet for publishing that fall in November 2015.

Within eight weeks of meeting with Lisa, my novel had a cover, and I was proofreading the galleys. I let the new reality sink in a little more every week, but I still felt unable to celebrate. This was partly because publishing had been a dream for so long that it felt too good to be true. Also, with many hands involved in its production, I fretted about whether the physical book would have the qualities I hoped for. And then there was the obvious: apprehension about how the novel would be received.

Another reason my excitement was subdued was that Sylvia, after a short remission, was not winning her fight with cancer. The July ablation she'd had on the small lesion on her liver appeared to trigger an inflammatory response, resulting in a new proliferation of cancer cells. By February, she was housebound, except when she needed to see her doctor, and was spending much of her days sleeping. One Saturday evening in mid-March, the water heater on the second floor of her house began leaking through the floor. The plumber who came on Monday used a blowtorch too close to a fire sprinkler, setting off a monsoon in the house. Sylvia's daughter Meredith, home at the time, called 911 and me. Then she led her bathrobed mother down into the street and helped her and their dog into their parked car. When I arrived, there was mayhem: two fire trucks, water everywhere, and my stunned sliver of a friend sitting in the car out front. I drove her to my house and set her up in bed.

Sylvia, her husband Peter, Meredith, and their golden retriever stayed with us for a week while their house dried out. It was profoundly affecting to witness the tender, complicated care Peter and Meredith gave Sylvia, and to have one of my dearest friends under my roof at the end of her life. When she was sleeping, I tried to carry on with the daily tasks that were moving my book forward, but my awareness of Sylvia's ephemerality kept me in the present moment. I didn't want to miss something important. I savored the times she asked me to help shift her tiny frame in the bed, each brief conversation we shared. "I don't want to keep going like this," she told me one day. We talked about what's within a patient's power when they are ready to stop suffering and say goodbye. What could be more important, and yet how many times in life do we get the chance to talk this way with someone we love? One morning, when we were chatting, she looked deep in thought for a few moments, and I braced myself for something difficult. Finally, she said, "I probably won't be able to eat it, but just in case, can you save me some of the Bolognese sauce you made for dinner?" She laughed. She was such a foodie. She'd been eating Gerber baby arrowroot biscuits, mashed potatoes, and ground chicken for days; no wonder she craved some zest!

That week, I barely thought about Parkinson's. But I thought a lot about what awaits me and everyone close to me at the end of our lives. During Sylvia's stay, I talked to Hadley, and she recalled her last days with her stepfather, Charlie. Our conversation about dying was disorienting, as if I were looking through a camera lens at the four of us—Hadley, Sylvia, Charlie, and myself, trying to adjust the focal length to correspond with our unspoken perceptions of where we were on the timelines of our lives.

In late March, I sat on Sylvia's bed, the bright California sunshine streaming through her bedroom windows. She was waifish, every bone explicit. Always meticulously groomed, she worried aloud about how long her fingernails had grown, and I asked her if she'd like me to cut them. Sylvia was a private person, and I felt honored when she said yes. As I held each of her cool, delicate fingers in my hand and clipped, I took my time, relishing the intimacy of this simple task, taking it in as Sylvia's last gift to me. She died several days later with Peter and Meredith by her side.

Winter and spring were a blur of proofreading the *Dream House* galleys, every word and every punctuation mark, six times. By the time the book went to print, I probably could've told you to pick any word, and I would've been able to turn to the page on which it appeared. At the behest of the publicist, I also needed to pull together promotional material. Among other things, this included setting up an author Facebook page and a website, which I was lucky enough to have our son, Tobias, design. I learned how to describe the book in as few, hopefully enticing, phrases as possible: "An architect of houses searching for home," "...how we shape and are shaped by our houses," and "What makes a house feel like home?" As tedious as the production period was at times, after years of editing *Dream House* with nothing but hope and encouragement to keep me motivated, I gobbled up the tasks before me, knowing that there would be a monumental payoff.

Lisa, my *Dream House* publisher, met me for lunch in July to present my printed book. When she passed it across the table, I was unprepared for the emotional rush that sent me diving for my napkin to brush away tears. To me, the book was an exquisite object. The quiet but evocative jacket, featuring an image of the Maine house where I was raised, perfectly captures the tone and landscape of the novel; the size and weight of the book are modest but inviting. I hadn't dared to hope that the physical embodiment of my story and the story itself, in which I explored everything that most moved me—space and architecture, love and motherhood, pain and healing, ocean, sky, and trees, would be so well integrated, so... right.

A week before the book's publishing date, in late October 2015, we threw a party. I dubbed it the "If not now, when?" party. I'd been casting about for an excuse to have a very big party for years, and a book event seemed more fun than waiting for a milestone birthday, which, especially when you have a progressive, degenerative disease, is not necessarily a cause for celebration. The party was a blast. Friends and family came, many of them from the east coast. I was especially honored that Dr. Bright came, that he chatted with my kids, and even purchased a book. Coming to the celebration was example of how he goes out of his way to show he supports his patients even when he's not wearing his white coat. Tobias' band played, and I danced with the freewheeling women in my writing group. Lisa set up a bookselling table, and friends generously stood in line to purchase books and have me sign them. While turning my Sharpie loose on book after book, it finally became real to me: my book!

Did I have Parkinson's? Not that night! I spoke into a microphone for the first time in my life and discovered it was fun! Being in that crowd of well-wishers was like soaking in a warm bath.

From November through April, I talked about *Dream House* in the West and New England at bookstores, private parties, newspaper and radio interviews, seven book groups, and an architecture school. Generous and genuinely excited family and friends from around the country facilitated opportunities for me to speak and sell books. Mindful of my energy's ebb and flow, I only scheduled events where I knew people who would fill the chairs.

I never stopped feeling nervous when approaching the podium, afraid I'd go blank in the middle of a thought. A couple of times, I did, but managed to recover well enough. After describing the inspirations for the novel, I would read a couple of passages and feel my anxiety drop away. Speaking the words I'd written, I re-experienced the passion I'd felt when I started the book years ago. It was powerful to feel I was engaging my listeners' emotions and imagination, not by selling plot or drama but simply through my choice and arrangement of words.

Finally, I was out of my room, playing my music. People were listening.

I didn't push much beyond my limitations to publicize *Dream House*, so the post-publication experience was entirely positive. Even at the event in my hometown, 3,000 miles away, where I feared God-knows-who would surface to scold me with a wagging finger for airing my family's troubles, people were warm, inquisitive, and even a little proud of their homie author. In addition to old family friends I hadn't seen in decades, two of my first childhood girlfriends were in that room, as well as my first love; their presence added a lovely if distracting, tenderness to the occasion. Everywhere I went, I was filled with gratitude for people's inquisitiveness, enthusiasm, and persistent pursuit of literature.

That Lewis was the best roadie ever made all the difference. It was as if he'd read a manual on how to support your Parkie wife while she's on a book tour. He hefted my carry-on into the overhead bin, took my hand in the airport when he saw my leg dragging, schlepped boxes of books, and ran peoples' credit cards at private events. While at our Airbnb, he dashed to the market for groceries, made me coffee every morning, and, in the evenings before my book talks, a mini margarita to boost my confidence. (Trust me, it works.) Each day, he rode a bike for an hour and a half but insisted he wasn't too tired to go back out and take a three-mile walk with me because he knew that exercise is what keeps my body from shutting down altogether. He was excited to greet the wonderful old friends who came out of the woodwork. Throughout the "season of *Dream House*," Lewis expressed no complaints. He had lost his partner-in-architecture years before but was now proud to crow about her book to anyone who'd listen. He was thrilled for me, but also, like many partners of those with debilitating conditions, he understood the importance of turning up the light on life's joyful passages and significant accomplishments.

So, how did it feel to finally be published at sixty? Besides joy, relief when I finished my book tour. Taking stock of my Parkinson's progression, I had a sense that publication came either not a moment or at least a year too soon. It was also a relief to be done with the story that had been parked in my brain like a claustrophobic RV full of family members and to clear out my cabinet filled with paper drafts, some dating back to the late 20th century. I could move on.

Parkinson's added to my life a new community of friends like Hadley with whom I can share the experience of our disease. The release of *Dream House* provided another avenue for making meaningful connections. Friends and total strangers have written to me about why the novel resonated with them; the territories that I'd burned to explore ignited in them vivid memories and powerful emotions. I've felt honored and delighted that they've shared, sometimes in intimate detail, tales of their complicated relationships with a house, with a parent, or with their children. This—touching the hearts and minds of my readers and, in return, being moved by their stories—was the least expected but greatest reward of realizing my long-time dream.

THIRTY-FOUR:
2023

My phone alarm wakes me at 7 a.m. Before being diagnosed with Parkinson's in 2009, I hadn't set an alarm for any reason since I was in my twenties and needed to get to my job on time. Now, the alarm goes off nine times daily, reminding me to take medications. As I emerge from sleep into wakefulness, I pass through a door into "the before," where, for a fleeting second, I am comforted by a vestigial sense that I am not alone in my house. I open my left eyelid with my fingers so that I can see well enough to connect a finger with the "stop" button on the alarm.

I am not alone. My sweet Rafa, a ten-year-old, mostly Spaniel rescue, is two floors below me. I know he is alert now, hanging on every sound that might signal that he will get his breakfast. Without fail, he will get breakfast. But first, some levodopa will need to find its way to my brain. I sit on the edge of the bed so I can take my first meds of the day. Eyes shut, I feel my way down the seven compartments of the plastic pill calendar that holds the dose. Each compartment holds three tablets that I have pre-sliced with a pill cutter to get what I hope is just the right amount, but the pills are chalky and hard to cut. By some miracle, I have never spilled the glass of water I sip from, even though my eyes are still shut. I will have to wait until they open so I can safely stand and walk to open the curtains. I am itching to check my email, but I will be sitting here for nearly half an hour, cradling my phone in my hand until my eyelids are ready to let me join the new day. "Eyelid opening apraxia," Dr. Google has told me, is very common in Parkinson's and other brain diseases.

Eyes that won't stay open, a dog that needs breakfast, the need to be medicated so I can take on two flights of stairs without falling: they have put an end to the luxurious routine I described in Chapter 29 when I could stay in bed until as late as nine-thirty and "peruse the New York Times" and "connect with the world of ideas and information." Don't ask me about current events. I'm frustrated and embarrassed about my ignorance that is a result of losing that hour or two I used to have in the morning, pre-pandemic.

When I finally stand on wobbly legs and pull back the curtains, I fill with doubt about whether I'll be able to manage what I have planned for the day: to work on this book, drive across the Bay Bridge to the Franchise Tax Board, take the car in to be serviced, pay a few bills. For the next thirty to forty minutes, I am in a crisis of self-doubt, a tiresome daily habit brought on by chemistry.

My finger is poised above my phone screen, prepared to cancel some part of my day. But then I remind myself that I felt this way yesterday morning, too, and the morning before that, yet I still managed to get nearly everything done that I needed to and had periods of feeling I had things under control.

It's especially apparent to those of us who ride levodopa's daily on-off rollercoaster that we are not necessarily the person we feel we are at any given moment. In a few more minutes, I can feel the dopamine treating my brain to a confidence-boosting bath. When it has fully kicked in, it's like an all-body sigh of relief.

I'm OK! Rafa will get his breakfast on time, and I haven't canceled anything.

I've had PD since my first symptoms presented themselves to me in 2007, sixteen years ago. I'm six years further along with this disease since I wrote about a day in a life with PD in Chapter 29. Yet, I have at least twice as much work to do each day than I did then, tasks that require physical, mental, and emotional exertion.

I am stronger than I was then.

I had no choice but to be stronger than I ever thought I could be.

In 2015, the year my novel *Dream House* was published, my agent asked what else I was working on. I sent him a detailed description of *An Alert, Well-Hydrated Artist in No Acute Distress*. He responded that while the story sounded dramatic, most publishers generally wanted to avoid "tales of misery" or "triumphing over misery," so I shouldn't plan on mine getting published. I was confused by this, hard-pressed to think of a book that didn't involve misery. But I understood that he was not interested in trying to sell this project.

My agent's rejection was not nearly enough to dissuade me from plunging ahead. The story had swept me into its current. Hadley's journey and my exploration of the workings of the brain continued to expand with power and poignancy. Besides, I was hooked on what seemed like a decidedly healthy habit; other than sleeping, writing is the only activity that allows me to completely tune out my body's chatter and the fear and sadness it can trigger. When you're writing what you're meant to be writing, expressing the ideas and emotions that feel most urgent, your mind is in heavenly flight from your body, except for the almost physical sensation of something tugging on your heart. It's that tug that kept me writing, not any vision of a destination. Destinations can be reached by way of shortcuts and formulas through unflagging determination or sheer endurance. Sometimes, goals can be met by abandoning something we care about to take up something someone else cares about. But when we focus too much on the questions—Where will my writing get me? For whom do I write?—we risk losing the tug.

In the months before *Dream House* was published, the publicist who'd instructed me to make a website suggested I start a blog to attract readers to my book. If only writing were as easy as baiting a fishing line with a little fish to catch a bigger fish! What more could I possibly find to write about? I wondered. I was 140 pages into *An Alert Well-Hydrated*, and between it and the novel, I'd written pretty much everything I had to say at the time.

The idea to publish *An Alert, Well-Hydrated Artist* online as a serial came to me quickly, as did my rationale. There was, of course, the problem of my agent thinking it was unpublishable. Then there was the fact that I conveniently had a place for it; I had blogger status at the *Huffington Post* since they'd published an essay and a book review. My son Tobias also introduced me to *Medium*, with its easy-on-the-eyes formatting. Between these two sites and *Facebook*, I had a potential audience who probably would be disinclined to pluck it whole, as a book, from a bookshelf but might be willing to read my story in ten-minute bites. Last but not least, I was happy that the "Blog" tab on my website would be able to deliver.

Having a regular schedule for publishing episodes of *An Alert, Well-Hydrated Artist* online every two weeks kept my mind engaged, and I enjoyed the immediate gratification of feedback I received from my readers, who were mostly family, friends, and Facebook friends. I learned who among them are, like me, fascinated with medicine. Some people didn't hesitate to tell me they enjoyed reading the "blog" more than my novel.

When I posted the last chapter of *An Alert Well-Hydrated Artist in No Acute Distress* online in early 2017, I pulled out the 187-page manuscript of a novel that I'd been sporadically working on during the years I was trying to get *Dream House* published. Working on it had always been compelling, and I thought I'd be excited to reconnect with the story. However, each time I opened it on my computer, I would sit and wait for that all-important visit from the muse that would keep moving the story along. I pictured Lewis sitting on his surfboard, staring out to sea, waiting for a wave. It didn't come. Why? Had I somehow outgrown the story in the four years since I'd last worked on it? Was my lack of interest the apathy that is known to afflict many people with Parkinson's?

Until this writer's block, Parkinson's apathy, or a paucity of thought that perhaps (gasp!) portended cognitive decline— whatever it was, struck, I had steered away from thinking about the future. I had heard enough about the wisdom of staying in the moment to know it was something I needed to do. And it worked. I continued to feel lucky; ten years post-diagnosis, people were still telling me they would never know I had PD. I'd never had a tremor, and levodopa, which I was gradually taking more of and more frequently as my PD progressed, worked well for me without causing dyskinesia. I still walked an hour a day and joined a new PD exercise class across the bridge on Marin that provided weekly contact with other people with PD. PD Connect challenged the full range of Parkinson's issues. And it was fun!

However, without my writing, something that every day for years I'd beaten back tedious tasks so I could get to, my future loomed. I imagined that as my disease progressed, my marriage would change because I would become more of a burden on Lewis. I dreaded the idea of becoming a burden on anyone, especially Lewis, who kept himself so busy and on the move that burdens weren't able to stick to him. I was a little afraid that he wouldn't notice that my needs were increasing. He was a fix-it guy, after all, and I was tweakable but not fixable.

Another thing that made me sad was imagining that by the time we had grandchildren—*if* I had grandchildren, I might not be able to safely lift them from their crib. I consoled myself with the thought that at least Lewis was strong and had the energy of three people put together. He could be the fun, physically active grandparent, and I would be the quiet grandparent who would cuddle, read, and listen.

I was obviously in a funk. Like most people, I was demoralized by a president whose words and policies seemed designed not only to undo everything vitally important and good that had been achieved over the previous decades but also to bring out the darkest sides of human nature. Against a landscape that has been scorched, drowned, or swept away by the extreme effects of climate change, we watched, marched, and even cried.

There was no shortage of things to make all of us very afraid about our future. But soon, a crisis would be brewing under my roof that would fully distract me from conjuring a doom and disaster scenario for our entire species.

THIRTY-FIVE:
FORGING RESILIENCE

I t's been ten years since Hadley was diagnosed with multiple system atrophy in 2013 at the age of thirty-seven. Worn out by years of having to prove she was sick with something serious, once she was diagnosed, she retreated from the medical world and stopped seeking care so she could focus only on the Women's Murals for the Montana State House. When she completed them in January 2015, she knew she would never again work at the grueling pace required for this commission. Every day, she suffered from profound fatigue and painful muscular spasms in all parts of her body. Finally, she went to see her neurologist, Dr. Reid, who treated the cramping with oral baclofen. The muscle relaxant helped, but chronic use caused unpleasant side effects.

In the summer of 2015, Hadley learned of a medical intervention that would end up having a huge impact on her quality of life: intrathecal baclofen therapy. ITB is a surgically implanted delivery system for baclofen that's brought great relief to some MSA patients. The device involves a pump, a round metallic disc about one inch thick and three inches in diameter, that's implanted under the skin of the abdomen.

A catheter connecting the pump to the spinal cord is also implanted under the skin to carry the medication directly to the spinal fluid. The pump is then programmed with a small computer that communicates with the pump via a wand placed over the skin. Because the baclofen has direct contact with the spinal cord and can be delivered continuously, it's much more effective than when taken orally and doesn't have as many side effects.

Yikes!" was my response when Hadley told me she was considering the surgery. "You know," she said, "I guess I've just gotten to the point where the idea of having foreign objects in my body and a tube going into my spine doesn't sound so bad. And accepting the help I need to feel better seems like a big moment of accepting my disease."

Hadley was scheduled to have the baclofen implant surgery on September 10, but she was worried. She'd been planning to travel with Sarah to meet her mother, Jana, in Prague on October 12. If she had the surgery, would she recover in time? But without the benefits of the surgery, she might not feel well enough to enjoy the trip. Considering her physical condition, "enjoying the trip" sounded like a long shot with or without the surgery. But I knew returning to the country of her ancestors with her mother and daughter could be a once-in-a-lifetime experience.

Intrepid as she is, Hadley decided to go for it and have the surgery. The several-hour procedure went well, but she endured a three-day spinal headache that was finally relieved by an epidural blood patch. She fainted several times during the first week of recovery in the hospital. This was not a major concern to her, a pro fainter, but she alarmed the nurses one day when she was out for so long that she turned blue. The good news was that with the baclofen continuously circulating through her system, she noticed less muscle rigidity right away.

The hospital kept Hadley for eighteen days, much longer than she'd expected. The many months of deferring health maintenance while working on her projects had taken a toll, and her doctors wanted to be sure she left the hospital equipped and in better shape than when she came in. They prescribed a full schedule of physical therapy and helped her come to terms with her need for a wheelchair. That wasn't easy, but she was pleased that her custom chair was designed to handle slopes and uneven ground and would have a "power booster" so she could hike on trails with her family.

While in the hospital, Hadley often expressed to me her appreciation for the people caring for her. It occurred to me that after working for so long to rise above her physical limitations, she'd finally given herself permission to put aside some of her responsibilities and receive the focused medical attention she badly needed.

Whenever we messaged each other, she was upbeat. One day, she texted me a photo of herself drinking from a big cup with a note that said: "I thought you should have a selfie of my alert, well-hydrated self in no acute distress!!!"

Another day, she surprised me with a photo in which she was painting in her hospital bed. She told me she had a show coming up in early October, just before she would leave for Prague. Of course, she did! She was unstoppable!

Hadley, Sarah, and Hadley's new wheelchair went to Prague in October as planned. It took them thirty-two hours to get there, but the time together with Jana was delightful. The wheelchair made sightseeing infinitely more comfortable, efficient, and safe. And Hadley was thrilled with how well the steady infusion of baclofen relieved the pain and exhaustion caused by her rigidity.

When she returned to Missoula, Hadley told me she felt that she'd had a wonderful life and had no regrets about things not accomplished. "I don't need a bucket list," she said. She was content being with her family and friends, painting, and making the most of each day. Sometimes, that meant sleeping a lot; other days, she spent much of her time at meetings for the nonprofit she'd founded, Summit for Parkinson's. Having given up driving because of a diminished ability to focus her visual attention, Hadley grew more concerned about what she perceived as an overall decline in mental functioning. She chose to undergo cognitive testing, which revealed significantly impaired executive function and spatial/visual skills, as well as audio memory. (I'm compelled to note I've never noticed these impairments; she always seems to be perfectly on her game.) Her neurologist prescribed Ritalin, a nervous system stimulant, and Aricept, a drug used to treat cognitive impairment related to Alzheimer's, both of which have been helpful.

A few months later, in February 2016, Hadley had the opportunity to work through some hard feelings she'd been lugging around for more than three years. She received a message from Dr. Youngman, the movement disorders specialist who'd diagnosed her with PD in 2010 and, two years later, had "fired" her when her diagnosis became unclear. He was going to be in Missoula and asked if she'd like to get together over coffee. Hadley gathered her courage and shared with him how confused and abandoned he'd made her feel. Dr. Youngman listened and let her know that he understood and felt bad about what had happened. Hadley was grateful and relieved to be able to close that dark chapter of her medical saga.

As many times as she's said, "I'm going to be careful about what I take on," Hadley continued to charge ahead with amazing initiative, energy, and productivity. That spring, she began a collaboration with the director of Missoula's Silver Foundation, Carolyn Maier, on an art installation that combines photographs, stories, and quotations to illuminate the journeys of people around the world living with Parkinson's. The centerpiece of the exhibit, titled *Forging Resilience*, is a life-size metal tree foliated with thousands of handmade leaves, each inscribed with a message from someone touched by PD. The installation premiered at the Montana Museum of Art and Culture in November 2015.

In September 2016, *Forging Resilience* traveled to Portland, Oregon, where it was exhibited at the World Parkinson Congress, a 3,000-5,000-person event held internationally every three years. Hadley and I arranged to meet in the WPC convention hall, and as I was waiting for her, I found myself remembering the first time we met in person in 2011, also in Portland, at a Parkinson's fundraiser. She'd struck me then not as a patient but an enthusiastic ambassador for her new disease. Now, as I watched her rolling toward me in her wheelchair, stopping to greet the many friends she'd made over the past six years, I saw the same: a highly effective ambassador, though now for her more complicated disease, multiple system atrophy. Unsurprisingly, she was asked to serve on the Board of the Multiple System Atrophy Coalition. I'm sure their community, too, has benefited from her creative and well-considered ideas.

THIRTY-SIX:

A HEALTHY APPEARING, APPROPRIATELY DRESSED ARCHITECT IN NO ACUTE DISTRESS

When Lewis turned sixty in 2017, he was perplexed that several of his oldest friends who were his age had chosen to retire from very successful careers and were enjoying themselves. "I will *die* if I have to stop working," he told me on more than a couple of occasions. I wondered why he chose such drastic language; it's not as if anyone were suggesting he retire or that we ever talked about retirement.

But soon, the man who jumped out of bed every morning with a zesty outlook on the day ahead started sleeping poorly. The longer his insomnia went on, the more anxious he became. "I don't get it! Why, when everything is going so well, when I'm at the top of my game professionally, am I feeling so out of it all the time?" he wondered aloud. He had his first panic attack while sitting with a perfectly congenial client in his office conference room. The client's voice seemed too loud, her lipstick too red. When the room began to tilt, Lewis excused himself and went and hid in the restroom until the panic passed.

In the spring of 2018, Lewis was out for dinner with his surfing buddies and choked on a piece of steak. Assuming the meat was stuck in Lewis' windpipe, his friend jumped up and gave him the Heimlich, which successfully dislodged it. A couple of months later, it happened again, but this time, Lewis noted to himself that he could still breathe; therefore, the meat must have been in his throat. He mentioned to me that his throat felt constricted, and I agreed with him that this could be attributed to his anxiety. I was focused more on his emotional state than his symptoms until his complaints about difficulty swallowing increased. Still, months passed. "It's getting better I think," he would report to me. But the next day, he would say he could tell the constriction was worsening.

Telling this story now, I am mystified why no one, especially Lewis and me, felt that a worsening problem with swallowing (dysphagia) was not something urgent to investigate. But friends and doctors alike told Lewis that dysphagia was very common and there were many different causes for it. They weren't wrong. One friend told us she'd had her esophagus stretched out by a gastroenterologist. I think all of us were eager to hear such reassuring histories. But at home, every night, the evidence was becoming scary. Lewis would have to get up from the dinner table at least once to cough up the food he couldn't swallow. Finally, in June 2019, he was referred for a barium swallow test that revealed a bone spur from his cervical spine that could've been restricting the passage of food through his esophagus.

By October, Lewis' voice had become noticeably softer. Since he was unable to eat any solid food, I'd invested in a fancy blender to make smoothies and pureed soups. Lewis was referred to an ear, nose, and throat doctor (ENT) who performed a flexible laryngoscopy to look at his larynx, which is located between the esophagus (throat) and the trachea (windpipe) and houses the vocal cords. The test, surprisingly, didn't turn up anything significant.

In December, six months after his first barium swallow test, I went with Lewis to have a second one that showed what the tech called an "outpouching" of his esophagus. She suggested that the pouch would cause swallowing difficulties and that food collecting in the pouch could be causing him to choke. While this finding and the bone spur that had been found in June were mysterious to us, they didn't appear to be setting off any alarms. They weren't, after all, *Cancer*.

Nearly two years after his first run-in with a piece of steak, on January 9, 2020, Lewis and I went to see the ENT he'd seen three months earlier. She performed a transnasal esophagoscopy in which she snaked a scope down Lewis' nose that went deeper into his esophagus than the flexible laryngoscopy she'd done in October. I was too squeamish to watch, so I busied myself recording the appointment.

"What's that?" Lewis asked, pointing at the screen.

"That is the sixty-four-thousand-dollar question," the ENT replied.

Lewis: "It looks like an oyster in there."

In the recording, there is a fat pause. Then the ENT says, "Mr. Butler, you have a growth in your esophagus."

"So, you're worried about cancer," Lewis said.

ENT: "Yes, sir, I am."

Lewis: "I've been told that cancer's typically not the cause of swallowing problems. That was what a friend who's a doctor said."

ENT: "Cancer is *not* usually the problem. It's very commonly something else, like the Zenker's diverticulum that we thought it was—the pouch? That's sort of what we thought it was. Even the swallow test you had looked pouch-like. But I wonder if the pouch-like aspect sort of masked this."

Me: "Are there things it could be other than cancer?'

There were, she told us, but usually more indolent things, like a benign muscular tumor, didn't grow so aggressively.

After the test, the ENT had us sit in her office while she arranged appointments for a biopsy and a CT scan. She shut the door so that the two of us were alone. I don't remember what we said to each other if anything. I was struggling with how to tell our kids about the "oyster," and Lewis was Googling "esophageal cancer" on his phone. When he finished, he said without looking up, "This is not a good cancer to have." After thirty-five minutes, the ENT let us know where Lewis should be for his biopsy the next day, and we left the building in silence. I suggested we stop in the park to digest the news. But Lewis beelined back to the office, so I kept a lunch date. It felt surreal to be socializing; however, my friend had had cancer, so she knew just what to say.

As soon as Lewis was diagnosed with esophageal cancer, things happened very quickly. A surgeon explained to us why he wouldn't recommend surgery. An oncologist told us Lewis would receive what he called "the most heavy-duty chemo and radiation we ever do."

How was this possible? was the question on everyone's lips. No one, including the doctors he'd gone to during the past year and a half, could fathom that Lewis would have cancer, just as they couldn't imagine I'd have Parkinson's at fifty-four and Hadley would have MSA at thirty-three. None of us fits the profile of our diseases. Esophageal cancer is known mainly as a disease of heavy smokers and drinkers. Lewis was famous on both coasts for his fantastic margarita recipe and enjoyed a shot of tequila a couple of times a week, driven in part by his desire to keep our unofficial "tequila cellar" (as the Margarita King, Lewis was the recipient of at least fifteen bottles of fancy tequila every year) from taking over the whole garage. He'd had a very short flirtation with smoking when he met me. In fact, "flirtation" might also describe the reason for his smoking, because I'd started smoking one or two cigarettes a day at the beginning of architecture school and, "Can I bum a cigarette?" was one way to get to know someone. Within a few months, we'd established our relationship, and smoking—a monumentally stupid, horrible habit to which we were subjecting not only our own lungs but also those of our studio mates, was no longer necessary.

Lewis might have done enough smoking and drinking to trigger cancer, but his habits didn't flag as risky to doctors used to seeing lifelong smokers and people who drink a six-pack a night. When trying to diagnose his swallowing problem, they were making an affective error by relying on their perceptions of him—as one doctor began his after-visit summary, "a healthy-looking, appropriately dressed architect in no acute distress." They were also paying attention to the symptoms that could confirm a positive outcome: a bone spur and later, what a radiology technician identified as a pouch (a void!) in his esophagus that would turn out to be—in the words of the ENT, "the pouchlike aspect that sort of masked" a tumor. So not a void, but rather, a very large solid!

This is another example of the common problem Dr. Jerome Groopman discusses in his book *How Doctors Think,* which I wrote about in Chapter 21: neither the patient nor his doctors ask, "What's the worst thing this could be?" We all know this is the question that's top of mind for both doctors and their patients. Are we patients so afraid of appearing to be hypochondriacs, and are doctors so averse to even suggesting possible bad news that we would rather hold off on getting to the truth?

This is not merely a rhetorical question. In the case of Hadley, the answer is no. She wanted to know from the time she first Googled MSA and called me to list the symptoms that matched hers. On the other hand, Lewis likely didn't want to know, so he didn't work too hard to get a diagnosis, instead taking in the reassurances from friends, doctors, and doctors who were friends, who were out in the orchard with him picking cherries. I admit that I did a little cherry-picking myself. With cancer, a delayed diagnosis could've made the difference between life and death. Once I'd learned how large his "oyster" was and had had a private freak-out about the void "masking" a solid, as well as the amount of time that had gone by, I could only take a kind of terrible comfort from learning fairly soon that the tumor was inoperable because it was so high in the esophagus and was also exceedingly aggressive.

There's another point to be made here: If Lewis had gone to the gastroenterologist when he began regularly choking on food, they likely would've seen a small tumor, which they would have monitored as it grew. He would've been receiving chemo and radiation starting in 2018 for two and a half years instead of in 2020 for eight months. This would mean that we wouldn't have rented that house in Arles, France, for three weeks in October 2018 and might've missed Elena's "white coat ceremony" at medical school. Most importantly, Lewis would've felt sick for a much longer time and would've been cut off from the people he worked with—which he had already declared would be, like retirement, a kind of death.

I wrote earlier about the distance Lewis had always kept from his mortality. After his serious bike accident in 2013, he told me he felt he lacked an inner warning system that would tell him when he was being too risky.

As a science lover, I'm not always a proponent of the mind-body connection. When it came to Lewis' cancer, though, I believe that his warning system was in full working order; that the bad seed of the tumor had planted itself in his psyche around his sixtieth birthday, and by eroding his trademark confidence and optimism, it was trying to make itself known to him. What other explanation could there be for why his insomnia and anxiety had come on so powerfully?

All the practitioners Lewis saw for treatment were very somber. Not one of them said anything about the possibility of beating the cancer. Still, family, friends, and colleagues, once they accepted he had cancer, believed that a man with such limitless energy was going to survive. I wondered how he processed their optimism. He knew he was not OK, and Lewis had never been OK with not being OK. After he started chemotherapy, he insisted on going to the office even though he was immunocompromised and there was a pandemic raging. "People in the office need to see that their boss is OK," he told me. This didn't last long, as he was soon too weak to make the trip.

THIRTY-SEVEN:
A DATE FOR DBS

A week after Lewis was diagnosed, I happened to have my semi-annual appointment with my movement disorders specialist, Dr. Bright. I asked him if he would order me a disabled parking placard so that I could park close to the entrance of the hospital where I'd be taking Lewis for treatment and fill out the form that would excuse me permanently from jury duty. Then, I asked him if I could be evaluated for deep brain stimulation surgery (DBS) as soon as possible. Two years earlier, I'd asked him when he guessed I'd be ready for the surgery, and he'd told me two to four years. He felt I would be an excellent candidate for the procedure. Now that I faced caring for Lewis and the probability of a future alone, I wanted to ensure I was in the best shape possible.

For a quick refresher on DBS, see Chapter 11. At the most basic level, it aims to do the work levodopa does without the same side effects. When electrodes are placed deep within the areas of the brain responsible for body movement and are connected to an implanted stimulator device, the stimulator uses electric pulses to regulate brain activity. This constant stimulation mimics the relief provided by levodopa with fewer fluctuations, meaning less wearing off and less dyskinesia.

I was given a date for DBS surgery in July with Dr. Philip Starr, who, along with his colleagues, Drs. Martin and Larson pioneered DBS for Parkinson's starting when it was given FDA approval in 2002. Before getting the green light to have DBS surgery, all patients undergo comprehensive prescreening to determine their eligibility. This can take several months. My screening included an MRI to make certain that there was nothing unexpected going on in my brain, such as structural abnormalities that would make implanting electrodes more challenging and testing to rule out more than mild cognitive deficits. If you ever have cognitive testing, I guarantee that no matter how sharp you believe your mind to be, you will suffer a significant loss of confidence from this testing! Finally, a neuropsychological evaluation by a neuropsychologist to rule out significant depression and/or anxiety is necessary since DBS has been known in some cases to exacerbate these conditions.

Once I'd passed the tests, there were decisions I was invited to weigh in on about the surgery itself. Perhaps the most difficult one was whether to participate in a study that Dr. Starr was leading that I knew was the future of DBS. At that time, in 2020, all DBS devices worked by connecting the electrodes that are implanted in the brain to a stimulator implanted in the chest. This "open-loop" system relies on a programmer or the patient to manually adjust the electrical stimulation to find settings that best treat symptoms.

Dr. Starr was implanting the hardware in his study participants that would receive the components of a "closed-loop" or adaptive DBS (DBSa) system. In this model, the DBS stimulator adjusts electrical current based on feedback it receives from the body instead of being operated by a remote device or programmer. Among other advantages, this innovation allows the DBS device to be off when it senses the body doesn't need the stimulation.

I was told I was a great candidate for the study because I was relatively young and had an uncomplicated case of PD with no comorbidities. Dr. Starr's team worked hard to recruit me, conveniently forgetting from month to month that I'd said no. Although I would've been honored to contribute my brain to the future of PD, ultimately, I decided the extra hardware that would be implanted in my brain and the frequent follow-up appointments required to be in the study were not right for me in my current circumstances. My partner was dying, which was, in a way, my comorbidity.

The second decision I was given the opportunity to contribute my thoughts about was which area of the brain I wanted the surgery to target. I read up on the two targets for DBS, the subthalamic nucleus (STN) and the globus pallidus interna (GPi), structures that are part of the basal ganglia near the center of the brain. In the basal ganglia, connections are made between different areas of the brain that, among other functions, allow the body to move. In Parkinson's Disease, the death of dopamine-producing neurons in the basal ganglia changes this important circuitry, affecting movement and causing other symptoms as the disease progresses. DBS's electrical stimulation interrupts the irregularly firing circuitry, regulating it so that symptoms are eased or, in some cases, disappear.

While the STN has been targeted more than the GPi in DBS, there has been evidence that one target might be better than the other for some patients. Both typically stop tremor and dyskinesia. In addition, rigidity, slowness of movement, as well as muscle cramping are greatly reduced after DBS, and one can usually also cut down on the amount of levodopa and other PD medications they're taking. Where the differences lie are in the non-motor symptoms.

The DBS team comprised the surgeon, Dr. Starr; the neuropsychologist who did my cognitive evaluation; and a movement disorders specialist who had evaluated my movement and met to discuss my case.

Dr. Starr called me in June to tell me that they unanimously agreed I would "do well with STN DBS." This might have been true, but I had read research comparing STN with GPi DBS and had arrived at the conclusion that targeting the GPi site would be a better choice for me.

Like many people with PD, I was fearful of the possible effect of DBS on my cognition. However, DBS has not been associated with significant cognitive decline, except in people who had more than mild cognitive deficits before surgery. This is why cognitive testing is used to determine whether the surgery is appropriate or in a patient's best interest. Verbal fluency is one area of cognition for which there is a statistically significant difference between STN DBS and GPi DBS outcomes. Specifically, in STN DBS, there is a greater decline in semantic fluency (tested by having the patient name as many words as they can from a single category, like vegetables, in sixty seconds) and in phonemic fluency (naming as many words as they can that start with the same letter, in sixty seconds). Studies have revealed inconsistent or insignificant differences between STN and GPi DBS in other areas of cognition, such as memory and executive function, which would impact quality of life to a much greater degree than the relatively benign effect on verbal fluency.

DBS programmers believe the differences between STN and GPi DBS outcomes are probably because the GPi region of the brain is larger than the STN. Its larger size makes it easier to place the electrodes where they will be most effective without the risk of the electrical stimulation spreading to adjacent areas where it could cause unintended, undesirable effects. An example of this "spreading" is with speech. About 90% of people with PD develop speech or voice disorders regardless of whether they've had DBS surgery; their voice might become quieter and their speech harder to understand. Research that compared the effects on speech of STN vs. GPi DBS was published online two months before my surgery in 2020. I hadn't yet seen it, but if I had, it would've made the choice between STN and GPi even easier. The study found that while GPi DBS worsened certain aspects of speech (like volume), it didn't compromise overall intelligibility, which was more likely with STN DBS. Since I was facing the probability of living alone and would need all the social activity I could get, the data on the effects of STN DBS on speech alone would've been enough to convince me to choose GPi DBS.

However, Google had a fair amount to say about the difference between STN and GPi DBS when it comes to mood. Once again, the research skewed in favor of GPi DBS. (One study reported that GPi patients were "happier, less angry and less tired" than STN patients, sounding more like an assessment of kindergarten students than a scientific observation. But it had this patient convinced!) There has been a lot of depression in my family of origin, and I have experienced it myself. Add to these factors that I had much more trauma and sadness ahead as I faced losing my partner, and choosing GPi seemed like a no-brainer (sorry!).

I told Dr. Starr all of this. I remember clearly how he responded: "Well, I was the agnostic in our group, but you've turned me into a believer. Let me take this back to the team and we will be in touch." The next day, someone from Dr. Starr's neuromodulation center called me to tell me they now agreed that GPi DBS would serve me best.

There were more decisions for me to make. One was whether I wanted to have "awake DBS" or MRI-guided DBS, which can be done while the patient is "asleep." Although there was a time when I thought having brain surgery while awake sounded like an intriguing adventure, now that DBS was upon me, I didn't consider it for more than a nanosecond.

If you're wondering whether DBS surgery is as scary as it sounds, the answer is no, at least not anymore. But twenty years ago, when Dr. Starr began performing DBS surgeries at the University of California San Francisco, patients were required to be awake, a challenge that could have come right out of the TV show Fear Factor. In awake DBS, a patient with advanced PD whose body is only not shaking when medicated is told to abstain from all medications and sit on a table in a semi-supine position with their head in a rigid headframe to keep it from moving. MRI is used to visualize the brain so that the electrodes to be implanted can be accurately inserted into the intended areas for stimulation. Since no general anesthesia can be given for awake DBS, local anesthetic is injected into the muscle on the top of the skull, where two burr holes are then drilled. (Since the brain has no pain receptors, it can't feel pain.) The leads, which are thin, insulated wires with four electrodes at the ends, are inserted through the holes into the STN or GPi brain areas. After the MRI confirms their correct placement, they are secured.

The advantage of awake DBS, which is still done, is that the patient can help the surgeon place the electrodes by providing feedback—for example, the patient might be asked to hold out their arm and tap their fingers together, a standard test we Parkies are given by our movement disorders specialist at every appointment. This movement is very hard to do for someone with advanced PD who's unmedicated, so if it's easy for the person having surgery, bingo! The surgeon knows they've hit their target with the leads.

The disadvantages of awake DBS are probably evident to everyone reading this! And now, enough MRI-guided DBS surgeries have been performed that it's clear they are as successful at alleviating symptoms as their more stressful prototype.

There were two other choices I was able to make. One was which of three devices I wanted implanted. I chose one that had directional leads, wires that hold the electrodes in place in the brain. I was told by a scientist who helped develop them that directional leads allowed greater flexibility and precision for delivering the stimulation to the brain. Last was my preference for having a replaceable or a rechargeable battery. This was an easy one for me as recharging my battery 30-60 minutes per week seemed simple compared to the invasiveness of having surgery to replace it every 3-5 years.

Now that my decisions had been made, I could relax, knowing that the surgery was going to happen. I went online shopping at Etsy and ordered some colorful cloth headbands that would cover the two-inch-wide strip where my hair would be shaved. A new look that would go with my new bionic self—I welcomed it!

THIRTY-EIGHT:
CANCER IN THE TIME OF COVID-19

U ntil 2020, my kids had been "kids." Lewis and I still took care of them, even though at thirty-three and thirty, they hadn't lived at home and had been financially independent for many years. Lewis took their calls about money, leases, and cars; I talked to them mostly about health and relationships. We were a good team because we both loved being parents to Elena and Tobias, and their well-being was our top priority. Lewis balanced my emotional sensitivity and physical vulnerability with his resilience and big energy. And at the end of the day, if we were troubled about one of them, we could worry together. We talked to and saw them often. The four of us took fun trips together, and we didn't need anything more from them than what they were giving. I had Lewis, my sisters, close women friends, and doctors to confide in about my health. I only talked about Parkinson's with Elena and Tobias if they asked. I liked the fact that I was able to protect them from the quotidian details of my disease so that they could remain on their exciting life trajectories without worrying about me.

This all changed overnight. When Lewis was diagnosed, Elena decided to fly out from Philadelphia the next weekend, and again over President's Day weekend. When it became clear to the world that we were in for a full-blown pandemic, the medical school where she was in her second year closed. I was surprised when she told me in March that she, her partner Matt, and Mickey, their dog, would be coming out to stay at our beach house fifty minutes away so they could quarantine. Then they planned to come to the city. I remember I asked Elena, "So you'll live at the beach?" "No," she said, "we're planning to move in with you." Looking back on that exchange, I realize I was still in a period of disbelief, inhabiting a life in which Lewis and I could take care of ourselves the way we always had. Elena's clear vision of the situation and her quick, proactive decision-making shook me out of that naïve state. It marked the beginning of the sea change that was about to occur in our family dynamic.

Elena was stepping up and would be calling the shots for our family. Because of COVID, she advised Tobias to move out of the house in Oakland he shared with five other people and move to an Airbnb close to our house in San Francisco so he could safely spend time with Lewis. Tobias did this, and his partner of seven months, Sasha, decided to move with him.

As for Lewis and me, we donned our masks and went to Manicini's Sleepworld to buy a queen-size Tempur-Pedic bed to put in the guest room for Elena and Matt. I felt numb, and I'm sure Lewis felt even more numb. But to the Mancini's salesperson, we probably appeared to be A Well-Nourished, Decisive, Sixty-Something Couple in No Acute Distress.

As COVID took control of our lives, I was worried that my surgery would be canceled because it might be considered elective. I didn't dare keep my hopes up during such a difficult time. As it turned out, I was very lucky to have two behind-the-scenes advocates, Dr. Bright and Dr. A, who I suspect were making sure my surgery stayed on the calendar.

After thirteen years, Dr. Bright is still my movement disorders specialist and has proved to be a consistently attentive and caring doctor. I long ago stopped obsessing about him telling Hadley not to obsess! I see him only every four to five months, but between appointments, I still send him emails that are sometimes long and filled with questions. Without fail, he has answered them before the end of the day. Emailing with doctors is unusual, especially since the advent of the patient online portal. Emailing with Dr. Bright gives me the privacy that the portal does not and allows me to write as much as I need to. Do I sometimes still wish that he probed more deeply some of the questions I bring to him? Yes! But I know he has a very heavy patient load, not only because he's known to be an extraordinary clinician, but also because he's warm and kind; he tracks what your kids are up to and how that project is coming along. He's still the doctor who dropped Lewis' travel cup off on our doorstep after my first appointment with him, the same generous person who came to my launch party for *Dream House.*

The other person who helped to shepherd my request for DBS through the system was Dr. A. Several months before Lewis' diagnosis, I had joined a study she was leading on the effects of mindfulness-based meditation on people with Parkinson's. I had no idea that Dr. A is a geriatric psychiatrist who works exclusively with people with Parkinson's who have had DBS surgery. Because she is especially warm and magnetic, months later, I was very happy to learn she was part of the DBS team and would see me through the evaluation and post-surgery follow-up.

My therapist also literally went out of his way to support me during cancer in the time of COVID. Since 2011, a year after I was diagnosed with PD, I have been driving across the

Golden Gate Bridge, a glorious, twenty-two-minute trip in each direction, to meet with Dr. S. in his office that looks out at a lagoon and the hills. In 2020, when shelter-in-place was recommended, Dr. S began to see clients on Zoom. However, he felt that Zoom might not be sufficiently therapeutic for me, given what was happening at home, so he offered to have in-person sessions outside his office building. For the next eight or so months, we sat opposite each other in folding chairs six to eight feet apart without masks because Dr. S thought masks would also be too distancing. When the fierce Bay Area winds came up in the spring, Dr. S set up a nylon windbreak that he would stake into the ground. One day, I pulled up next to our meeting spot just in time to see the blue windbreak sailing across the lagoon! It would be hard to overstate how comforting Dr. S's care has been.

In the spring and early summer, Lewis was in and out of the hospital on an outpatient basis to receive chemo and radiation. The tumor wasn't shrinking, though, and the radiation burned a fistula (hole) between his esophagus and trachea, necessitating the surgical insertion of a stent.

Elena wanted to oversee Lewis' case both at home and during his four hospital stays so she could talk to his doctors. It was a marvel to watch her in her new role as doctor-in-training. She ordered what seemed like a truckload of equipment and supplies. When we moved Lewis out of our bedroom into Elena's old room, she cleaned out most of the drawers in the maple desk I'd designed for her when she was ten. I'd been asking her to tackle this job once a year for at least ten years, without results. But now, she wanted to have all the necessary tools—gauze, scissors, tweezers, medicines, in a place where we could always find them. She bought a whiteboard so that we could keep track of when he had been nebulized (a nebulizer turns medication into a mist that is inhaled through a mouthpiece) and given food and medications through his feeding tube. She ran a tight ship! She became the mistress of the machinery that all day was grinding and humming and hissing, belching a medicine-y miasma that stuck in my nose. Ever resourceful, and always on call to help, Tobias found the perfect rolling cart online (it was actually sold as a "gift wrapping cart") to hold the smaller machines and their parts that were used throughout the day and night. It was heartbreaking to watch my children transform one of the safe spaces of their childhood into a hospital room for their dad.

On two more occasions, Lewis panicked about being unable to breathe and had to be taken by ambulance to the Emergency Department. The hospital runs were very stressful for him, so in June, when Lewis felt his breathing had become too restricted by the growing tumor, he underwent a tracheostomy, a procedure that creates an alternative airway by making an opening in the neck. During her time with Lewis at the hospital, Elena was tutored in how to properly dress a wound as well as how to assemble, use, and then clean the many parts of the apparatuses she was sent home with. It was a lot to learn, even for a medical student; Elena and I pondered how someone less educated, willing, or able could be expected to learn everything she had to in order to take care of their loved one.

I was relieved when Elena carved out a new space for herself in the tiny bedroom next to hers that had been Tobias' as a young boy. There, she could be within earshot of Lewis while she learned a new craft, knitting. In no time at all, it seemed, she graduated from knitting simple scarves to making hats for her friends with babies and sweaters with patterns and interesting textures. In the evening, while Lewis slept or plugged into his laptop to watch *Longmire,* she would snuggle up to Matt and Mickey, their miniature dachshund, on the couch, and Rafa and I would fill up the other end of the couch. Elena would knit while we watched my favorites, *Homeland* and *Ozark,* or her TV comfort foods, *The Bachelor* and *The Great British Bakeoff.* She knit while visiting Lewis for hours in the hospital and whenever her hands weren't otherwise occupied. After a few months, she needed something more, so she pulled my old Singer sewing machine out of the closet, read the instruction book, and started making clothes for herself. Now, the whir of the sewing machine joined the orchestra of machinery keeping Lewis alive.

Monday through Friday, Matt Zoomed from the dining room table with his colleagues and prospective collaborators, allowing me to witness the professional side of this confident, articulate, and sweet young man who I had a feeling would be in my life for a very long time. He took over many jobs around the house, including feeding and walking the dogs, putting out the trash, and answering the front door when Elena and I couldn't. Once or twice a day, he'd take in groceries, gifts of food from friends, and the almost daily packages of yarn, fabric, patterns, and other sewing and knitting accouterments.

Though they were both working full time at their apartment, Tobias and Sasha came over often to help and offer their sunlight. These four young people's lives had been turned upside down by a pandemic that had isolated them from many of the most important people in their lives. On top of this, they were also witnessing Lewis' death. But there was not a complaint to be heard from them. When we five would eat dinner together the room would often fill with laughter, an important reminder to me that as scared as I was, life would go on.

THIRTY-NINE:
IT IS BRAIN SURGERY

July 2020 arrived, and with it, my DBS surgery.

In an email to a friend I wrote, "I am neither brave nor strong, and I hope I don't end up proving it to all those who tell me I am."

We didn't talk much about my surgery at home. Although my kids didn't express this, it had to be very scary for them to have one parent headed to have brain surgery while the other was sick with cancer. The night before, I took a shower, washed my hair with the antiseptic I'd been given, and packed a bag, feeling as if I were sleepwalking. I hid my Parkinson's and sleep medications in a sock, as I was advised by people in the PD Facebook group: "When you check in, they will figure out a way to steal any meds you bring in! So, hide them, or you'll suffer when they don't have the meds you need when you need them." Tobias dropped me off at the front door of the hospital. Except when I gave birth, this was my only stay in a hospital, and the same adrenalin rush propelled me toward the check-in desk. There's no going back when you're in labor; I felt the same about DBS.

The surgery went so smoothly that afterward when I was kept awake most of the night by nurses coming in and out of the room, I asked—more like begged, the resident to let me go home. Typically, a DBS patient spends two nights in the hospital, but she said she'd see what she could do. A couple of hours later she gave me the OK to go home. I was ecstatic to see Tobias stroll into my room and amazed that I had no problem walking out of the hospital.

When I got home and saw myself in the mirror, I was surprised that Tobias, Elena, and Matt hadn't visibly flinched at the sight of my partially shaved and bloody bandaged head. I don't remember having any pain. In fact, I don't remember any recovery at all.

A week later, I went back to the hospital for part two of the DBS procedure. Dr. Starr implanted a neurostimulator, a rectangular box about three by three inches, just below my collarbone. The neurostimulator contains a battery that generates the electrical signals that are delivered to the brain. To connect the stimulator with the leads in my brain, he tunneled an insulated wire under the skin from the stimulator, up the side of my neck, to the leads. I hadn't thought through how the leads would get their power, and the new bumpy landscape of my neck and head surprised me. I found myself fingering the new neck "tendon" and wondering just how Dr. Starr managed to bury it so neatly under my skin.

Ten days later, Elena and her knitting went with me to meet with Monica Volz, one of the DBS programmers at the neuromodulation center. I'd been told not to take my PD meds and I was nervous and a bit claustrophobic in her small, windowless room. After removing the staples from my scalp, Monica sat at her desk in front of the programming machine. "Are you ready?" she asked, smiling. A nurse practitioner in her fifties, Monica is undoubtedly the most experienced

DBS programmer in San Francisco. When she sits at her desk, turns the dials on her mysterious machine, and then hands you an incomprehensible electrical diagram of what she's done as if I might actually understand it, she reminds me of a mad scientist. In fact, although she is a very serious scientist, she's not a mad one; she is lovely, down-to-earth, and empathetic.

The big moment arrived when she turned on my stimulator for the first time. For people with a disabling tremor or dyskinesia, this event is dramatic, a kind of resurrection, because the body that has never stopped flailing and shaking becomes suddenly still. For someone like me, who's never had a tremor and had only very mild dyskinesia in my right foot that wagged when I was sitting down, it's harder to see or even feel the changes when the electrodes are turned on. Monica turned a dial or two and then looked at me to see if I was responding. I wanted to be able to report on some change! I was also worried about how Elena was doing, trapped in a small, windowless room while her mother was having her electrical circuitry altered. And then, finally there it was: after a year of my right foot wagging, it was now totally still, and my left foot began to wag. (This has continued, but because it's not bothersome, I always forget to ask Monica why this switch happened.) The other noticeable effect her adjustments had was I became lightheaded when I stood up to walk. For me, this is always the clearest sign that the stimulation is turned up too high.

After nearly two hours, Monica sent me home with Boston Scientific's DBS operating instructions, my new remote control with which I can alter the stimulation, and two battery chargers, one for the stimulator and one for the remote control. A whole year went by before I noticed I had a couple of phone messages from Boston Scientific asking to set up a time for me to meet with their rep to discuss the equipment. Luckily, the use of the various components is very straightforward.

Since having surgery, people always ask me if it has made a big difference in my symptoms. I have one clear memory from the first week after my DBS was turned on, of my neighbors asking me how it was going. I was struck by the fact that I was sweeping the sidewalk. It wasn't the sweeping that surprised me, but the timing of it at 11:45 a.m. Typically, 11:30 – 12:30 was an hour during which I never would've attempted a task so physical, as it was one of my difficult "off" times during the day when my PD medication hadn't kicked in. Almost three years later, I am still finding DBS very helpful for my bradykinesia (slowness), and I'm still walking three miles every day.

When Monica turned on my stimulator, I started having constant tingling and numbness in the bottom of my feet, but it hasn't gotten worse in three years. Also, my balance, which was always very good, even after eleven years with PD, became an issue within a year after my surgery. I have had to hire a dog walker because Rafa will sometimes lunge at other dogs, and he pulled me to the ground a few times. But I can manage some spectacular falls all by myself when bending over or doing anything that puts me in an unstable posture. The classic way for people with PD to fall is backward. I was glad no one was at my house to witness the fall I had a year ago, when I took a heavy cast iron pot full of soup out of the refrigerator with both hands and stepped backward. When my foot bumped into a grocery bag I had just packed for the weekend, I started falling back and knew I wasn't going to be able to stop myself. I had to drop the pot of soup, which went everywhere, and I fell hard on the wood floor. The good news is I didn't hurt myself, and a fall like that is an excellent learning experience.

FORTY:
A BRIGHT FLAME IS EXTINGUISHED

S oon after Elena and Matt moved in in March, she, Lewis, and I were sitting around chatting and she abruptly let out a wail followed by unbridled sobbing, "Elena!" Lewis barked. "What are you crying about?"

Lewis was always uncomfortable when any of us cried. This brings me to the threshold of a room I'm hesitant to take you into. In this room, Lewis was dying and didn't want to talk about it. With anyone. He didn't talk to those of us caring for him except to make requests. He didn't tell his oldest friends who lived outside of San Francisco that he had cancer, even though he continued to be in occasional touch with them. I didn't realize this until two weeks before he died when one of his dearest friends called me and burst into tears. Of course, by March he didn't have vocal cords that could sustain a conversation, which worked in his favor. Lewis especially didn't want to see anyone, another way the pandemic allowed him to be sick the way he preferred—without a lot of attention on him, or the messiness of other people's grief.

Before he moved from our bedroom to the hospital bed in Elena's old room, in the evenings, I would often sit on our king bed as close to him as I could while he wrote emails. Our two dogs sprawled on the bed with us, and Elena sat in the chair by the window, knitting. Lewis didn't ever reach out for me, let alone hug me, but I tried not to take it personally. What did I know about how it feels to be dying? Besides, his body was not his own. He had a hole in his neck (his trach) to breathe through, a hole in his chest (the port for chemo), and a hole in his abdomen (his G-tube), where he took in his liquid nutrition. These new orifices made him vulnerable because they were at risk for infection, and the tubes attached to them could easily get yanked, making it hard to get physically close to him.

Once Lewis moved to his hospital bed, there were just a few times he invited me to sit with him. Each time, I felt my hopes rise: Maybe this would be the moment he'd say something about life, about dying, about us, or our kids. Really, anything more intimate than "Can you find my Airpods?" would do. The first time he patted the bed for me to sit down, he put his hand to his trach to begin speaking and then stopped. He shook his head and lay back again. I wondered later if he'd had something important he wanted to tell me but was afraid he'd cry. This would have been scary for someone who had to have mucous suctioned from his throat multiple times a day to be able to breathe. Another time he beckoned me to perch next to him, he said, "The nurse will be here in less than an hour, and I want to sleep before then."

"I think Lewis is just furious that this is happening and probably feels horrible that you will be alone with your Parkinson's," a wise friend told me. I knew she was probably right. I didn't expect Lewis to find the kind of equanimity that the Renaissance man, Oliver Sacks, had in his last six months of life. But I would be lying if I said I wasn't hurt that he didn't share just a tiny bit about how he was feeling. I was sad on behalf of our kids, his father and sisters, as well as our closest friends. He made it clear that he didn't want to see anyone, but toward the end I told him there were a few people he needed to let in because even though he didn't need to say goodbye, *they* needed to. After all, we were the ones who had to go on in life without him.

Whenever Elena was with Lewis at the hospital, she would always send me a short video of Lewis and her, reporting on the latest trachea news. At the end of each video, she would audibly prompt Lewis to tell me he loved me, words he'd always had a hard time saying. It made me laugh to watch my child instructing her father on how to be a good partner in his last months of life, but I also felt grateful for her thoughtfulness and proud of her courage to take on this role.

Half an hour after getting home from his last visit to the hospital in early September, Lewis patted the bed, and I went to sit down next to him. "There's nothing more they can do for me," he said.

In drought-stricken California, fires caused by lightning strikes merged to become the state's largest wildfire in history. The August Complex fire burned over a million acres in four months. On Sept 9, we woke up and put up the shade to a day that never dawned. Smoke had blotted out the sun. The word "apocalyptic" has never seemed more appropriate.

Lewis died at home on a sunny afternoon, September 17, 2020, with his family around him.

FORTY-ONE:
SILVER LININGS

D eath can bring with it new experiences of love.
Make no mistake—food that is delivered to your front door by the person who made it is a kind of love! Masked friends and neighbors frequently dropped off meals and treats. Chandra, Butler Armsden Architect's CEO, created a calendar so that for more than a month around the time of my DBS surgery, the firm's employees could sign up to bring dinners for the five of us.

Women friends from near and far generously kept in close contact with me by taking walks and texting. One family with whom Lewis and I have always been very close not only regularly delivered gorgeous, professional-level home-baked confections but also, during 2021, agreed to form a pandemic pod with me so that we could go to our beach house together for indulgent, maskless getaways. Their door in the city was always open for me, which was especially comforting after my kids moved out.

At the beginning of every single month since Lewis' death, I have received flowers from an anonymous someone. I have no idea who it could be, but this is an extraordinary gift from someone who knows that while the trauma of Lewis' dying recedes with time, the mourning never stops. The only way I could think to thank them was to post a photograph of every month's bouquet on Facebook.

When Lewis was diagnosed with cancer, Lewis' father, Lew, was devastated. He was still missing my mother-in-law, Sheana, since her death in 2016. I've always heard that the most terrible thing in life is to lose your child, and I believe this is true. Lew has told me many times, "Lewis wasn't just a great son; he was my best friend. The biggest honor of my life was when he asked me to be the best man at your wedding." It must have been terribly lonely to be a ninety-three year-old widower during a pandemic that made it very dangerous for him to be with any of us, let alone his dying son. Fortunately, Lew lives only ten blocks from us and has a large, sunny garden where the kids and I would go and sit with him. He was, and still is, key to Elena and Tobias' feelings of security now that Lewis is gone. He wasn't with us when Lewis died, but an hour or so afterward, Elena drove over to his house and, in Lew's words, "Fell into my arms and sobbed." My one-on-one relationship with Lew has continued to be very comforting. After having dinner together at my house, though, it's hard to know which of us—he, with his ninety-six year-old legs or I, with my Parkinson's, should be helping the other get down my front steps!

In November 2020, Matt flew east to spend the holidays with his family before returning to the house he would share with Elena in Philadelphia. Elena slept on the Tempur Pedic until the end of December, and then it was time for her to return to medical school and the rest of her life.

Anticipating Elena's departure was almost the toughest part of everything I'd been through. For the eight months she was living with me, every night when I went to bed, she would come in to give me a hug and we'd exchange "I love yous." I treasured that routine as much as I had when I tucked in her and Tobias when they were little. I also needed it, and she knew it.

Not only would I miss her immensely, but also, as a mother, I grieved for Elena and Tobias' loss of their fun and loving dad, which I knew would hit Elena very hard once she'd left. She would miss the intimate family pod we'd had with Tobias, Matt, and Sasha. Finally, I knew she had to be afraid of leaving me with my PD and without Lewis. This octopus-like mourning was too hard for us to talk about, so we tiptoed painfully around each other in a way we never had before. Mostly, we carried our loads silently, but we did deal each other a couple of ferocious emotional blows that hurt us both.

Before Elena left, though, she and I did something together that was wonderful and very healing—we shopped for a wedding dress. She and Matt had been quietly making plans for their wedding which would be in the spring of 2022. In a boutique on San Francisco's Hayes Street, Elena tried on five or six dresses. I was careful to keep my opinions in check until she slipped into one that seemed made for her. It took my breath away. "It's perfect!" I blurted. She asked me to put down a deposit on it, possibly the happiest money I've ever spent.

On December 28, 2020, Elena left for Philadelphia in a rented van packed to the roof with both a rowing and a sewing machine; the new wardrobe she'd sewn and knitted for herself, mounds of fabric and yarns; her dog, Mickey; and her medical school friend, Hannah, who flew out to share the cross-country adventure. Tobias and Sasha took over the Tempur Pedic that same night, a tremendously generous move to keep me company, one I hadn't requested. There were a few perks for them, like not having to pay rent for a few months and having separate workspaces. And there was Rafa, my funny dog whom they both adore. The best thing about having them as roommates was hearing their non-stop, animated chatter when they were finished working. How was it possible, I wondered, that they could still have so much to talk about when they'd been with each other 24/7, nearly exclusively for a year? Tobias was falling deeply in love, and I had a front-row seat! Over the four months they lived with me, I grew to love Sasha as I had Matt.

This was the biggest cancer-in-the-time-of-COVID silver lining: not only did the pandemic strengthen Tobias' and Elena's bonds with each other and with their partners, but it was also the privilege of my lifetime to have many intimate months with my two adult children, to see them take on responsibility and caring with such grace, to have a window into their professional lives, and to be able to get to know their extraordinarily mature, delightful and kind partners. There was a lot of love shared in our house, and while we are still adjusting to our new roles, it has deepened in the three years since we lost Lewis.

On Lew's ninety-fifth birthday, a sparkling day in April 2022, he walked his granddaughter Elena across the deck of the family beach house that Lewis had designed decades ago, delivering her to Matt at the driftwood altar in the dunes. In the crowd of over 130 there were tears of profound sadness and exuberant joy. After so many months of not being able to celebrate, everyone there had earned this spectacular, cloudless day.

To me, it felt like a miracle.

FORTY-TWO:
HADLEY'S IMPLANTS
AND PROCEDURES OLYMPICS

D uring 2020, the year that Lewis was sick, Hadley and I weren't in contact much; like most people, the pandemic gave us an extra excuse to hibernate. In contrast to my pre-pandemic days of having a house to myself until Lewis got home after work, I had a full house of people, and a partner to take care of. Time had become more precious to Hadley, too, as she was sleeping seventeen to eighteen hours a day and had a full schedule of appointments nearly every day. As anyone with a chronic disease knows, being sick is very time-consuming!

Nevertheless, Hadley managed to stay connected with the same activities she had been involved with in 2018: running meetings for her non-profit, Summit for Parkinson's, Zooming with the Michael J. Fox Foundation Patient Council twice a year, and creating paintings for her shows at the Radius Gallery, where she's been exhibiting since 2017. She was also still contributing her paintings to organizations to use for fundraisers and doing special smaller commissions for private clients and businesses.

After climbing on scaffolding to paint large murals in public spaces for many years, Hadley needed to adjust to making work that wasn't so physically demanding. In 2017, she was given an opportunity to create a public artwork that was a perfect fit: a license plate for Montana that would be sold to raise funds for MoFi, a Missoula lending company that serves Montana businesses. Hadley chose to paint a quintessential Montana landscape featuring a ranch against a backdrop of the Mission Mountains.

In October 2019, Hadley was honored when the Forging Resilience Tree, which she'd co-created with Carolyn Maier and had been featured at the 2016 World Parkinson Congress, was permanently installed in one of the conference spaces at the Michael J. Fox Foundation in New York City. While creating the tree, Hadley met a multimedia artist, Stoney Samsoe, who had volunteered to help make the leaves. Stoney had participated in artist residencies and approached Hadley about helping her start such a program in Montana. Hadley was excited about the idea and the two artists founded Open Air. The program differs from most residencies in that it places artists in a particular place in Montana, where they are expected not only to engage the community in their art-making, but also to refer to the landscape or history of the place through their work. When the pandemic hit in 2020 and residencies were no longer possible, Stoney and Hadley modified the program, finding artists who could work locally. Hadley found starting Open Air very rewarding, but she was spread too thin and ultimately had to let go of her role in the organization.

Because Hadley has so much weakness and discomfort, she paints and conducts most of her business from her bed in her studio on the second floor of the house she shares with her husband, John, and sixteen-year-old Sarah. She leaves the house to attend her show openings, artist talks and appointments and to go on special occasion outings with her family. Since she's only awake six or seven hours a day, she makes a special point of spending ninety minutes every night and every weekend with her family.

Once a week, Hadley goes to the auditorium of Loyola Sacred Heart High School where, in 2011, she had begun work on her largest commission to date: four murals depicting the history of the Missoula Catholic schools. She had completed two panels and sketched in two more when she had to put the project on hold in order to create the Women's Murals for the Montana State House. In the years since 2015, she has hired five artists to finish the panels under the guidance of her discerning eye. From her wheelchair, Hadley shines a laser pointer on the enormous eight by twelve-foot murals to direct Lillian Nelson and Ann Carp, the two artists currently working on the project. "I think you need more shadow here," she instructs. She is pleased by how well they've been able to match her style. Panels three and four are coming to life and will be finished by the fall of 2023.

Throughout 2021-2022, Hadley was also busy preparing for, enduring, and recovering from procedures to address new or worsening MSA symptoms. The baclofen pump, which had been so helpful for her rigidity when it was implanted in 2015, hasn't been able to keep up with her increasing stiffness; she can only extend her hips and knees to a forty-five-degree angle. In order for her to be flexible enough to move any part of her body, including hands, elbows, shoulders, knees, and hips, every three months, in one day, she's given twenty-one shots of Botox to relax her muscles. After this treatment, she will sleep up to twenty hours a day for the first few weeks and it takes four to five weeks for her to fully recover. "Even with all this—and they've added fentanyl and morphine to my baclofen cocktail, my pain level from my rigidity is a six," Hadley told me.

Finding herself constantly tired all of 2018, Hadley discovered that her heart rate was in the high thirties and low forties, and her blood pressure, which has always been very low, had dropped even further. At the cardiologist's, she found herself in the uncomfortable position of having to convince him that her exceedingly slow heart rate was not due to her being a super athlete but rather, was an autonomic dysfunction caused by MSA. With the cardiologist, she planned to have a pacemaker implanted. When she went in for surgery, she took an article she'd read about MSA and anesthesia to the doctors. They followed the protocol recommended in the article to a T, using a short-acting anesthesia, Propofol. Despite the precautions taken, Hadley didn't come out of the anesthesia for eighteen hours. The anesthesiologist was very alarmed, as were John and Jana. The whole time she was out, she couldn't move any part of her body or speak, but could feel and hear everything people in the room were saying. Her family was understandably worried that Hadley would never emerge. Hadley could only lie there, wishing she could reassure them that she would be back. At one point, when the surgery team moved her from the table to do a CT scan, she was as limp as a ragdoll, and her head flopped, hitting the CT machine.

Since swallowing had become more and more difficult for Hadley, 2021 brought her yet another bodily invasion: a gastrostomy tube, or G-tube, which would deliver nutrition directly into her stomach. But something went terribly wrong. Once the tube was placed, Hadley's stomach began to spasm as if it were trying to reject the foreign body. While MSA causes all of her muscles to go into spasms at different times, the pain she was experiencing now was different.

Hadley has a very high threshold for pain. So, reading between her always copious exclamation points in her texts, I knew she was suffering enormously. Four days after implanting the G-tube, they discovered it had migrated into her lower intestines, and they had to put it back in place. After eight days, the hospital sent her home with the expectation that she would use the G-tube. However, anything that was put into it, even water, made Hadley's abdominal pain worse. She was back in the ER eight days later because she had lost nine pounds in those eight days.

Hadley stayed in the hospital for five weeks. She had become very weak, and since she couldn't walk or do the most basic things, she was checked into rehabilitation for four weeks. After stabilizing her with IV nutrition, the hospital encouraged her to try another type of feeding tube called a MIC-KEY button, which eliminates the four inch long tube coming out of the stomach and uses a port, or hole, that's flush with the skin

Unfortunately, the MIC-KEY tube was not any more effective than the G-tube. A speech therapist in the rehab center asked Hadley what she liked to eat at home to see how different the formula used in the feeding tube was from what she was used to eating. He had Hadley pick out a recipe, and John came to the hospital with all the ingredients, a blender, and their Instapot. The therapist's theory was that if Hadley tasted what was going into her feeding tube, her brain would be triggered to prepare her stomach for what was coming in. John is a great cook, and Hadley loved the curried butternut soup with ginger that he made. But her stomach was not having it!

Hadley needed a way to eat! She felt certain that if she couldn't eat, she would die, but the doctors were running out of ideas. For three days, Hadley, her doctors, John, and Jana sat with the horrific possibility that Hadley could starve to death.

There was only one option left: total parenteral nutrition (TPN) or intravenous (IV) feeding. Doctors don't like patients to be on TPN on a permanent basis because it's hard on the liver, but Hadley was given special permission to use it indefinitely. Unlike a feeding tube, which delivers nutrition to the stomach, Hadley's TPN, which is placed in her right bicep, sends a nutritious blend of protein, carbohydrates and vitamins through a catheter into her bloodstream and on to her heart. To add interest and calories to her "meals," Hadley supplements with small bites of delicious sides that John and Jana make: curries with soft, saucy rice, a little roast salmon; and soft, buttery potatoes.

Hadley has become used to eating a little food by mouth and getting the rest from the IV. The idea of using the G-tube was abandoned two months after Hadley left the hospital, but it was capped off and left in place because they thought if the TPN failed, they might need to go back to using it. After a year, she was doing fine with the TPN but still in extreme pain because of the G-tube. They decided not to remove it since they suspected it might have been entangled with a nerve.

This was not the end of Hadley's trials with procedures. In January 2022, she had a colonoscopy to see if something had been overlooked that could be causing her continued abdominal pain. This was followed a couple of months later by an endoscopy, and in May she underwent surgery to have the battery in her baclofen pump replaced. Both tests were normal, and the battery replacement went well, but in all three cases, it took her eight hours to wake up from the short-acting anesthesia.

In May of 2023, the G-tube tube was finally removed without complications; still, Hadley describes considerable pain at times, rating it a seven when it peaks instead of a ten. She is hopeful that the pain will continue to lessen as she heals from the surgery.

If there were an Implants and Procedures Olympics, Hadley would surely get a medal!

FORTY-THREE:
A NEW PROJECT

In 2021, Hadley traveled to Oregon Health and Science Hospital (OHSU) in Portland, Oregon, where she has gone for medical care many times. This was the first time since her diagnosis of MSA that she was there to be treated specifically for MSA. During the long appointment, her movement, cognition, and speech were evaluated to determine what kind of home help she would be eligible for through Medicare. She reported to me a few days later, "They told me I was in late stage MSA and shouldn't use my energy to exercise." When she said "late-stage MSA," I felt a thud in my stomach. I expected her next words to address how hearing this made her feel. Instead, she said, "I found myself thinking. "Wow! I really do have this disease, and finally, the system is treating me like I do."

When I asked Hadley how she felt about being told she was in "late stage," she didn't miss a beat. "Oh, well, the life expectancy for regular MSA is seven to ten years post-diagnosis. But they figured out a few years ago that for people diagnosed with MSA when they're under forty, it can be as much as eighteen years. But you can be in late-stage for many years."

I couldn't bring myself to ask for clarification, but I believe Hadley's multiple autonomic failures—heart rate, blood pressure, swallowing, might be why doctors consider her late-stage.

When Hadley returned to Missoula from OHSU, she watched an episode of *Diagnosis,* a TV and New York Times Magazine series written by Dr. Lisa Sanders. Fired up by stories of patients like hers who've struggled to get diagnoses, all her experiences with doctors came back to her. She decided to read *An Alert, Well-Hydrated...*from front to back. It gave her a new perspective on her ordeal. "This time it was like I was reading about someone else, not me," she told me. "I was thinking about what that one doctor said to me, about how he could see how I fooled all my doctors, and how it's stuck with me. No patient should have to deal with that!"

With her challenging health issues and her history with physicians, it's easy to see why, in 2012, when one of the doctors at The Mayo Clinic said, "I can sure see how you fooled all your doctors," it hit Hadley very hard. He could have said, "This is a very complex case. I can see why your illness has stumped doctors." But the words he carelessly chose made it sound as if Hadley had been trying to trick doctors. If he was trying to add some levity to the situation by teasing her, it was, at best, inappropriate and insensitive. But for Hadley, who'd come to The Mayo Clinic because she'd exhausted many medical resources and would be leaving a few days later without a diagnosis, it was devastating.

Hadley told me recently that what she'd said to me eight years ago, in 2015—that she'd accepted her disease, wasn't completely accurate. She had been enormously relieved to stop spending energy on the search for a diagnosis so she could focus on the Women's Murals for the Montana

State House. However, she'd remained anxious after the whole ordeal. As a result, for nearly two years following her experience at The Mayo Clinic, she hadn't sought medical care with the exception of seeing her Missoula neurologist, Dr. Reid.

When Dr. Reid referred Hadley for a two-hour baclofen epidural test to determine whether she would be a responsive candidate for the implant, it wasn't the procedure itself Hadley was nervous about. She was afraid that if the epidural didn't improve her symptoms, this would cast doubt on her diagnosis of MSA. She was relieved that the epidural significantly helped with her painful rigidity because it was an affirmation that she did, in fact, have a "real" disease.

"It was how I felt about the swallow test I had back in 2013, remember?" I remembered well how oddly excited she had been, telling me about how initiating a swallow was normal, but there was a delay when the food got farther down her throat. The doctor had explained that this part of swallowing is an autonomic function that a person has no control over; therefore, she couldn't have caused this dysfunction by having a functional disease or emotional problems.

Even after she'd finally been given a clear diagnosis of MSA by Dr. Truitt in Houston in 2013, Hadley carried the humiliation and self-doubt that had been planted in her early on by doctors who didn't believe her symptoms indicated anything serious was wrong with her. I had wondered why she didn't talk to me much about *An Alert, Well-Hydrated Artist in No Acute Distress* when I was publishing it online in 2016-2017. I assumed she was feeling too unwell or too busy to read. I know now that she worried that if she talked about my blog with family and friends, some of whom had been on the fence about whether to believe she had MSA, they would feel validated by reading about the doubt Hadley's doctors had expressed for so many years.

In April. 2022, Hadley sent me a mysterious text saying she had an idea she wanted to discuss. But first, she had to talk to Dave Iverson, a retired NPR journalist, documentary filmmaker, and author of a memoir, *Winter Stars.* Dave also has Parkinson's Disease, and Hadley had met him in 2016 when she joined the Michael J. Fox Foundation Patient Council. As promised, she called me the next day after she had talked to Dave about making a short film documenting her life with MSA and her career as an artist. Dave said he'd think about it and suggested that, in the meantime, she should find a videographer who was local. Hadley immediately thought of her next-door neighbor, Damon Ristau, a documentary filmmaker. Damon was excited to get involved, partly because his father has Parkinson's.

Hadley asked if I'd be willing to get *An Alert Well-Hydrated* published as a book, which she had also talked to Dave about. Her idea was to have the book be a "companion piece" to the film. I hadn't ever heard of a tandem arrangement like this, but Hadley seemed clear on the concept. She told me, "I decided that my story needed to be told. I see the film and book as being teaching tools." When she said she thought it would also be a good project for her and me, I realized she'd been thinking about how I'd been at loose ends for several years without a writing project to anchor me, as well as my day-to-day struggle as a new widow. As always, I was amazed that with all she had going on, she was still thinking about how she could help jumpstart my creative juices.

Dave, who lives in the Bay Area, agreed to be the director and editor for a short film about Hadley. He read *An Alert, Well-Hydrated Artist...* and felt that the blog wouldn't need much editing to be published as a book. Everyone, including me, began referring to the "epilogue" I would add to cover Hadley's and my lives from 2018 through 2023. I realized very soon that this was a much heftier project than anyone realized. So much had happened in my life since 2018! It was almost too soon to write about all I've been through and all the ways in which my life has changed. On many days, I was unable to.

FORTY-FOUR:
HADLEY AT HOME

On August 14, 2021, Hadley texted me:

"HI, Catherine!!! I'm so sorry about the lack of communication, but this has been one crazy month!!! My status is that since the end of May I have gained four pounds and am now at 103. The days feel busy even though I'm not doing anything, but I'm happy to have all the help with care. I am lucky to have a great care team. Over the last month there have been a few switches out from some people that weren't hearing my needs and how MSA is different from what they are used to. Almost every visit for the first month, people were telling me I had sixty days total with the home health therapists and then I was on my own. There were a lot of tears, and it caused a ton of stress which doesn't help anything. Sure, we can hire all that out, but we only have so many resources, and the future was looking extremely overwhelming. I finally got a good

PT, and after working on me for several weeks, she realized what my body needs is someone trained, and it wasn't going to be so easy to train family, friends, and bath aides to do what I needed. So, the last two weeks they stopped talking about my timeline which has helped. PT was supposed to take over the lower half of my body and OT the upper half. I was told yesterday that next week is my last week with OT, and I will have to figure something else out with my upper body. At this point, I just feel like I will take what I can get and be grateful for that!!! Some super positives are that we got the asphalt poured, the ramp installed, and the power chair!!! John and I have gone out for an hour on the weekends around the campus and neighborhood which has felt great, and I'm happy I have the chair to be able to use. We are still waiting on the van, but that will be another exciting moment, and we can actually drive someplace for us to walk in a different area. So life is about the small things these days and I am very grateful for each moment. It's a new normal, but I'm happy to have it. I know you have been adjusting to your new normal as well, and I keep you in my heart every day!!!!!"

When to apply for home health services is a big decision. Once a patient starts an at-home program, they are not allowed to get the same services elsewhere. Through Medicare's Home Health Services, Hadley has been receiving occupational therapy that helps her, in her words, "find the easiest way to get the job done." This includes tasks that require hand coordination, such as opening packaging, getting dressed (think buttons and zippers), and using certain tools, like scissors, all of which are difficult for Hadley because of the extreme stiffness in her hands. The occupational therapist also advises Hadley on ways to conserve her energy and how to keep her home safe so she can avoid falling and having other accidents. A physical therapist comes to Hadley's home twice a week. PT is split between stretching and dry needling, which involves inserting needles into Hadley's tight muscles to help stimulate blood flow and alleviate pain.

Also included in Home Health is cognitive speech therapy. Hadley's cognition was tested in 2014 because she was having trouble with executive function while doing research for the Women's Murals. She was also finding it hard to recognize people she'd run into whom she knew but couldn't place. Since then, she's been taking Aricept, a medication used to treat cognitive impairment, which has been helping, but the therapist has also taught her some "tricks" to help her identify people.

Once a week, a nurse comes to the house to change the dressing on Hadley's TPN IV site, and once a month, she comes to do a blood draw. In addition, twice a week, a certified nursing assistant (CNA) comes to help Hadley with showering, dressing and hair.

Hadley has once-a-week sessions with her wonderful psychotherapist, whom she's been seeing for years. She also sees her PCP once a month via telehealth and twice a year in person. Every other week, she goes to a physiatrist, who provides Botox treatments and gives her body a workout on his table, stretching her uncooperative muscles and manipulating her spine.

There are rules that must be followed in order to keep Medicare's Home Health Services; Hadley can only leave the house to go to doctors' appointments or to have her hair done, to church, or special occasions.

I asked Hadley if she was ever lonely. She said, "Oh my gosh, no! I have all these people around me all the time!"

FORTY-FIVE:
PARKINSON'S PANIC

Hadley, Dave, Damon, and I planned to meet at the end of April 2023 in Missoula, where Dave and Damon would begin our three days of filming with Hadley's and my reunion. We had last seen each other in 2016 at the World Parkinson Congress in Portland, Oregon.

Because this is a story about living with neurological disease, I would be remiss if I didn't include certain details about living with PD. I am probably speaking for anyone with a progressive, chronic condition (like aging!) when I say that flying becomes more difficult every year. This is one of my biggest frustrations because family members and many of my friends live on the East Coast.

I have never been an anxious flier. But since 2020, anxiety has been part of my life with Parkinson's. It's stressful enough to travel alone because of the physical rigor of getting through large terminals, standing in lines, and hefting bags into overhead bins. With anxiety now one of my symptoms, I no longer fly alone. As soon as I knew I'd be flying to Missoula, I asked Tobias to go with me. He was very happy to do so, citing long solo hikes and craft beer as two of his reasons.

In one of the most flagrant mistreatments of airline passengers I have experienced, what should have been an efficient trip to Montana became an ordeal that validated my recruiting Tobias to travel with me. We were due to be in Missoula by 8:00 p.m. and didn't get there till the next morning at 10:00 a.m. A delayed departure from San Francisco set up a domino effect of stresses, starting with having to run to the gate in Seattle, where our connecting flight had just pulled away despite there being six people from our flight who were supposed to be on it. Tobias and I joined a line of angry passengers at the service desk where he searched on his phone for alternative flights to Missoula. I had just taken my 5 p.m. PD medication when we landed in Seattle, and I could feel myself getting tenser. I had the thought that if I were alone, I would be too anxious to make my fingers work on my phone to do the task Tobias was taking care of.

There were no other flights to Missoula until the morning. By the time we got our voucher for a room at the Comfort Inn and arrived at baggage claim, the bags had been removed from the carousel and I knew I was headed into one of my twice-a-week panic attacks, an affliction I never had before 2020. My chest and throat became constricted, my breathing was shallow, and my body became enervated, so I had to give my carry-on bag to Tobias. When he asked someone official looking where we could pick up our bags, he was told we'd have to come back in two to four hours because they would "have to locate them." This was the second time I had the thought that if I were alone and having a panic attack, I wouldn't be able to navigate finding the hotel, and then a couple of hours later, returning to an unfamiliar airport to (hopefully) pick up my bag. I was in a kind of stupor while waiting the forty-five minutes for the Comfort Inn shuttle. When I have a panic attack, I am useless. It's hard for me to walk or think. I can't distract myself by talking, reading, writing, meditating, or watching a screen. For the 45-120 minutes the anxiety lasts, I feel despondent and totally alone in the world. When I'm home and have one of these episodes, I often pace or just sit and stare into space until something shifts. Sometimes, I will take a small amount of an anti-anxiety medication which can help, and other times, if the anxiety lasts long enough, my next dose of levodopa will help.

When we arrived at the hotel, Tobias and I retreated into our separate rooms for half an hour. My sister texted us the name of a good restaurant near the airport, and on the way there, I felt my body easing its way to a more comfortable place. At the restaurant, I sat facing a large window that looked out on a pretty grove of aspens. The beer tasted good, and Tobias was cheerful. He talked about his and Sasha's developing plans to get married, which made my whole insides smile. After dinner, we walked around a small lake, where there were kids still swimming at 8:30. When your life becomes limited by physical disability and you no longer have a bucket list that involves exotic travel, this is one way to expand your experience—by slowing down your gaze to take in more detail. Together, the pleasing aspects of the scene I had been intently focusing on helped to restore my equilibrium.

After we returned to the hotel, Tobias went back to the airport, where he waited forty-five minutes to get our bags.

In the morning, we arrived at the airport at 7:00 for our 8:00 flight. Tobias punched our confirmation number into a machine, but it would not accept it. We had to run to find customer service, where they fixed the issue. The airline employee the night before had given us an invalid confirmation number! This was yet another moment for me to feel very grateful that Tobias was with me.

I related this tedious story for three reasons. One is to acknowledge that this is the kind of thing elderly and disabled people go through all the time. Even if they don't have panic attacks, when stressed, they feel vulnerable and incompetent at something that they used to handle with ease. They get rattled when someone in line behind them is waiting for them as they fumble for their money or IDs, or they suddenly feel weak and must sit down. They feel humiliated when they fall in public. They become afraid. All of us will be here at some time. But when you're sixty-eight and not visibly disabled, people don't expect this dysfunction. Perhaps people with invisible disabilities should have a placard to hang around our necks like the one we hang on our car mirrors. It could say, "Parkinson's! Please Be Patient." Of course, using a wheelchair at the airport would also send this message. I might just swallow my pride and order one next time.

The second reason I made a point of describing this is that many people with PD who struggle with anxiety and depression—known as "non-motor symptoms" of PD, don't talk about them. Since recently learning that not enough levodopa and too much levodopa can both cause anxiety, I have been trying to manage the wearing off as well as the "stacking" of levodopa by making small adjustments to the seven doses I take every day. So far, my tweaking has been paying off.

FORTY-SIX:
MISSOULA!

When Tobias and I arrive in Missoula, Dave texts me to let me know they've set the scene for my reunion with Hadley. Hadley would be waiting for me in her wheelchair in her garden, and I would come through her back gate. I'm expecting it to be awkward to reunite in front of a camera, knowing that the intention is to capture something intimate. But it's going to be a performance no matter what. I've decided not to anticipate or plan what I will say or do. As I reach to open the gate, I feel a shiver of excitement despite the eighty-degree day.

The moment I see Hadley, I totally forget that Dave and Damon are there recording our every movement and word. Tobias stands back to give us some space. So much has happened to Hadley and me since we last saw each other seven years ago. Yet, at forty-seven, she looks the same. She is wearing a cool, furry, pale green vest over an ivory blouse. When I hug her, I feel our boniness and realize we are both smaller—only a combined 216 pounds, it turns out.

I don't remember what I say to Hadley or what she says to me; later, I have to ask Dave. But in her embrace, I can't hold back tears.

During our three days together in Missoula, Hadley appears so mentally alert and directed still that it's hard to fathom that she needs to sleep seventeen or eighteen hours a day or has cognitive issues. I also knew that several weeks before, she'd received twenty-one shots of Botox near every joint in her body so that she could move. This treatment, which she gets every three months, usually wipes her out for weeks, and this time was no different. Just a few days before we arrived in Missoula, she had been sleeping twenty-one hours a day. I worried about the impact our busy days of filming would have on her. In typical Hadley style, though, she rallies and is able to keep the schedule Dave has set for us, and she even adds more to it. I am the one who can't always keep up the pace! Like Dave, Hadley has scenes in her head that she'd like to include in the documentary. Having never worked with her, I hadn't witnessed firsthand how determined and precise she is about how she does things. I'm impressed but not surprised.

Recently, I told Hadley she was relentless. I don't remember the context, and I was laughing when I said it. But it made her feel bad. She thought I meant she'd been pushing us too hard on the film and book project. I hadn't meant that at all. But as I began backpedaling and thinking more about the word "relentless," the more I realized that it truly fits her.

Hadley is soft-spoken and physically delicate and has a genuine sweetness to her, so I doubt many people would associate the word "relentless" with her. But that's because they might think only of the word's negative uses, like "ruthless" or "uncompromising." There are many more positive words that are synonyms. One of them, "persistent," was made famous in 2017 by Sen. Mitch McConnell when he called out Sen. Elizabeth Warren because he'd been unable to silence her on the Senate floor. "She had appeared to violate the rule," he said. "She was warned. She was given an explanation. Nevertheless, she persisted."

Whether or not you agree with McConnell's criticism, it can't be denied that, in this case, using a word meant to imply that Sen. Warren was pushy and unruly backfired. And the rest is herstory.

It had only taken Dave, Hadley, and me about five minutes to come up with a working title for the film *Hadley Ferguson: Passion to Persist.*

In the twelve years I have known Hadley, the word I have used most often to describe her to people has been "extraordinary." I've used this word so much that I fear it's lost its impact. After all, anyone can see this extraordinariness just by looking at all Hadley's accomplished. When I first met Hadley, I was amazed by how many mural commissions she'd completed before she was even thirty-five. When I started writing about her quest to get a diagnosis, I understood that the head-on way in which she approaches obstacles is what has made her career as an artist so unusual. It's what makes her *uniquely* extraordinary.

Writing the first version of *An Alert, Well-Hydrated…*, I had plenty of material to cover, with Hadley's and my own diagnosis stories. I didn't realize until 2015 that I was writing a story that would have a second thread: two alert, well-hydrated artists completing the most fulfilling projects of our careers. It was a happy narrative coincidence that Hadley's Women's Murals at the Montana State House and my novel *Dream House* both debuted in 2015. How lucky was I, as a writer, to be able to end my story about degenerative disease in this joyful way!

Eight years later, I have been given a chance to write another ending to our story. I have wanted to offer a more precise picture of who Hadley is. This would not be easy, I knew, because Hadley has very little time to herself when she's not sleeping. With home health caregivers coming and going, her outside appointments, the time she spends with her family, and the still active projects she's working on, in the past year, we've only had time for a few long phone conversations. I'm certain I wore her out, drilling her with questions until well after 11 p.m. mountain time. Not that she even once complained. I don't think I've ever heard her complain. *This is Hadley.*

When I was writing about Hadley's struggle with the failed G-tube implant, I was feeling uninspired by my dry reportage, shocking as the details were. In an a-ha! moment, I scrolled back through our texts to 2021 and found the one in which she described the whole debacle four days after the surgery. It was this text, one quintessentially Hadley, that gave me the clues I'd been looking for.

> Hi, dear Catherine!!! How is it that I am always in that very rare category? Can we bring on a laugh about this now?!?!? So... I had the surgery, but I had a 1/1,000,000 complication... of course!!! I just had a bad feeling going into it, and my intuition always seems to prove right...darn it!!

The exclamation points! *This is Hadley.* She went on to describe what happened with the surgery and closed the text with:

> This is the first time I could text because I've been so doped up on Morphine. The nurses have done all of my tube feeding so far, so we shall see how this goes at home... fingers crossed we can pull this off!!!!!

The text was accompanied by a video she'd taken for me of her stomach muscles visibly spasming. She wrote that the spasms brought on pain that, on the scale, was 17/10. Even given this number, I had to work to understand just how much pain and fear she was feeling because of her spunky presentation style. *This is Hadley:* relentlessly good-humored. Her ability to joke about all that her body is going through while still taking her health very seriously is why, when we were first getting to know each other, we would find ourselves laughing. It's why I felt comfortable naming a chapter full of descriptions of invasive, excruciatingly painful procedures that left her wondering if she might die, something as silly as *Hadley's Implants and Procedures Olympics.*

However, I thought Hadley might bristle at being described as "relentless," so I wrote the following pre-emptive text to her:

> "Extraordinary" is someone who, at the age of 39, wins a commission to paint two very important murals that will hang permanently in the Montana State House. "Relentlessly can-do" is the person who took on the project only five months after being diagnosed with a deadly neurogenerative disease. "Relentlessly determined and optimistic" is the person who, after being awarded the commission, defended her ability to complete the project to a concerned member of the selection committee despite feeling increasingly unwell.

> "Relentless" means you are unstoppable, which implies that there are forces that will try to stop you. All of your life, your body has been trying to stop you, but you haven't let it because you have relentlessly high

expectations for yourself. You are going to pull off whatever endeavor is important, not only to you but also to your community, no matter what. What's the word for someone who has already contributed so much meaningful (and permanent!) content, as well as love and fun to the world, someone who's been told she's in late-stage MSA but who wakes up and decides she's still not done and wants to give the world a film and a book about her life that will help other people?

Girl, the word is either "crazy" or "relentless!" To be called "relentless" is perhaps one of the highest compliments there is, because it's only applicable to very hard-working people who have a strong vision for how to get things done."

This, without any exaggeration, is Hadley.

FORTY-SEVEN:
EVERY DAY IS A NEW DAY

P erhaps the most important thing I've learned while writing this book is that it is not for lack of trying that there won't be a cure for Parkinson's or MSA in my lifetime! Many brilliant scientists and their generous funders are highly motivated to discover the next Big Breakthrough for neurological disease. But it seems the more they know, the more they know about how much more they still don't know. There's an expression people in the Parkinson's community use a lot: "If you've met one person with Parkinson's disease, you've met one person with Parkinson's disease." Some scientists are now describing PD not as a single disease but a combination of many.

When people ask me about the future, how I answer depends on where I am in the five cycles of my daily dopamine fluctuations. At 7:00 a.m., 11:30 a.m., 2:30 p.m. or 5:00 p.m., I will tell them to wait at least forty-five minutes and ask me again. Otherwise, they will get an answer that might sound like this: Where do I start with all the things I am terrified about? How about the fact that the days are still getting longer, but in a week, they will begin getting shorter and shorter, and then winter will come? And this will happen every year! You get the idea.

However, if they ask me about my outlook when the dopamine has fully kicked in, I tell them I will never stop missing my fun and multi-talented partner, Lewis, but I am deeply grateful for the forty extraordinary years I had with him. I have never felt more attuned and appreciative of the goodness and beauty in my life. I have formed new relationships with my children. With friends, I have more of the floor now that my loquacious, impatient buddy is no longer here to interrupt my too-long, too-slow stories with his short, faster ones. I have also learned new skills having to do with house and car maintenance and finances, which has often felt overwhelming but empowering, too. I have even had a romance going for a year, something that I didn't think would be possible for me, sixteen years into Parkinson's. It has restored some youth to these bones.

In a few months, I will have an elevator in my three-story house that will allow me to get from my ground-floor garage and laundry room to the kitchen and up another floor to my bedroom and study. This will make it possible for me to go away without having to worry about how I will safely get bags up and down my very long, narrow, and steep stairs.

Within the next two years, a liquid form of levodopa/carbidopa that can be self-administered under the skin will be approved by the FDA. The continuous infusion will eliminate fluctuations in motor and non-motor symptoms and the interference of food with levodopa absorption. This could be a game-changer for me. I will be able to throw away my pill cutter!

Very soon, a baby boy will be born to Elena and Matt—my first grandchild!

Tobias and Sasha are planning their wedding!

And Hadley? She has another show at the Radius Gallery coming up. I expect she will make her typical twenty to thirty paintings without leaving her bed and that she will likely sell all of them.

There will be an important and beautiful film, and this book will proudly keep it company.

Four new murals illustrating the history of Missoula's Catholic schools will be unveiled—work created with energy seemingly summoned from a place neither corporeal nor celestial but somewhere in between.

This is my remarkable friend, Hadley:

> I have been public through the arts, but my true passion lies with my people. I feel very content because I know I am connected to the people I love, and that connection lives and breathes beyond my physical presence. I will always be present in some way; I don't see my time as ever ending.

THANK YOU

To Hadley Ferguson, for trusting me to tell your story and creating the imperative that it become a published book, and most importantly, for your friendship. You have always been an inspiration to me, and I'm excited that I can play a role in bringing that inspiration to the world.

To the first readers of this work, my writing group, Anita Amirrezvani, Eli Brown, Carolyn Cooke, Laurie Fox, and Tess Uriza Holthe, who insisted I weave in my own story with Hadley's. Your enthusiasm was great fuel; when I took detours to explore topics like illness and optimism and alpha-synuclein, rather than trying to rein me in, you pressed for more.

To Laurie Edwards, who has written brilliantly and extensively about living with chronic illness. Thank you for your wisdom and insightful feedback early on.

Thanks to my two editors: Josh Model, for telling me I should never change the title and for not being shy about telling me what I should cut, and Meghan Bowker, for your leniency about what I could keep. A special thank you to Dr. Jessica Ng and Dr. Phuong Hoang, movement disorders specialists, who so generously fact-checked the medical material in the book. To my sisters, Gay Armsden and

Beverley Daniel, who provided feedback, support, and put up with my hours of working during their visits, when they probably suspected my sessions on my laptop yielded very little usable writing.

Dave Iverson, journalist, filmmaker, author, and helpful friend, you make the world seem a little kinder. Thank you for connecting me with Betty and Wally Turnbull and Jori Hanna at Light Messages Publishing Torchflame Books, whose empathy I'm sure helped with their decision to take on this book and also gave them the patience to generously respond to my requests for more time. Finally, a shout-out to my close friend, Karen Jaffe, for writing the book forward. Karen, I am so grateful you are in my life! You know I can't do this PD thing without you.

The author and Hadley Ferguson (2013)

Visit catherinearmsden.com to view photographs of the 2015 unveiling on Hadley's murals for the Montana State House.

ABOUT THE AUTHOR

Catherine Armsden grew up in coastal Maine and was educated at Brown University (AB, Art) and Harvard University Graduate School of Design (MArch). In 1983, she moved to San Francisco with her husband, the late Lewis Butler, where they co-founded Butler Armsden Architects.

Catherine was less active with the firm after 2000, eventually abandoning it altogether when she became possessed by an idea for a novel inspired by her work designing houses. *Dream House* was published in 2015.

At 54, a diagnosis of Parkinson's Disease provided Catherine with the inspiration for *An Alert, Well-Hydrated Artist in No Acute Distress*.

To nourish her lifelong love for making art and supporting artists, Catherine has served on the Board of Directors of Southern Exposure, Emergent Art Space, and the Lewis W. Butler Foundation.

Printed in the USA
CPSIA information can be obtained
at www.ICGtesting.com
LVHW090346290624
784273LV00003B/285